Modernist Literature and Postcolonial Studies

Postcolonial Literary Studies

Series Editors: David Johnson, The Open University and Ania Loomba, University of Pennsylvania

Visit the Postcolonial Literary Studies website at
www.euppublishing.com/series/epls

Modernist Literature and Postcolonial Studies

Rajeev S. Patke

EDINBURGH
University Press

© Rajeev S. Patke, 2013

Edinburgh University Press Ltd
22 George Square, Edinburgh EH8 9LF

www.euppublishing.com

Typeset in 10.5/13 Sabon
by Servis Filmsetting Ltd, Stockport, Cheshire, and
printed and bound in Great Britain by
CPI Group (UK) Ltd, Croydon CR0 4YY

A CIP record for this book is available from the British Library

ISBN 978 0 7486 3992 2 (hardback)
ISBN 978 0 7486 3993 9 (paperback)
ISBN 978 0 7486 8260 7 (webready PDF)
ISBN 978 0 7486 8261 4 (epub)

The right of Rajeev S. Patke
to be identified as author of this work
has been asserted in accordance with
the Copyright, Designs and Patents Act 1988.

Contents

Series Editors' Preface

Postcolonial Literary Studies foregrounds the colonial and neo-colonial contexts of literary and cultural texts, and demonstrates how these texts help to understand past and present histories of empires. The books in the series relate key literary and cultural texts both to their historical and geographical moments, and to contemporary issues of neo-colonialism and global inequality. In addition to introducing the diverse body of postcolonial criticism, theory and scholarship in literary studies, the series engages with relevant debates on postcolonialism in other disciplines – history, geography, critical theory, political studies, economics and philosophy. The books in the series exemplify how postcolonial studies can reconfigure the major periods and areas of literary studies. Each book provides a comprehensive survey of the existing field of scholarship and debate with a time line, a literature survey, discussion of key critical, theoretical, historical and political debates, case studies providing exemplary critical readings of key literary texts, and guides to further reading. At the same time, each book is also an original critical intervention in its own right. In much the same way that feminism has redefined how all literary texts are analysed, our ultimate aim is that this series will contribute to all texts in literary studies being read with an awareness of their colonial and neo-colonial resonances.

DJ and AL

Acknowledgements

I am grateful to David Johnson and Ania Loomba for the opportunity to join this project, and to Jackie Jones and Jenny Daly at Edinburgh University Press for their support. David and Ania have been enormously helpful in bringing the manuscript to some kind of order. David's care and patience have been exemplary, Nicola Wood's vigilance in copy-editing, and Matthew Gale's in reading proof-copy and preparing the index have kept me from many typographical and bibliographical sins of omission and commission. The anonymous reviewers who commented on an early draft of the book proposal were helpful in revising the plan, as was my friend and former colleague, Robert Lumsden, and as were Lily Rose Tope and Vince Serrano, who commented on parts of the manuscript, and Petrus Liu, who drew my attention to relevant materials in the nick of time. I am grateful to my colleagues in the Department of English Language and Literature at the National University of Singapore for help in countless ways, over many years of working together, and especially to my dear friend Susan Ang; to the Faculty of Arts and Social Sciences for the grant of sabbatical leave for the early part of 2011; to Pericles Lewis and Charles Bailyn at Yale-NUS College for making it possible for me complete work on this book; and to the Central Library of the National University of Singapore for providing unfailing access to research materials. The image used on the cover is reproduced by kind permission of Aboli Salunke, Pune (and readers can guess what it represents that might be pertinent to the argument of the book). The terrains of modernism and of postcolonial writing are vast and many: I am grateful to the enormous body of writing that has made this modest undertaking easier. My bibliography is the tip of what lies beneath, the citations and notes only a token of a much greater debt owed to the fellowship of scholarly writing. Finally, I am grateful to my wife Rithu – loyal friend and companion – for more than what words can express.

Timeline

Year	Events in History, Politics, Science and Technology	Events and Publications in Literature and the Arts
1803	First steamship	
1804	Independence for Haiti	
1807	Prohibition to traffic in slaves in British ships or to British colonies	
1813	English East India Company loses its trade monopoly	
1815	Ceylon (Sri Lanka) taken over by the British from the Dutch	
1833	Britain abolishes slavery throughout the British Empire	
1852		Karl Marx starts his dispatches on British India to the *New York Tribune*
1853	First railways and telegraphy in British India French colonisation of New Caledonia	
1857	Mutiny in India Transatlantic cable completed	

1858	Dissolution of the East India Company	
1859		Charles Darwin, *On the Origin of the Species*
1860s		Brazilian Castro Alves writes abolitionist poems
1863	Maxwell formulates theory of electro magnetism	Charles Baudelaire, 'The Painter of Modern Life' Manet exhibits *Le Déjeuner sur l'herbe*
1865	Rebellion in Jamaica	Manet exhibits *Olympia*
1866	Nobel invents dynamite	
1867		Karl Marx, *Das Kapital*, vol. 1
1869	The opening of the Suez Canal	
1870		The Metropolitan Museum founded in New York
1872		Friedrich Nietzsche, *The Birth of Tragedy*
1874		First Impressionist Exhibition (Paris)
1875	Alexander Bell patents telephone	
1879		Henrik Ibsen, *The Doll's House*
1880	Start of the First Boer War in South Africa	Cézanne begins his series of paintings of Mont Sainte-Victoire
1882	First large-scale migration of Jews from East Europe to Palestine; occupation of Egypt	
1883	Colonisation of south-west Africa by Germany	
1884	Start of the Berlin Conference (on the colonisation of Africa by European nations)	Friedrich Nietzsche, *Thus Spake Zarathustra*

1885	Congo colonised by Belgium Formation of the Indian National Congress Parts of East Africa colonised (until 1917) by Germany	Van Gogh buys Japanese Ukiyo-e woodcuts in Antwerp
1886	Slavery abolished in the Spanish colonies	Georges Seurat finishes work on his large Pointillist canvas, *La grande Jatte* Henri Rousseau begins exhibiting in Paris Jean Moréas, first Symbolist Manifesto José Rizal, *Noli Me Tangere*
1888	First Kodak camera Slavery abolished in Brazil	Rubén Darío, *Azul*
1890		James George Frazer, *The Golden Bough*
1891		José Rizal, *El filibusterismo*
1893	Henry Ford builds his first car	
1894		Claude Debussy, *Prélude à l'après-midi d'un faune*
1895	The cinematograph invented by the Lumiere brothers X-rays discovered by Roentgen	
1896	José Rizal executed in the Philippines by the Spanish	
1897	J. J. Thomson discovers the electron The Dreyfuss Affair (France)	Stéphane Mallarmé, *Un Coup de dés*
1898	Spain cedes Puerto Rico and Cuba to the US	Joseph Conrad, *Heart of Darkness*

1899	Start of the second Boer War in South Africa The US take control of the Philippines from Spain The War of the Thousand days in Columbia West Samoa colonised by Germany	Anton Chekov, *Uncle Vanya* Arnold Schoenberg, *Verklarte Nacht*
1900	Boxer Rebellion in China Max Planck formulates quantum theory The Cook Islands annexed by New Zealand	José Enrique Rodó, 'Ariel' Sigmund Freud, *The Interpretation of Dreams*
1901	The annexation of the Asante kingdom by Britain	Picasso in Paris: start of his Blue Period (1901–4) Thomas Mann, *Buddenbrooks*
1902	Benin colonised by the French End of the Boer War in South Africa Laying of the first trans-Pacific communication line	Alfred Stieglitz co-curates the first exhibition of photography held in New York Henry James, *Wings of the Dove*
1903	First silent movie, *The Great Train Robbery* The first successful air flight by the Wright brothers The US occupies Panama	Guillaume Apollinaire, *Les Mamelles de Tirésias* Thomas Mann, *Tonio Kröger* W. E. B. du Bois, *The Souls of Black People*
1904	Roger Casement reports to the British Foreign Office on abuses in the Belgian Congo Roosevelt declares the US to be the policeman of the Caribbean Start of the Russian-Japanese War The massacre of Herero tribesmen in German south-west Africa	Anton Chekhov, *The Cherry Orchard* Henry James, *The Golden Bowl* J. M. Synge, *Riders to the Sea* performed Joseph Conrad, *Nostromo*

1905	Einstein proposes the special theory of relativity 'Swadeshi' movement in India	German Expressionist group *Die Brucke* formed in Dresden Matisse and friends described as 'les fauves' (the wild beasts) Rubén Darío, *Cantos de vida y esperanza* Sigmund Freud, *Theory of Sexuality*
1906	Muslim League established in India The first radio broadcast (from Massachusetts) The term 'suffragette' comes into use for the first time	Matisse buys a small African sculpture (from the Congo) in Paris, shows it to Picasso (the start of Primitivism in painting and sculpture)
1907	Britain's 'white' colonies are granted autonomy and dominion status Lumiere brothers manufacture commercial colour film	August Strindberg, *The Ghost Sonata* J. M. Synge, *Playboy of the Western World* Joseph Conrad, *The Secret Agent* Picasso begins to make frequent visits to the African collections at the Trocadéro (Paris) Picasso, *Les Demoiselles d'Avignon* Rainer Maria Rilke, *New Poems*
1908	Ford introduces Model-T cars	Ezra Pound, *A Lume Spento* Ford Madox Hueffer (later Ford) starts *The English Review*
1909	Plastic invented by Leo Baekeland	Braque and Picasso develop Cubism F. T. Marinetti, 'The Futurist Manifesto'
1910	Annexation of Korea by Japan (occupation lasting until 1945) Start of the Mexican revolution Union of South Africa	A. N. Whitehead and B. Russell, *Principia Mathematica*, vols 1–3 First performance of Mahler's Symphony 8 First Post-Impressionist Exhibition (London) Frank Lloyd Wright builds Robie House, Chicago Wassily Kandinsky, *Concerning the Spiritual in Art*

1911	Revolution in China The French and the Spanish divide Morocco	Joseph Conrad, *Under Western Eyes* Founding of the Blue Rider group in Munich (start of Expressionism)
1912	Stainless steel comes into use	C. G. Jung, *The Psychology of the* *Unconscious* First performance of Mahler's Symphony 9 Harriet Monroe's *Poetry* magazine begins publication Gropius creates the International Modern style in architecture Marcel Duchamp submits *Nude* *Descending a Staircase*, No. 2 to a gallery in Paris Rilke begins work on the *Duino* *Elegies* Schoenberg, *Pierrot Lunaire* The term 'expressionism' first used by a critic in *Der Sturm*
1913	Henry Ford creates the manufacturing assembly line	Armory Show, New York D. H. Lawrence, *Sons and Lovers* Ezra Pound, *A Few Don'ts by an* *Imagiste* Igor Stravinsky, *The Rite of Spring* Joseph Conrad, *Chance* Marcel Proust, *Swann's Way* Rabindranath Tagore, *Gitanjali* Sigmund Freud, *Totem and Taboo* Thomas Mann, *Death in Venice*
1914	The opening of the Panama Canal The start of World War I	*Des Imagistes* (anthology), ed. Amy Lowell Dorothy Richardson, *Pointed Roofs* Gertrude Stein, *Tender Buttons* James Joyce, *Dubliners* Robert Frost, *North of Boston* Vorticist periodical *BLAST* first published (London) W. B. Yeats, *Responsibilities*

1915	Einstein proposes the general theory of relativity	D. H. Lawrence, *The Rainbow* Ezra Pound, *Cathay* Ford Madox Ford, *The Good Soldier* Franz Kafka, *Metamorphosis* Joseph Conrad, *Victory* Virginia Woolf, *The Voyage Out*
1916	Easter Rising in Ireland Arab revolt in the Middle East	Ezra Pound, *Certain Noble Plays of Japan* Guillaume Apollinaire, *Le Poète assassiné* James Joyce, *A Portrait of the Artist as a Young Man* Le Corbusier uses reinforced concrete for building houses Vladimir Lenin, *Imperialism* Wyndham Lewis, *Tarr* serialised in *The Egoist*
1917	The Russian Revolution The Balfour Declaration promises a homeland in the Middle East for Jews Rutherford splits the atom	Edward Thomas, *Poems* First public Dada exhibition, Galerie Corray, Zürich Guillaume Apollinaire, *The Breasts of Tiresias* (first performance) Joseph Conrad, *The Shadow-Line* Sigmund Freud, *Introduction to Psychoanalysis* T. S. Eliot, *Prufrock and Other Observations*
1918	End of World War I	Oswald Spengler, *The Decline of the West*, vol. 1 Lytton Strachey, *Eminent Victorians* Tzara, first Dada Manifesto
1919	Treaty of Versailles	César Vallejo, *The Black Messengers* Ezra Pound, *Homage to Sextus Propertius* Franz Kafka, *In the Penal Colony* John Maynard Keynes, *The Economic Consequences of the Peace* Ludwig Wittgenstein, *Tractatus Logico-Philosophicus*

1920	Women get the vote in the US	Claude McKay, *Spring in New Hampshire*
		D. H. Lawrence, *Women in Love*
		Edith Wharton, *Age of Innocence*
		Ezra Pound, *Hugh Selwyn Mauberley*
		F. Scott Fitzgerald, *This Side of Paradise*
		Wilfred Owen, *Poems*
		Stravinsky collaborates with Picasso on *Pulcinella*
		T. S. Eliot, *The Sacred Wood*
1921	Civil War in Ireland	Marianne Moore, *Poems*
	Marconi makes the first radio broadcast	Luigi Pirandello, *Six Characters in Search of an Author*
1922	The League of Nations awards Britain the Mandate for Palestine and Iraq	Alban Berg completes work on opera *Wozzeck*
		Arnold Schoenberg, *Theory of Harmony*
	Partition in Ireland, and the creation of the Irish Free State	James Joyce, *Ulysses*
		Katherine Mansfield, *The Garden Party*
		Rainer Maria Rilke completes *Duino Elegies* and writes *Sonnets to Orpheus*
		T. S. Eliot, *The Waste Land*
		Virginia Woolf, *Jacob's Room*
1923	End of the Ottoman Empire in Turkey	e. e. cummings, *Tulips and Chimneys*
		Georg Lukács, *History and Class Consciousness*
		Le Corbusier, *Towards a New Architecture*
		Rainer Maria Rilke, *Duino Elegies*
		Rainer Maria Rilke, *Sonnets to Orpheus*
		T. S. Eliot, '*Ulysses*, Order and Myth'
		Virginia Woolf, 'Mr Bennett and Mrs Brown'
		Wallace Stevens, *Harmonium*

1924	Large-scale Jewish migration into Palestine	André Breton, *Surrealist Manifesto*
		E. M. Forster, *A Passage to India*
		Oswald de Andrade, *Brazilwood*
		Pablo Neruda, *Twenty Love Poems and a Song of Despair*
		Thomas Mann, *The Magic Mountain*
1925	Imperial Conference defines 'dominion' status	Alan Lock (ed.), *The New Negro*
		André Breton, The first *Surrealist Manifesto*
		André Gide, *Les Faux-Monnayeurs*
		Eugenio Montale, *Ossi di sepia*
		International Exhibition of Industrial and Modern Decorative Arts, Paris (Art Deco)
		Scott Fitzgerald, *The Great Gatsby*
		Virginia Woolf, *Mrs Dalloway*
		W. B. Yeats, *A Vision*
1926	First televisions	Ernest Hemingway, *The Sun Also Rises*
		Fritz Lang, *Metropolis*
		Gertrude Stein, 'Composition as Explanation'
		Hugh MacDiarmid, *A Drunk Man Looks at the Thistle*
		Langston Hughes, *The Weary Blues*
		Wassily Kandinsky, *Point and Line to Plane*
1927	Chiang Kai-shek becomes nominal leader of China	Laura Riding and Robert Graves, *A Survey of Modernist Poetry*
	Stalin comes to power in Russia	Marcel Proust completes *In Remembrance of Things Past*
		Martin Heidegger, *Being and Time*
		Sean O'Casey, *The Plough and the Stars*
		T. S. Eliot, *Ash Wednesday*
		Virginia Woolf, *To the Lighthouse*

1928	Colour TV comes into use	Bertolt Brecht, *The Threepenny Opera*
	Discovery of penicillin	D. H. Lawrence, *Lady Chatterley's Lover*
	Modernisation begins in Turkey	Leonard Woolf, *Imperialism and Civilisation*
	Women get the vote in the UK	Virginia Woolf, *Orlando*
		W. B. Yeats, *The Tower*
		Wyndham Lewis, *The Childermass*
1929	Stock Market Crash in the US	André Breton, The second *Surrealist Manifesto*
		Claude McKay, *Home to Harlem*
		Jean Cocteau, *Les Enfants terribles*
		William Faulkner, *The Sound and the Fury*
1930	Gandhi leads civil disobedience movement in India	Sigmund Freud, *Civilisation and its Discontents*
		Sol Plaatje, *Mhudi*
		William Faulkner, *As I Lay Dying*
1931	British Commonwealth of Nations created	Artaud attends a performance of Balinese dancers in Paris
		Edmund Wilson, *Axel's Castle*
		Eugene O'Neill, *Mourning Becomes Electra*
		Fritz Lang's feature film: *M*
		Victoria Ocampo founds the magazine *Sur* (Argentina)
		Virginia Woolf, *The Waves*
1932	James Chadwick discovers the neutron	Archibald MacLeish, *Conquistador*
		An Objectivist Anthology, ed. Louis Zukofsky
		Aldous Huxley, *Brave New World*
1933	Hitler appointed chancellor in Germany	Pablo Neruda, *Residensia en la tierra*
	Nazis denounce 'degenerate' art	Gertrude Stein, *The Autobiography of Alice B. Toklas*

1934	Mao Zedong begins the Long March	Evelyn Waugh, *A Handful of Dust* Jean Rhys, *Voyage in the Dark* *Negro: An Anthology*, ed. Nancy Cunard Samuel Beckett, *More Pricks than Kicks*
1935	First analogue and digital computers Italy invades Abyssinia John Maynard Keynes suggests New Economic Theory	Aimé Césaire first uses the term *négritude* Christopher Isherwood, *Mr Norris Changes Trains* Mulk Raj Anand, *Untouchable* (*Coolie*)
1936	Beginning of Spanish Civil War	Djuna Barnes, *Nightwood* William Faulkner, *Absalom! Absalom!*
1937	Japan invades China	David Jones, *In Parenthesis* John Steinbeck, *Of Mice and Men* Pablo Picasso, *Guernica* Wallace Stevens, *The Man with the Blue Guitar* Wyndham Lewis, *Blasting & Bombardiering* Zora Neale Hurston, *Jonah's Gourd Vine*
1938	IRA bombings in England	Antonin Artaud, *The Theatre and Its Double* Bertolt Brecht, *Mother Courage and Her Children* C. L. R. James, *The Black Jacobins* Exhibition of Surrealism, Paris Jean-Paul Satre, *Nausea* John Dos Passos, *USA* Lewis Mumford, *The Culture of Cities* Raja Rao, *Kanthapura* Samuel Beckett, *Murphy*
1939	Start of World War II	Aime Césaire, *Cahier d'un retour au pays natal* James Joyce, *Finnegans Wake*

1940	Fall of France	Richard Wright, *Native Son*
		Walter Benjamin, 'On the Concept of History'
1941	Japanese attack on Pearl Harbor	Jorge Luis Borges, *The Garden of Forking Paths*
		Virginia Woolf, *Between the Acts*
		Orson Welles, *Citizen Kane*
1942	The building of the first nuclear reactor	Albert Camus, *The Myth of Sisyphus*
		Albert Camus, *L'Étranger*
		Wallace Stevens, *Notes Toward a Supreme Fiction*
1943		Jackson Pollock's first one-man show in New York
1944		Bertolt Brecht, *The Caucasian Chalk Circle*
1945	End of World War II First nuclear device used against humans (in Hiroshima) Establishment of the UN	Léopold Sédar Senghor, *Chants d'ombre* T. S. Eliot, *The Four Quartets*
1946	Beginning of the Cold War Independence for the Philippines	W. E. B. du Bois, *The World and Africa*
1947	Independence and the partition of India and Pakistan	Albert Camus, *The Plague* Jean Genet, *The Maids* Thomas Mann, *Doktor Faustus*
1948	The National Party in South Africa adopts apartheid policy	Ezra Pound, *The Pisan Cantos*
1949	NATO is set up	Alejo Carpentier, *The Kingdom of this World* George Orwell, *Nineteen Eighty Four* Miguel Ángel Asturias, *Men of Maize* Simone de Beauvoir, *The Second Sex*

1950	Start of US–Korean War	Charles Olson, 'Projective Verse' Eugène Ionesco, *The Bald Soprano* Le Corbusier begins work on designing a new city (Chandigarh, India) Samuel Beckett, *Waiting for Godot*
1951	Independence for Libya	Albert Camus, *The Rebel* Samuel Beckett, *Molloy*
1952	First hydrogen device exploded Mau Mau uprising in Kenya	Amos Tutuola, *The Palm-Wine Drinkard* Frantz Fanon, *Black Skin, White Masks*
1953		James Balwin, *Go Tell it on the Mountain*
1954	Algerian war of independence End of war with the French in Vietnam	
1955	The Bandung Conference (Indonesia)	Aimé Césaire, *Discours sur le colonialisme* Juan Rulfo, *Pedro Páramo*
1956	Independence for Morocco and Tunisia Suez Crisis	Allen Ginsberg, *Howl* Eduard Glissant, *Soleil de la conscience* John Berryman, *Homage to Miss Bradstreet*
1957	Independence for the first black African colony: Ghana	Samuel Beckett, *Malone Dies* and *Endgame*
1958	Formation of the West Indies Federation	Chinua Achebe, *Things Fall Apart*
1959	Cuban revolution	Carlos Fuentes, *La región más transparente* Frantz Fanon, *A Dying Colonialism* Robert Lowell, *Life Studies* Wole Soyinka, *The Lion and the Jewel*
1960	Independence for the French colonies in Africa	George Lamming, *The Pleasures of Exile*

1961	The creation of the Non-Aligned Movement	Amiri Baraka, *Preface to a Twenty Volume Suicide Note* António Agostinho Neto, *Poemas* Frantz Fanon, *The Wretched of the Earth* George Lamming, *The Pleasures of Exile* V. S. Naipaul, *A House for Mr Biswas*
1962	Cuban missile crisis Independence for French Algeria Independence for Jamaica	Alejo Carpentier, *Explosion in a Cathedral* C. L. R. James, *The Black Jacobins* Carlos Fuentes, *The Death of Artemio Cruz*
1963	Independence for Kenya	Mario Vargas Llosa, *The Time of the Hero* Thomas Pynchon, *V*
1964	Nelson Mandela sentenced to life imprisonment	Christopher Okigbo, *Lament of the Masks* Ngugi wa Thiong'o, *Weep Not, Child* Wole Soyinka, *The Interpreters*
1965	Independence for Rhodesia Singapore declares independence	K. Nkrumah, *Neo-Colonialism*
1966	Independence for Barbados, Botswana, Guyana, Lesotho	Amilcar Cabral, *The Weapon of Theory* Jean Rhys, *Wide Sargasso Sea* Mario Vargas Llosa, *The Green House*
1967	Che Guevara executed in Bolivia Civil war in Nigeria Six-day war in the Middle East	Aimé Césaire, *A Season in the Congo* Gabriel Garcia Márquez, *One Thousand Years of Solitude* Kamau Brathwaite, *Rites of Passage* Ngugi wa Thiong'o, *A Grain of Wheat*
1968	Invasion of Czechoslovakia	Jack Kerouac, *The Dharma Bums*

1969	First man on the moon	Mario Vargas Llosa, *Conversation*
	Woodstock music festival	*in the Cathedral*
1971	'Coloured' peoples	Kofi Awonoor, *This Earth, My*
	forced into 'homelands'	*Brother*
	in South Africa	Roberto Fernández Retamar,
	Idi Amin comes to power	'Caliban'
	in Uganda	
1972	Marcos declares martial	
	law in the Philippines	
1973	Britain joins the ECC	Ayi Kwei Armah, *Two Thousand*
		Seasons
1975	End of the Vietnam War	Chinua Achebe, 'An Image of
	Independence for	Africa: Racism in Conrad's *Heart of*
	Angola, Mozambique,	*Darkness*'
	Cape Verde	G. Deleuze and F. Guattari, *Kafka:*
		Towards a Minor Literature
1976	Riots in Soweto	Cheikh Anta Diop, *The African*
	township in South Africa	*Origin of Civilisation*
1977	Military coup in Pakistan	Elaine Showalter, *A Literature of*
		Their Own
1978	Martial law in Iran	Edward Said, *Orientalism*
1979	Ayatollah Khomeini	Ayi Kwei Armah, *The Healers*
	takes over in Iran	Kamau Brathwaite, *History of the*
	The Soviets invade	*Voice*
	Afghanistan	
1980	Independence for	
	Zimbabwe	
	Start of Iran–Iraq war	
1981	AIDS identified	Edouard Glissant, *Le Discours*
	Personal Computers	*antillais*
	introduced by IBM	Salman Rushdie, *Midnight's*
		Children
1982	Falkland Islands invaded	Isabel Allende, *The House of the*
	by Argentina	*Spirits*
1983		Benedict Anderson, *Imagined*
		Communities
1986	Chernobyl nuclear	
	accident	
	Marcos overthrown in	
	the Philippines	

1988	'Fatwa' against Salman Rushdie	Salman Rushdie, *Satanic Verses*
1989	End of Pinochet's dictatorship in Chile The Berlin Wall dismantled Tiananmen Square massacre	Bill Ashcroft, Gareth Griffiths, Helen Tiffin, *The Empire Writes Back*
1990		Derek Walcott, *Omeros*
1991	Collapse of the Soviet Union Operation Desert Storm South Africa repeals apartheid laws	
1993	Terrorist attack on World Trade Center	Edward Said, *Culture and Imperialism*
1996	'Truth and Reconciliation Commission' set up in South Africa	
1997	Hong Kong returned to China by Britain	

Outline

It takes a heroic constitution to live modernism.

Walter Benjamin

In this book, I have tried to provide a revisionary account of modernist writing informed by insights derived from postcolonial studies. The undertaking is premised on the belief that 'modern' is not read often enough in conjunction with 'colonial', though each has long been implicated in the characteristic preoccupations and repressions of the other. Depending on the authors and texts we select, the two notions can prove highly interactive, reminding us that we live in a contemporary world riddled with difference and asymmetry, dominated equally by a will to power and a will to change.

There are several ways of defining key terms. I have chosen to follow the historian and political essayist Perry Anderson, for whom 'modernity' is 'neither economic process nor cultural vision but the historical experience mediating the one to the other' (1984: 97). From this it follows that 'modernisation' identifies the process that transforms individuals, communities and nations through interaction with evolving technologies, and 'modernism' describes a set of tendencies, practices and beliefs specific to literature and the creative arts.

The transformations in outlook and circumstance associated with modernity became international in asynchronous fashion. Their narrative is woven tightly into the fabric of colonialism and neo-colonialism, with modernist creativity as the thread that works with and against the weave. In the aftermath of modern imperialism, which is also the era of new nationalisms, uneven economic development, rapid urbanisation, religious and racial violence, and the impact of new technologies and media, 'modern' has shaded off into an assortment of 'postmodern' predicaments and strategies.

A postcolonial perspective can muster evidence for the argument that wherever modernist strategies were adapted and modified under the pressure of the turbulent and volatile realities of colonies struggling to stabilise as new nations, each striving for a modernity of its own, this afterlife produced some of the most compelling writing and art of the twentieth century. Such developments make it possible to argue that modernist writing is better read in a broadly transnational rather than a narrowly European or Western context.

The task is inflected by two recent developments. An old assumption that each of the terms derived from 'modern' had a globally uniform application has come under question. It is now more common to hear of modernisms rather than modernism. Modernity too is now addressed as alternative and plural rather than singular. As remarked by the Mexican writer Carlos Fuentes, 'the clocks of all men and women, of all civilisations, are not set at the same hour' (1988: 199). It is now commonplace to recognise that there might be as many paths to modernisation as there are social formations. Progress or failure on any of these paths depends more on the political, economic, religious, ethnic, technological and cultural contingencies of a given time and place than on the logic of a singular template that equates modernisation with 'progress'. Such recognitions help us focus on all manifestations of the 'modern' as culture-specific phenomena.

The earliest instances when the terms 'modernity', modernisation' and 'modernism' came into use are by now easy to identify. The changes in societies and cultures as well as perceptions and attitudes to which they allude had been under way for some time before they were recognised under those names. Even today, the exact sense of each term remains open to debate. When did 'modernity' begin? Are we still part of the 'modern age'? The answers depend on who is included in that 'we', and on what 'we' expect from the answers. Likewise, the matter of endings is open to debate. Is 'modernity' a project still ongoing? Is 'modernism' over and done with?

Other questions ensue. How do we accommodate the bewildering variety of associations conjured up by a host of 'postmodern' nominations into any account of 'modern', 'modernity' and 'modernism'? How do the connotations discovered in 'postmodern' connect to those covered by 'postcolonial'? In each case, there is no simple answer. My own argument presents the relation of 'modern' to 'colonial' as a tangle of complicity, ambivalence and resistance. I agree with Jed Esty that any claim to 'an ideological chasm between modernism and colonialism' is as implausible as any claim of 'direct ideological correspondence' (2007: 70).

The book comprises three chapters, each consisting of three sections. Chapter 1 provides an account of 'becoming modern' in the context of imperialism and postcolonial studies. Conventionally, it is said that modernism was constituted through an aesthetic break with preceding European traditions. The first chapter outlines the argument that this account needs supplementing by awareness of the transformation of European (or Western) sensibilities through the influence of colonialism on attitudes to other cultures, identity, race, sexuality and ideas concerning the exotic and the primitive. These transformations involved the appropriation of motifs from non-Western civilisations by modernist writing and art, and such motifs were brought within the purview of the modernist by the colonial.

In Chapter 2, a set of debates highlights significant aspects of the interrelations between modernity, modernism and colonialism. The first section covers disagreements within the intellectual Left, which contribute to an understanding of the antithetical relation between realism and modernism. The second addresses the seeming paradox that a number of Anglophone modernists, including W. B. Yeats (1865–1939), Ezra Pound (1885–1972) and T. S. Eliot (1888–1965), were progressive in their aesthetics but reactionary in their politics. The third examines the question of whether modernist writing is complicit in, or resistant to, racism. This debate allows us to place the anti-Semitism of Eliot and Pound in the broader context of racial prejudice as a frequent though incidental concomitant to colonialism, while also recognising that modernist texts generally betray mixed feelings about imperialism as well as social modernity.

Chapter 3 aims to demonstrate a number of vital connections between modernist and postcolonial writing. In the first section, Virginia Woolf (1882–1941) and Jean Rhys (1890–1979) are read together in the context of a discourse concerning gender and sexuality. In the second, the use of allegorical modes by Franz Kafka (1883–1924) is treated as a precedent to the postcolonial writers' search for alternative modes of narration to realism and naturalism. Nick Joaquin (1917–2004) from the Philippines and Arun Kolatkar (1932–2004) from India are discussed together in the final section to show the complex elements that tie modernity in the former colonies to the problem of faith amidst 'modern' predicaments.

I hope that the cumulative effect of the debates and case studies presented in this book enables fresh insights into the strategies and problems of modernist literature, and provides grounds for a more informed assessment of its relevance to our own times and places. In showing how certain features of modernist practice acquire special significance from a postcolonial perspective, the aim is to bridge the two discourses. However, not every modernist writer is equally apt to the demonstration of a significant interaction between 'colonial' and 'modern'. Therefore, the book is selective in what it highlights from authors, texts and topics. For reasons of space, references to modernism in the arts are few, and allusions to modernist writing in languages other than English are largely confined to Kafka (and Kolatkar) in translation. Likewise, though modern drama is no less significant than modernist fiction or modernist poetry, there are fewer references in this book to dramatists. There is no such thing as a definitive account of modernist practices; there is only the need to rethink the issues raised by modernist writers and artists as they apply to our own times and places, wherever and whenever that might be, in a world that has been concurrently and unevenly 'colonial' and 'modern' for the last several hundred years.

For Nikish and Meghan

and in memory of

Laxmibai Ghugle and Parvatibai Patke

Chapter 1

Introductory Survey

Becoming 'Modern'

> What we have in common is *the irruption into modernity*.
>
> Edouard Glissant

Baudelaire and the modern city

It is often said that we live in a modern world, or that we seek to become modern. How did this manner of thinking come about? For an answer, we turn not to a dictionary but to mid-nineteenth century Paris. There we encounter the primary source for the use of 'modern' among authors and artists, Charles Baudelaire (1821–67).[1] In his essay 'The Painter of Modern Life' (1863), we are introduced to Constantin Guys, who becomes the symbolic protagonist in an allegory concerning the role of art in relation to its times. This artist loves incognitos and crowds. He hardly ever moves in intellectual or political circles. The 'mainspring of his genius is *curiosity*' (Baudelaire 1995: 7). His modesty is 'touched with aristocratic reserve' (8–9), and he would qualify as a dandy except that he lacks detachment. Instead, he shows 'an insatiable passion' for 'seeing and feeling' (9). He confesses to an excessive love of being in 'the ebb and flow of movement, in the midst of the fugitive and the infinite' (9). As an urban solitary, he is the augury of much that is to follow in the writing and art of the ensuing century, because he brings out what is latent in the experience of feeling alone in crowds and cities.

Baudelaire gives us the artist as an epicure of the senses who cherishes the mutability of experience. This 'solitary gifted with an active imagination' is 'looking for that quality which you must allow me to call "modernity" [. . .] He makes it his business to extract from fashion whatever element it may contain of poetry within history, to distil the eternal from the transitory' (12). Baudelaire articulates a paradox: the artist captures the moment for eternity. That brings him to one of the decisive crystallisations of the idea of modernity for art: 'By "modernity" [*modernité*] I mean the ephemeral, the fugitive, the contingent, the half of art whose other half is the eternal and the immutable' (13). This idea recurs in subsequent writers. W. B. Yeats, for example, in 'Sailing to Byzantium' (1928), prays to be gathered 'Into the artifice of eternity' (Yeats 1997: 197).

Baudelaire's exalted tone half conceals and half reveals the recognition that the experience of reality in European cities has become fugitive, fragmented and anxious. In the 1930s, the cultural critic Walter Benjamin (1892–1940) analysed Baudelaire's preoccupation with the artist, anonymous among crowds, as part of the need for people 'to adapt themselves to a new and rather strange situation, one that is peculiar to big cities [. . .] the obliteration of the individual's traces in the big-city crowd' (Benjamin 1973: 37, 43). The 'modern' intuited by Baudelaire had presentiments of more than what he could be expected to have realised. A 'modern' that began in Europe soon showed a potential for growth and intensification that would eventually encompass all aspects of life, all over the world, bringing with it the impulse to render difference exotic. What has this quintessential European modernist to do with colonialism?

As a young man, Baudelaire was sent by his parents to India. He broke off his sea voyage and returned to France after a short and involuntary delay on the islands of Mauritius and Réunion. The trip led to a clutch of poems, including 'Le Cygne' (The Swan) and 'La Belle Dorothée'. They show that his sympathies remained embedded in an old European habit of binary thinking which represented the colonised 'native' as the antithesis to modern European civilisation. The quintessential European progenitor of modernism may have derived his critique of modernity from his formative experiences in the colonies, but he did not quite manage to shed the assumptions of his culture (cf. Lionnet 2008).

When did we become 'modern'?

Nevertheless, with Baudelaire beside us, we can attend to the nuances of 'modern' on which all notions of modernity and modernism depend, which in their turn determine what is included in the idea of modernist writing. The word had a modest origin in the sixth century AD as a derivative of the Latin *modernus* (the moment of the 'now'), a sense it continues to retain amidst the accretions of later centuries. It has since become a polar element in a variety of antitheses. From the Middle Ages to the Renaissance, 'modern' has served as the opposite of pre-modern, ancient, classical, pagan, or medieval, and since the seventeenth century, of anything that is thought antiquated and outmoded. Since then, it has also served as an antithesis to the primitive, the undeveloped and the under-developed.[2]

We can distinguish between three current uses of 'modern'. The first refers to society (in terms of its characteristic milieu), the second to cultural production, as in writing and the arts (in terms of shared attributes), and the third to the 'contemporary' element in experience (an equation between 'modern' and 'new'). A loose synonymy between 'modern', 'new' and 'contemporary' might seem a simple way of separating a 'now' from its past.[3] But the association is not as straightforward as it seems. The American poet Ezra Pound gave the implied congruence between 'modern' and 'new' a sense of excitement and urgency in his book of essays, *Make it New* (1934). By 1960, however, the British poet D. J. Enright could make the opposite claim, that 'To be contemporary now, whatever it may be positively, is pretty obviously *not* to be modernist' (Enright 1960: 8).

Any simple equation of 'contemporary' and 'modern' remains unsatisfactory: everything contemporary is not necessarily new; and everything new is not necessarily significant. The British critic Frank Kermode remarked that while 'The New is to be judged by the criterion of novelty, the Modern implies or at any rate permits a serious relationship with a past, a relationship that requires criticism and indeed radical re-imagining' (Kermode 1990: 65). The potential for confusion in how we use 'modern' is compounded by the fact that it has proved capable of contrary references. On the one hand, as noted by the British Marxist critic Raymond Williams, the word attributes a kind of 'perpetual present tense for experimental writing' (Williams 1989: 38).[4] On the other hand, 'modern' is also used to mark the onset of an epoch, and thus provides the name for a new historical period.[5]

'Modern' marks time in relative rather than absolute terms, as a mode of contrast and differentiation. Fredric Jameson, for instance, describes the use of 'modern' to represent both a radical break with the past and a sense of constituting a distinctive period as 'a dialectic of the break and the period' (Jameson 2002: 23). This is a process in which 'the seamless passage from past to present, slowly turns into a consciousness of a radical break; while at the same time the enforced attention to a break gradually turns the latter into a period in its own right' (24).

If scope is an issue, so is field of application. The dates proposed for the beginning of the 'modern' age vary, depending on the field. The German philosopher G. W. F. Hegel (1770–1831) picked 1500 'because of three events: the discovery of the New World, the Renaissance, and the Reformation' (Cascardi 1992: 26). By the time we reach Jameson, the candidates for an inaugural date for the modern age have become more numerous. He lists as many as fourteen alternatives for the possible inauguration of the 'modern' in Europe and the West. In chronological order they are as follows: (1) The 'discovery' of the New World, and the subsequent conquest of the Americas; (2) The Protestant Reformation; (3) Galileo and the birth of the new sciences; (4) Descartes and the self-reflexive split of subject from object; (5) the Enlightenment; (6) the Industrial Revolution; (7) The French Revolution; (8) Adam Smith and the emergence of capitalism; (9) nineteenth-century historicism; (10) Nietzsche and his notion of 'the death of God'; (11) Max Weber and his rationalisation of the monopoly stage of industrial capitalism and new bureaucratic processes; (12) aesthetic modernism; (13) the Soviet revolution of 1917; and (14) the postmodern turn of the 1960s (Jameson 2002: 31–2). Such a huge plurality confirms the sense that the epochal function of the term determines the date we choose to recognise as the beginning of the 'modern' age.

Modernism and progress

During the European Enlightenment, and as part of the consolidation of the industrial revolution in Europe, 'modern' and 'modernity' became closely associated with various ideas of progress. These included new ways of narrating historical process, increasing secularism, the application of science and technology to the harnessing of nature for human benefit, urbanism, industrialisation, transformations in the notions of the rights and freedom owed to 'ordinary life', transformations in the processes of administrative and bureaucratic governance, and an intellectual commitment to building a body of knowledge about nature and human institutions along lines of rational inquiry.

Many contemporary disciplines now use the term 'early modern' to refer to the period from the fifteenth century to the end of the eighteenth century. The term 'late modern' then comes in to refer either to the nineteenth and twentieth centuries as a whole, or to the period after World War II, when many of the practices and institutions concerning international trade, finance, as well as the role of media and digital technology, became established as defining features of the global contemporary. The

European idea of modernity developed in several, not always compat-ible, directions. The British academic Peter Osborne suggests 'three distinct but connected approaches' to the idea: 'modernity as a *category of historical periodisation*, a *quality of social experience*, and an (incom-plete) *project*' (Osborne 1992: 23). The first represents the approach of the historian of ideas, the second the approach of the social scientist, and the third the approach associated with those, like the German soci-ologist and philosopher Jürgen Habermas (b. 1929), who believe that modernity was a process of social emancipation and transformation. Habermas has argued consistently over the years that its logic remains viable, though its implementation fell short of the ideal. He also believes that we need to resuscitate the ideal for our times. The process went astray after the French Revolution, and humanity needs to re-establish a utopian vision of the future through the use of what he calls commu-nicative rationality, which he believes will safeguard humanity against pessimism, cynicism, or postmodernist ennui.

A debate from the 1980s between Perry Anderson and the American academic Marshall Berman provides two rival accounts of how moder-nity and modernisation might relate to modernism. Anderson criticised Berman's book *All That is Solid Melts in the Air: The Experience of Modernity* (1982) for its view of the allegedly unlimited potential for self-development in modernity. Instead, he invoked a Marxian concep-tion of human nature, which stressed the role played by the 'onrush of capitalist economic development' in contributing to the creation of 'a brutally alienated and atomised society, riven by callous economic exploitation and cold social indifference, destructive of every cultural or political value whose potential it has itself brought into being' (Anderson 1984: 98).

Berman rejected what he regarded as Anderson's excessive pessimism, and reiterated his belief that 'To be modern [. . .] is to experience per-sonal and social life as a maelstrom, to find one's world in perpetual disintegration and renewal, trouble and anguish, ambiguity and con-tradiction: to be part of a universe in which all that is solid melts into air. To be a moder*nist* is to make oneself somehow at home in this maelstrom' (Berman 1984: 114). The debate illustrates the difference between those who treat modernists as either at-home or ill-at-ease with social, technological and economic modernity. The debate does not show a sense of detailed engagement with the global expansion of modernity, and the implications of colonial histories for the idea of the modern. Nevertheless, Anderson's critique underlines 'the gigantic objective transformations of society unleashed by the advent of the capitalist world market' allied to 'the momentous transformations of individual life and personality which occur under the impact' of capitalism (Anderson 1984: 98).

'Modern' in the European seventeenth century

Various conceptions of what 'modern' might signify keep occurring frequently over a large span of European history, from the end of the Middle Ages to the latter half of the twentieth century. The period of the European Renaissance came to be seen, in retrospect, as the inauguration of an early modern period. Some commentators regard this period as characterised by the development of the idea of a transcendent individual or human essence. In the seventeenth century, several writers from France and England distinguished their era as the age of the 'Moderns', and claimed that the merits of their contemporaries compared favourably with those of the 'Ancients'. Their act of self-nomination helped consolidate the sense of change they wished to foreground. The positive values they attached to being modern transformed it from a term of temporal differentiation to a term enlisted in cultural polemics.

The polemics began in France in 1687, and soon spread to England in what became known as the 'Quarrel between the Ancients and the Moderns'. The specifically English component of that 'Quarrel' became known, after the English satirist Jonathan Swift (1667–1747) wrote about it, as 'The Battle of the Books'. The self-appointed advocates for the Moderns set themselves in opposition to the Ancients, while the defenders of the Ancients scoffed at the presumption underlying the contemporary challenge to authority and tradition. The Moderns laid claim to 'Progress'. Their idea of progress turned its back on the classical and pagan European past, and they celebrated their own sense of modernity. The debate continued to retain its topicality for the twentieth century. This is shown in Ezra Pound's translation of a dozen of the thirty-six *Nouveaux Dialogues des mortes* (1683) by Bernard le Bouyer de Fontenelle (1657–1757). Pound's translations were published during 1916–17 in the periodical *Egoist*, and developed a dialogue of his own invention, 'An Anachronism at Chinon' (1917). In this dialogue, a fictional version of the French novelist François Rabelais (1494–1553) converses with an American student (modelled after Pound). The critic Robert Longenbach remarks that the dialogue leaves 'Rabelais's and Pound's claims for the superiority of each other's centuries balanced in counterpoint' (Longenbach 1988: 195).

'Modern' in the European eighteenth and nineteenth centuries

In the eighteenth century, the new value attached to 'modern' was taken up by a small number of *philosophes* (public intellectuals) in France, Scotland and England, followed later by Germany and other parts of Europe. By the mid-eighteenth century, it had become a loose confederation of like-minded ideas and attitudes. By the late 1780s (that is, by the time of the French Revolution and the rise of Romanticism), a large part of the initial optimism and utopianism surrounding this idea of modernity had been subverted. However, in a major work titled *An Inquiry into the Nature and Causes of the Wealth of Nations* (1776), the Scottish social philosopher Adam Smith (1723–90) described contemporaneous economic transformations in such a way as to ensure that ideas of progress remained focused on the socio-economic dimension of capitalist modernity. The European colonies had a major role to play in these transformations, both as sources of raw materials, and as markets supporting the economic expansion of Europe. Book IV of Smith's work analyses at length the economic advantages of possessing colonies.

The commodity as an object of luxury consumption came into its own during this period, especially as an import from the colonies. In *Eighteenth Century British Literature and Postcolonial Studies*, Suvir Kaul notes that 'the consumption of imported goods, and the social changes that were seen to follow from their increased circulation, allows us to think about the ways in which people experienced the overlapping energies of capitalist and colonialist expansion' (Kaul 2009: 86). At the same time, the fundamentally exploitative nature of colonialism did not go unnoticed, at least as far as the more discerning and conscientious intellectuals were concerned. A sense of expansionist hubris could combine with awareness of injustice. This is evident in a work by the Marquis de Condorcet (1743–94). In *Sketch for a Historical Picture of the Human Mind* (1793–4), he asks rhetorically:

> Can we doubt that either common sense or the senseless discords of European nations will add to the effects of the slow but inexorable progress of their colonies, and will soon bring about the independence of the New World? And then will not the European population in these colonies, spreading rapidly over that enormous land, either civilise or peacefully remove the savage nations who still inhabit vast tracts of its land? (Kramnick 1995: 28)

We have only to remove the inconsequentially lame 'peacefully' to get a blueprint, not only for the colonisation-modernisation of the Americas, but also of Australia and New Zealand. Yet, in the very next paragraph, the author went on to sketch the most clear and concise case for the logic of eventual decolonisation:

> Survey the history of our settlements and commercial undertakings in Africa or in Asia, and you will see how our trade monopolies, our treachery, our murderous contempt for men of another colour or creed, the insolence of our usurpation, the intrigues or the exaggerated proselytic zeal of our priests, have destroyed the respect and goodwill that the superiority of our knowledge and the benefits of our commerce at first won for us in the eyes of the inhabitants. (Kramnick 1995: 28)

The idea of progress promised by reason as applicable to the field of science was attractive and timely for an age mindful of the larger significance of recent achievements by Descartes in mathematics and philosophy, Locke in several types of philosophical reasoning, and Newton in physics and astronomy. Behind these luminaries, there was the cumulative scientific progress represented by the work of Galileo Galilei, Robert Boyle, Nicolaus Copernicus, Lord Bacon, Johannes Kepler and William Harvey, to mention the most obvious European innovators in their respective fields of inquiry. How this led to a utopian conception of progress can be sampled from a letter dated 8 February 1780 by the American scientist and statesman, Benjamin Franklin (1706–90), to his friend and fellow-scientist, Joseph Priestley. Franklin writes in a context in which the liberal, secular and rational dimension of the Enlightenment, as fed by scientific progress, had an enormous influence on some of the leading thinkers in North America, just as the founding of the American nation, in its turn, lent support to the cause of Enlightenment and the French Revolution:

> The rapid progress true Science now makes, occasions my regretting sometimes that I was born too soon [. . .] O that moral science were in as fair a way of improvement, that men would cease to be wolves to one another, and that human beings would at length learn what they now improperly call humanity! (Kramnick 1995: 74)

Precisely what Franklin feared came about in the French Revolution of 1789. The optimism nourished by eighteenth-century intellectuals about the benefits of systematic rationality did not survive. As modernity took on the savage aspect of violence, war and Napoleonic dictatorship, the idea of progress receded into the distance. The composer Beethoven removed the dedication he had intended to Napoleon in the score of his Third Symphony, which became, instead, *The Eroica*.

For Europe in the nineteenth century, modernity entailed the transformation of living conditions and attitudes to experience by three major forces: the industrial revolution, capitalism and colonial expansion. The analysis of society from the perspective of political economy acquired a new and powerful new exponent in Karl Marx (1818–83). We are indebted to Marx, and his collaboration with Engels, for many of the insights and approaches that continue to address the consequences of industrial capitalism and colonialism on society and individual life. These include the emphasis on the material bases for consciousness and society; the dynamics of class struggle; the distinction between use-value and exchange-value; the exploitative and alienating aspects of industrialism and colonialism; the utopian drive towards a rational distribution of economic productivity; the hallucinatory quality to life produced under capitalism; the deluding aspect of ideological deformations of social perception; the damaging effects of reification on individual and collective life; and the dominance of commodity fetishism in industrialised societies. Such insights continue to inform contemporary modes of social and cultural analysis, regardless of the fate suffered by communism in the late twentieth century.

In the work of later nineteenth-century intellectuals, scepticism acquired an intensive and analytic quality, leading to the outright rejection of rational utopianism by those who responded to the influence of the philosopher Friedrich Nietzsche (1844–1900). In the pioneering sociological work of Max Weber (1864–1920), it led to a sombre recognition of the effects of industrial capitalism at the levels of work psychology, the rationalisation of economic productivity, and the growth of new bureaucratic processes. It also gave Weber impetus to argue for a necessary 'connection of the spirit of modern economic life with the rational ethics of ascetic Protestantism' (Weber 1958b: 27).

Not everyone agrees with Weber's explanatory model, nevertheless, his arguments are helpful in relating issues of economic development and attitudes to work to their cultural matrix in religion. When we make those connections, we recognise that (1) the specific kind of modernity which arose in Europe spread globally, not by virtue of its use of reason as a transcendental faculty but through its purposive, instrumental and exploitative use in capitalism, industrialisation and colonialism; (2) the attempt to adopt the European template in other parts of the world proved slow and problematic, except in North America, because it went against the grain of the entrenched belief systems of the other major world religions.[6] It is also crucial to add that 'in Weber's account, the triumph of reason culminates not in the establishment of the kind of rational utopia imagined by the Enlightenment philosophers but in the forging of an "iron cage" of economic compulsion and bureaucratic control' (Gaonkar 2001: 8).

'Modern' in the twentieth century

In 1784, a German periodical invited leading thinkers of the time to address the question 'What is Enlightenment?' The distinguished German philosopher Immanuel Kant (1724–1804) answered the question with a rallying call for his times: '*Sapere Aude*! (dare to know) "Have courage to use your own understanding!" – that is the motto of enlightenment' (Kant 1996: 58). His call, and its underlying reasoning, has continued to evoke discussion and debate to this day. One of the most influential reflections on the Kantian question came from the French philosopher Michel Foucault (1926–84). In 'What is Critique?' (1978), he describes the inauguration of the Enlightenment as a type of rationalisation that would eventually characterise all 'social relations, state organisations, economic practices, and perhaps even the behaviour of individuals' (Foucault 1996: 390). For Foucault, the significance of the eighteenth-century apotheosis of reason could not be stressed enough because it represented:

> a moment in the formation of modern humanity [. . .] a period without a fixed date, with multiple entries because one can define it just as well by the formation of capitalism, the constitution of the bourgeois world, the establishment of the state system, the foundation of modern science with all its correlative techniques, the organisation of an opposition between the art of being governed and that of not being governed in such a manner. (1996: 392)

In a later essay on the same topic, 'What is Enlightenment?' (1984), Foucault underlined the continuity of concerns between the eighteenth and the twentieth century: 'modern' Europe is 'historically determined, to a certain extent, by the Enlightenment' (43), compelled towards the same kind of philosophical interrogation as the eighteenth century, 'that simultaneously problematises [. . .] man's historical mode of being, and the constitution of the self as an autonomous subject' (42).

This condensed account of the European history of the idea of modernity shows four overarching trends in the shift from medieval to modern. First, the progressive secularisation of society. Second, a progressive challenge to hierarchic modes of social organisation. That is, it shows awareness that equality and freedom are rights that should not be denied to any man – though woman, child, slave, or other races lagged behind in gaining the same rights – by tradition, prejudice, law, or the powers vested in a ruler or a state. Third, an increase in the growth in knowledge about the material world (through the development of the natural sciences), which had the capacity to affect all aspects of life.

The diminished hold of religion over all walks of life, the growth of individualism, and the rise of science and technology are the three main trends. To them one must add a fourth in order to complete the differentiation of modern from medieval: the gradual and thoroughly unequal transformation of the world, especially at the level of economics, and at the level of the psychology of self-perception (in individuals as well as in collectivities), because of the experience of European colonialism. The first three features are distinct from the fourth: their emphasis on human betterment remained at odds with the exploitative logic of colonialism. Modernity à la Europe became a problematic category of social transformation because of a stark contradiction. The very processes by which Europe laid claim to modernity were accompanied by the acquisition and governance of colonies in a manner that denied the colonised proper access to the same model of modernity.

Perhaps the most useful contemporary approach to the use of modernity as a period concept is that proposed by the Canadian philosopher Charles Taylor (b. 1948). He suggests that we ought to distinguish between two types of 'modernity' theory. He describes one kind as 'acultural' theories. These are the more common and dominant variety. They treat modernity as a unitary idea with a uniformly global application. He describes the second type as 'cultural' theories of modernity. He supports this type as the better explanatory model. It distinguishes the approach to modernity adopted by one society or culture from that of another. He explains that 'a "cultural" theory of modernity is one that characterises the transformations that have issued in the modern West mainly in terms of the rise of a new culture [. . .] By contrast, an "acultural" theory is one that describes these transformations in terms of some culture-neutral operation' (Taylor 1995: 24). To support cultural theories implies that ideas of modernism are 'translated' to non-Western cultures. There, as noted by Peter Osborne, they undergo a change of reference and 'enrichments of sense' consequent upon their association 'with a radically extended range of forms of cultural experience of temporal difference' (Osborne 2000: 61).

The European 'modern' and colonial history

The many associations of the word 'modern' were at first confined to Europe. However, as European exploration and trade expanded, the associations of 'modern' too expanded to include meanings beyond Europe. As exploration and trade originating from Europe became international and then global in scale, this family of notions took to the seas, and spread far and wide, its European origins either disguised, or open to emulation. That is how the progression of the 'modern' family gets intertwined with a development that was already under way: colonisation. Exploration, trade, overseas conquests and overseas settlements brought home to European nations a sense of the advantages they possessed over the many peoples they encountered. These advantages represented two kinds of modernity: specific technologies (especially those concerning navigation and armaments) and specific dispositions (organisational, mercantile, industrial and capitalist). Both types of modernity were geared to the accumulation of material and psychic benefits: territory, wealth and the self-aggrandisement that went with both. Modernity was thus an enabler of colonial profiteering, and of territorial annexation, settlement and control. The process started with the Portuguese and the Spanish after the arrival of Christopher Columbus at the Bahamas in 1492. Portugal and Spain acquired vast territories in the Americas, while the Portuguese also went round the Cape of Good Hope to explore and trade in Asia, and the Spanish went round the tip of South America to colonise the Philippines. The two nations were soon followed in both directions by the other sea-faring nations of Europe. The most successful were the Dutch, the British, the French, the Belgians and the Italians; the least successful were the northern nations of Scandinavia and Germany.

Since both 'colonialism' and 'imperialism' refer to empires, using either term to encompass a diversity of practices, policies, experiences and histories entails an inevitable degree of simplification. One way of avoiding confusion in the use of the two terms is to follow Edward Said, who in *Culture and Imperialism* (1993) uses 'imperialism' to cover 'the practice, theory, and the attitudes of a dominating metropolitan centre ruling over a distant territory', and 'colonialism' to refer, more narrowly, to 'the implanting of settlements on distant territory' (8). As noted by the British historian Steven Howe, '"imperialism" has undergone a sharp decline in popularity, while "colonialism" has zoomed up the citation charts' (Howe 2002: 25). Though the two terms seem almost interchangeable, they have had very different histories. The American anthropologist Nicholas Dirks notes that 'imperialism' is often used to 'focus on the economic, and specifically capitalist, character of colonial rule', while the term 'colonialism' 'has sometimes been reserved for cases of settler colonialism' (Bennett et al. 2005: 42). The term 'imperialism' became current after the late 1850s (*OED*), though its Roman ancestry in the idea of the *imperium* is ancient. Its contemporary capacity to speak of the 'new global form of sovereignty' created by 'a series of national and supranational organisms' (Hardt and Negri 2000: xii) shows that the term has renewed its relevance for our times, even if the type of colonialism practised by Europe and the US before World War II have long since lost their political and moral viability.

The British historian J. A. Hobson (1902), and the leader of the Marxist revolution in Russia, V. Lenin (1917), gave the term 'imperialism' prominence with reference to the ideology and economic drive underlying European expansionism of the nineteenth century. The authors of *The Empire Writes Back* draw attention to the mixed motives at work in the creation and sustenance of the modern European empires through the British explorer David Livingston's phrase 'Christianity, Commerce, Civilisation' (Ashcroft et al. 1998: 127). They remind us that 'colonialism, far from disappearing as the [twentieth] century goes on, too often merely modified and developed into the neo-colonialism of the post-independence period' (1998: 51). The term 'neo-colonialism' acquired currency from *Neo-Colonialism: The Last Stage of Imperialism* (1965) by the Nigerian political leader Kwame Nkrumah (1909–72). The term refers to 'all forms of control of the ex-colonies' by the advanced capitalist nation-states of the contemporary world through 'international monetary bodies, through the fixing of prices on world markets, multinational corporations (controlled from the U.S. or Europe) and cartels and a variety of educational and cultural institutions' (Ashcroft et al. 1998: 162–3).

Decolonisation

Our survey of the European and colonial refractions of modernity brings us to the era of global decolonisation and the topics that will be covered in the next section, to which the following is meant to provide a bridge. While North America, parts of South America, South Africa, Australia and New Zealand became settler colonies, the ecologically dense, tropical and equatorial colonies of Europe remained possessions prized, not for settlement, but for the economic profit to be extracted from them. Modern European colonialism lasted until the early decades of the nineteenth century in South America; the European empires on other continents and islands lasted longer, and crumbled after World War II. European imperialism ran parallel to but only partially congruent with the history of modernity. It contributed directly to the development of European modernity, from the early seventeenth century to the end of modern colonialism in the twentieth century. Imperialism was morally untenable, and sustained through sheer – or mere – force. Decisive change occurred on a global scale with decolonisation and independence. Such change was accomplished either through violent or passive resistance. This were generally preceded and enabled by the gradual corrosion of the claim associated with Rudyard Kipling's notion from 1899 that colonising others was 'The White Man's Burden' (Kipling 1982: 602–3).

The narrative of global decolonisation comprises a long series. It starts with the American declaration of independence in 1776, followed by independence for the colonies of Catholic Europe in Latin and Central America during the early nineteenth century, then by gradual autonomy for the settler colonies: Canada, 1867; Australia, 1901; New Zealand, 1907; South Africa, 1910; and the Irish Free State, 1921. This process was followed, more belatedly, by independence for the non-settler colonies of the Protestant European nations, and independence for the Philippines from American control in the decades following World War II. The series comes to a kind of close with the return of Hong Kong to mainland China in 1997, although if we look towards Northern Ireland, the first overseas territory colonised by England remains its last colony.

The nominal end of modern colonialism was followed by self-rule for former colonies as newly autonomous nation-states. It did not necessarily bring an end to the dominative-dependency axis set in place by colonialism. In the era of new nationhood, the claim to universal applicability that had been enjoyed for so long by the 'modern' family began to wear down. By the end of the twentieth century, it had become as common for the idea of 'modernity' in the Western mode to be met with searching questions, reformulations, resistance and downright rejection. For example, M. K. Gandhi rejected the Western model of progress for India. Ngũgũ wa Thiong'o rejected English as a creative medium because, he argued, it was not apt for a writer from Kenya. Instead, he chose to write in his tribal language Gikuyu. For anticolonial intellectuals and activists, modernity did not represent a matter of choice, or an individual attitude towards life; it was a condition thrust upon entire populations by colonial rule. Becoming modern was a matter of involuntary propulsion for individuals and for nations.

The intertwined histories of 'modern' and 'colonial' show that most ideas of 'modern' are far too deeply rooted in European colonial history to sustain without discomfort the claim to universal applicability often made on their behalf, either as terms of description or prescription. Any attempt to speak of modernist literature must take particular care in how it defines relations between creative practices – whether in Europe, the Americas, or elsewhere – and the discursive category of modernity.

Likewise – though this is less obvious – any account of modernity becomes more plausible when based on recognition that narratives of modernity are inseparable from the history of the last six hundred years of overseas European settlement, colonisation and empire. The process may have begun in exploration, encounter and trade. What it led to was various forms of domination, whose impact is felt to this day by many regions and peoples. These forms include territorial, ecological, technological, economic, religious, cultural, intellectual and psychological domination. The history of becoming modern is also at the same time, in major part, a history of modern imperialism, and its complex influence on how we live today, wherever that might be in terms of place, community, culture, or nation.

'Modern' in a Postcolonial Perspective

> Modernity is more about ideas than about periods.
>
> Rabindranath Tagore

Twentieth-century anti-colonialism

The range of meanings we might extract from the idea of 'postcolonial' has been a matter of much debate in the last three decades. I use 'postcolonial' to signify the continuing effects of colonial habits and institutions on cultural orientations and economic as well as political practices among groups and individuals no longer colonised in the formal or political sense. As Edward Said remarked in 1994, 'the effects of colonialism are much deeper and go on much longer than when the last white policeman leaves' (Said and Ali 2005: 101). The study of postcolonial predicaments and practices entails recognition of the pitfalls, traps, detours and dead-ends that have impeded the processes of cultural and psychic decolonisation.

The establishment of postcolonial studies as an academic discipline took place during the 1980s and 90s. It was preceded by several kinds of anti-colonial writing from Europe's colonies and the United States. Writers such as Rabindranath Tagore (1861–1941), W. E. B. du Bois (1868–1963), Sol Plaatje (1876–1932) and Mulk Raj Anand (1905–2004) grappled for ways to narrate the encounter between European modernity and their respective colonised worlds beyond Europe during the early decades of the twentieth century. Their work disseminated ideas concerning European cultural practices and forms as well as modernist practices to the colonies. As shown by an essay on 'Modern Poetry' by Tagore, their reaction to this modernity was not without ambivalence: 'The subject matter of today's verse does not wish to seduce with loveliness. What, then, is the source of its strength? It is in its confident selfhood, what in English is called *character*' (Tagore 2001: 284); and yet, it was worrying that this modernity was a consequence of the fact that 'The world they view and show is crumbling, dustblown, and choked with *rubbish*. Their minds today are morbid, discontented, unsettled' (2001: 290).

Du Bois was a pioneer in the cause of civil rights, and in resisting racism. Platje's *Mhudi* (written 1919, published 1930) was the first novel in English by an African. Tagore's varied creativity applied a discerning modernity of spirit to his Indian materials in a manner that continues to inspire writers internationally. Anand's novel *Untouchable* (1935) dramatised the Gandhian struggle to dismantle the caste system in India. In subsequent decades, other intellectuals from the colonies showed acute awareness of the need to critique colonialism in texts such as C. L. R. James's *The Black Jacobins* (1938), Fanon's *Black Skin, White Masks* (1952), Aimé Césaire's *Discourse on Colonialism* (1955), Éduard Glissant's *Soleil de la conscience* (1956), George Lamming's *The Pleasures of Exile* (1961), Amilcar Cabral's *The Weapon of Theory* (1966) and Roberto Fernández Retamar's 'Caliban' (1971). As an example, let us look a little further into the Caribbean writers from this group.

Caribbean anti-colonialism

From Trinidad and London, C. L. R. James (1901–1989) allied anti-colonialism with communism during the 1930s while leading the Pan-Africanist movement. His major historical work, *The Black Jacobins* (1938), drew attention to the importance of Toussaint l'Ouverture (1743–1803) in his role as the leader of the Haitian revolution of 1791, which led to independence for Haiti by 1801–4, and brought the ideals of liberty and equality promoted by the French Revolution to the Caribbean. Aimé Césaire (1913–2008) made a sustained and varied contribution to the creation of a vital link between modernist practices and awareness of how colonialism had shaped Western civilisation. In the 1930s, in association with Léopold Senghor (1906–2001) and Léon Damas (1912–78), he promoted the idea of 'Négritude' as a way of fostering pride in racial identity among peoples of African descent. A second contribution took the form of a turbulent medley of verse and prose, *Cahier d'un retour au pays natal* (*Notebook of a Return to My Native Land*, 1939).

The work uses an assortment of modernist techniques to grapple with a sense of cultural dislocation in the context of Martinican colonisation. It also showed what could be done by the adoption of various Surrealist techniques, which he described in a later work, *Discourse on Colonialism* (1955) as 'a process of disalienation' (Césaire 1972: 26) in a specifically colonial context. Césaire became a tutelary figure for younger contemporaries. *Discourse on Colonialism* provided a succinct critique of the brutalising effects of colonialism on Western civilisation through its production in the West of a type of 'modern barbarian' characterised by 'excess, waste, mercantilism, bluff, gregariousness, stupidity, vulgarity, disorder' (Césaire 1972: 23).

We owe to another intellectual from Martinique, Frantz Fanon (1925–61), an incisive psychoanalytical critique of racism, which diagnoses it as an internalisation by the colonised of what he called 'Manichean delirium' (Fanon 1967: 44–5, 183; 1963: 41–2). His writings provide cautionary reflections on the difficulties faced by colonised societies in sustaining the will to new nationhood in the aftermath of colonialism. He questioned the efficacy of 'Négritude' as a recuperative strategy for peoples of African descent, and he distinguished between political decolonisation and cultural and psychic forms of decolonisation. His ideas and arguments continue to lend themselves to a variety of postcolonial reinterpretations. Homi Bhabha, for instance, treats Fanon's notion of blackness as 'the shadow of colonised man, that splits his presence, distorts his outline, breaches his boundaries, repeats his action at a distance, disturbs and divides the very time of his being' (Bhabha 1986: xiv). Others, such as Benita Parry or Henry Louis Gates, Jr, recuperate a somewhat different Fanon, who wrote not as an academic but as a displaced Martinican psychiatrist adopting the cause of Algerian independence in his resistance to the Europe he had looked up to during the period of his intellectual development as a psychiatric physician, an aspect of Fanon's work that is surveyed with insight in David Macey's biography of Fanon (Macey 2000: 1–30).

The semi-autobiographical early novels of George Lamming (b. 1927), *In the Castle of My Skin* (1953) and *The Emigrants* (1954), focus on the ambiguities of living in metropolitan England as West Indian expatriates, while *Of Age and Innocence* (1958) and *Season of Adventure* (1960) treat the Caribbean experience of displacement in a fictional island setting. In *Examination of Another World* (1967), the Cuban poet and essayist Roberto Fernández Retamar (b. 1930) redefined *modernismo*, the Latin American version of literary modernism, as a form of latent political activism resistant to American and other forms of imperialism. In *Calibán* (1971), Shakespeare's character becomes a symbol of Latin American marginalisation. It has the potential to energise regional culture on its own terms. More recently, in an interview published in 1995, Retamar demurs at the currency acquired by 'postcolonial', preferring 'neocolonial' as a more accurate representation of global realities:

> I can't hide the fact that the term postcolonial which is so fashionable today, and which Latin American thinkers like Martinez Estrada also began to use in the sixties, does not satisfy me. The world that used to be colonial is not so much postcolonial now, but rather neocolonial. It's not just a matter of words. That heavily inflected post – so much a part of a certain postmodernist taste – suggests that colonialism has been left behind; but this simply isn't so. Neocolonialism, by contrast, insists on the perpetuation of a colonial condition; it names the form assumed by colonialism in the age of imperialism. (Retamar 1995: 421)

Édouard Glissant (1928–2011), from Martinique, made his mark as a novelist, poet and essayist from the 1980s. In works such as *Poetics of Relation* (1990), *Treatise on the Whole World* (1996) and *Philosophy of Relation* (2009), he has provided some of the most sophisticated articulations in French of a sustained postcolonial critique that grounds itself in a Caribbean context but aspires to a more general applicability. His continual search for a language adequate to the uniqueness of the Antillean quality of experience is balanced by his development of the concepts of 'relation', 'métissage' (cultural mixing) and 'tout-monde', which are meant to capture a sense of interrelatedness between the localised and the complexly global dimensions of modern postcoloniality. The example of such writers provided postcolonial studies a rich and diverse intellectual legacy.

Postcolonial studies

The political dissolution of Empire and the work of anti-colonialist intellectuals was followed at the academic level by the development of Commonwealth literary studies in Britain during the 1960s, and in its former colonies thereafter. It created a context of awareness that Western metropolitan literary traditions could be supplemented by creative writing in English from the former settler and non-settler colonies. However, Commonwealth literary studies had no theoretical vocabulary of its own. Nor did it possess a polemical edge to the promotion of what was sometimes referred to as 'new' literatures.

The edge came with *Orientalism* (1978) by Edward Said (1935–2003). The book proved very influential in the dissemination of political, cultural and moral awareness concerning the cultural consequences of European imperialism. The approaches associated with postcolonial studies derive from Said a sense of the totalising power of Orientalist discourses. The development of the academic discipline, however, has not always taken note of how suspicious Said was about the self-empowerment of theory divorced from action in the political realm; and how insistently he spoke from the position of a privileged individual acculturated in Western humanism, practising his profession in a culture and society of which he was critical. He wrote as a Palestinian living in the US, in a spirit of opposition that bespoke a mix of anger, sadness, dispossession and a desire for redress. While his specific contributions to the interface between colonialism and modernism are particularly acute for a writer such as Conrad, or Yeats, his work also retains a larger import for how we interpret the relation between texts and the semblances of reality they evoke.

The impact of Said gathered momentum with Ashcroft, Griffiths and Tiffin's *The Empire Writes Back* (1989), which disseminated a method designed specifically for reading texts from the colonies and former colonies of Europe. Postcolonial studies caught on rapidly after that. Its institutionalisation in the US has followed a slightly different path from that in Britain, and in Europe's former colonies. As an academic discipline, it allows an eclecticism of approach and method to focus on an analysis of many kinds of discourse and practice. Its multi-disciplinary approach to the interface between residual forms of imperialism and incipient forms of emancipative modernity takes the risk of reducing its objects of study into a cultural ghetto of its own making.[7]

At its best, however, postcolonial studies continues to offer the promise of combining analysis, diagnosis, disclosure and critique in a manner that is implicitly, and often explicitly, both political and ethical. A postcolonial perspective on the study of culture and literature entails alertness to several aspects of the current situation at regional and global levels: (1) resistance across the entire spectrum of dominative practices: psychic, economic, political, cultural and literary; (2) complicity between resistance and collusion, or resistance and assimilation in colonial and post-independent societies; (3) interactions between the global and the regional at the level of social and cultural change and identity; (4) the gap that separates the nations which modernised and colonised from those which were colonised. The latter lagged behind in the race for a modernity as defined by the West.[8]

Modernism as a crisis of creativity

European and Anglo-American creative practices at the end of the nine-teenth and the start of the twentieth century experienced two kinds of crisis: one reactive, the other internal to the history of art forms. The two were closely interconnected. The reactive element concerned the response of art to the numerous changes that were part of social moder-nity, including industrialism, urbanism, colonialism and the continual impact of technological change on the patterns of individual and collec-tive living. It found expression as resistance to Enlightenment ideas of progress. It was induced by what the American art historian T. J. Clark describes as 'a social order which has turned from the worship of ances-tors and past authorities to the pursuit of a projected future – of goods, pleasures, freedoms, forms of control over nature, or infinities of infor-mation' (Clark 1999: 7).[9]

The second form taken by the sense of crisis was internal to the history of art. It was mediated by two factors. Both were indirect results of social modernity: access to new materials; dissatisfaction with inherited ways of using an art-medium. The Spanish philosopher José Ortega y Gasset (1883–1955), writing in 1925, described the modern-ist sensibility as driven by a 'will to style' (Ortega y Gasset 1948: 25) which rejected 'an ever growing mass of traditional styles' because they hampered 'the direct and original communication between the nascent artist and the world around him' (44). The modern artist – the Cubist and the Expressionist, for example – inverted the traditional conception of art as an idea of representation that sought to reproduce physical reality through its chosen medium. Instead, such art worked on the premise that 'if, turning our back on alleged reality, we take the ideas for what they are – mere subjective patterns – and make them live as such, lean and angular, but pure and transparent; in short, if we deliberately propose to "realise" our ideas – then we have dehumanised and, as it were, derealised them' (37–8).

Given the reaction against various forms of mimeticism or represen-tational realism, it is easy to suppose that the modernist revolution was primarily a matter of form and technique. But there was more to the avant-garde element of modern art and writing than technical experi-ment. The German playwright Bertolt Brecht, for instance, rejected the Hungarian critic Georg Lukács's account of modernism as a form of formalist anti-realism. The key element of modernist art, Brecht emphasised, was not formal experiment for the sake of experiment, but the abandonment by modern authors and artists of the function taken on by traditional art: the desire to achieve a close correspondence with reality. We will attend to this debate in more detail in the first section of Chapter 2.

Self-reflexivity became the new mode of aesthetic self-individuation.[10] Tradition could be modified and added to only by rejecting old habits and conventions, by embracing new materials (both in the sense of revisions to the material cause of an art-medium, and in the sense of openness to new modes of experience). Ideas about what was apt subject matter for art underwent radical change. Ceaseless experiment ensued. Artists and writers became more and more willing to risk alienating large sections of the public, in a spirit of deliberate risk and challenge. In architecture, metal, concrete and glass supplied a combined new material cause; geometry and the needs of industrialisation supplied new shapes and functions; while urbanism showed the scope for new structures that mediated new relationships between the traditional concept of home and modern concepts of urban workplace and workspace. In painting, the rise of photography provoked painters into re-examining the relation of their art to the traditional function of mimetic realism: the impression, the symbol, the geometrical and the abstract shape, shade and colour became the new vocabulary; fragmentation the new syntax, rupture a new component of style.

Ortega y Gasset notes that avant-garde art promoted the recognition that 'From painting things, the painter has turned to painting ideas' (Ortega y Gasset 1948: 38).[11] Likewise, fiction learned to re-examine its notions of reality, realism, identity, consciousness and the relation of language and narrative to experience. In consequence, it produced a new sense of reality as subjective interiority: private, fragmented and ineluctably fugitive.[12] Drama too, like fiction, broke away from realism in representation; it abandoned the inherited notion of the 'well-made play'. It became more self-reflexive and experimental, as in *Six Characters in Search of an Author* (1921) by the Italian playwright Luigi Pirandello (1867–1936). In poetry, *vers libre* broke the back of traditional rhetoric and prosody; the lyric fragment prospered where once there had been epic and verse narrative. T. S. Eliot, in 'A Preface to Modern Literature' (1923), treated new developments positively: 'it had a curiosity, a *recklessness*, which are in violent contrast with that part of the present which I denominate as the already dead' (Longenbach 1988: 170). In music, atonality, dissonance and regressive rhythms replaced the traditional grammar of tonality, sonata form, harmony and structure. Those elements had flourished from Franz Joseph Haydn (1732–1809) to Richard Strauss (1864–1949), finding in the gigantic symphonic works of Gustav

Mahler (1860–1911) a bridge between the traditionalism of the nineteenth century and the imminent modernism of early twentieth-century music.

The myth of a singular modernism

Let us consider the manner in which Anglo-American academic writing developed the idea of a singular modernism, and how that approach has become pluralised in recent years. Modernism is a discourse about practice conceived primarily by critics and historians rather than by writers or artists. With the rise of academic disciplines that give attention to the formerly marginalised (whether on grounds of race, gender, or geographical location) a grudging recognition has grown that there could be alternative ways of looking at modernism. The British cultural critic Paul Gilroy, for instance, argues in defence of an Afro-modernist counterculture in *The Black Atlantic: Modernity and Double Consciousness* (1994), and in *Postcolonial Melancholia* (2005), he protests against the weakening of contemporary notions of cosmopolitanism 'by the inability to conceptualise multicultural and postcolonial relations as anything other than risk and jeopardy' (Gilroy 2005: 4).

We can illustrate the mono-cultural approach to modernism by identifying the influential texts and critics who helped consolidate a highly selective canon for literary modernism. The American critic Edmund Wilson's *Axel's Castle* (1931) created a genealogy for symbolism, grouping together Arthur Rimbaud, Auguste Villiers de l'Isle-Adam, W. B. Yeats, Paul Valéry, T. S. Eliot, Marcel Proust, James Joyce and Gertrude Stein: a Franco-American-Irish avant-garde elite with no reference to England; comprising more poets than prose writers, with only one woman, and no dramatist. His book was followed from England by F. R. Leavis's *New Bearings in English Poetry* (1932), an acute but aggressively Anglocentric book, which made heroes of Eliot and Pound, and added Gerard Manley Hopkins to the canon in belated reparation for the neglect he had suffered in his lifetime. The books by Wilson and Leavis were the first two studies to promote literary modernism, though they differed in terms of the canon they selected, and the qualities they praised. They were followed quickly from the US by works such as Cleanth Brooks's *Modern Poetry and the Tradition* (1939). The American New Critics fostered the assimilation of modernist poetry into the academic curriculum, an undertaking helped by their emphasis on close reading, the high value they placed on complexity and irony, and their assertion of art as autonomous.

In the 1940s, the English scholar C. M. Bowra consolidated the Symbolist genealogy with *The Heritage of Symbolism* (1943). The modernist personnel in his book are Valéry, Rilke, Stefan George, Alexander Blok and Yeats: the Americans were out; two Germans and one Russian were in; and women and other races were omitted, giving us a European poetic canon with Yeats as the only Anglophone representative. Wilson, Leavis and Bowra wrote as critics, the latter two from within the academy. Leavis was the most fervent, and the most conscious that he was writing about contemporary writing at its most promising; Wilson and Bowra wrote about what they regarded as a development that was recent, but largely over. They treated Symbolism as a movement, the central element in literary modernism, with an origin in French literature, and with Arthur Symons in the role of a mediator of French trends to Anglophone readers and writers. They paved the way for a reception that the academy would ingest later, from the 1960s onwards, when the idea of a specific movement such as Symbolism was absorbed into a much larger, more portentous concept of a modernist literary tradition.

Consolidation of the mono-cultural approach

The subsequent consolidation of a singular modernist narrative was accomplished by two influential compilations. Both were academic and pedagogic. The first was an anthology from the US, Richard Ellmann and Charles Feidelson's *The Modern Tradition* (1965). It announced a tradition based on the rejection of tradition (an irony noted by reviewers such as Frank Kermode and Paul de Man). Ellmann and Feidelson provided a sourcebook of ideas, statements and manifestos aimed at breadth of coverage, stretching back to include Blake and Goethe among the founders of a large and miscellaneous Euro-American fellowship. The book stands out in retrospect for its reliance on discursive statements from artists and authors in its jigsaw puzzle approach to modernism, its relative marginalisation of women writers and its thematic approach to topics. The second compilation was from England, Malcolm Bradbury and James McFarlane's *Modernism: A Guide to European Literature 1890–1930* (1978). It was aimed even more unabashedly at a student market along the lines that Lionel Trilling had worried about in the 1960s.[13]

Bradbury and McFarlane divided their book according to geography, movements and genres. That enabled them to imply that modernism was afoot more or less concurrently (well before the term as such had been coined or gained currency) in poetry, fiction and drama, from a variety of metropolitan locations in Europe and the US, and comprised a series of movements, from Symbolism and Impressionism to Imagism and Vorticism, Futurism, Expressionism and Surrealism. Their composite literary narrative represented a consensus for the 1960s and 70s about a European canon, leavened with some Americans. Their account of modernism was held together by increasingly unifying claims about what might be said to hold all this diversity together under the umbrella of a singular '-ism'. With varying degrees of updating, this pattern of literary history prevailed from the mid-1960s to the 1990s. In comparison, accounts that relate modernism in literature to modernism in the arts are less common. Christopher Butler's *Early Modernism: Literature, Music and Painting in Europe 1900–1916* (1994) represents a circumspect venture of this kind.

Meanwhile, the English academic Alan Sinfield, in *Literature, Politics and Culture in Postwar Britain* (1989), noted a small but significant nuance. The critics associated with the periodical *Scrutiny* in England promoted writers such as Eliot, Yeats, James, Conrad and Lawrence for their literary innovativeness, while their mentor, F. R. Leavis, laid stress on their ethical worth. He had a minimal interest in several features that are by now regarded by many academics as central to literary modernism: 'cosmopolitanism and internationalism; self-conscious experimentation with language and forms; the idea of the artwork as autonomous; and the concept of the artist as alienated' (Sinfield 1989: 182). The Leavisite canon, and the predilections it was based on, was disseminated through the critical work of many of his followers, and through journals such as *Critical Quarterly* and Boris Ford's seven-volume set, *The Pelican Guide to English Literature* (1954–61).

Thus, in post-World War II Britain, certain modernist authors were assimilated into the canon, but not modernism as such. The concept of a modernist movement remained largely a foreign and un-English phenomenon. Concurrently, a reverse trend occurred in the US, which saw the American establishment celebrate modern art as central to American creativity before and after World War II. Special attention was given to its international and cosmopolitan elements, as well as its role in Marshall MacLuhan-type effects of technological globalisation by avant-garde art practices. Though 'not uncontested' by 'middlebrow culture', such narratives liberated Americans from 'a longstanding anxiety that U.S. culture was unsophisticated and provincial' (Sinfield 1989: 186). The growth of New Criticism in the US paralleled the Cold War. The two phenomena might seem unrelated but, as Sinfield points out, the formalism that characterises some accounts of modernism 'was congenial to Cold-War ideology, since it discouraged political, economic and social ideas among writers and critics [. . .] [and] imagined the poetic text as autonomous' (188). Thus, when modernism was put back into the British academic canon during the 1950s, it was as brought in as 'a U.S. construct' (191).

If we turn to more recent attempts along the lines established by Ellmann and Feidelson, and Bradbury and McFarlane, such as *Modernism: An Anthology of Sources and Documents* (1998), edited by Vassiliki Kolocotroni et al., we notice that the compilation merely updates the 1960s and 1970s approach. The only major difference is that women writers get a generous representation, and Langston Hughes makes an appearance as one of only two representatives of non-white American modernism. In other respects, the collection retains a largely unaltered idea of the modernist tradition: a phenomenon confined to Europe and the US, with its roots in the Romantic period (or even earlier), and an implicitly Caucasian racial identity. The youngest authors in the 1998 compilation are George Orwell and Richard Wright, each represented by writing from 1940.

The implication is that modernism came to an end, more or less, by the end of the 1930s. Ellmann and Feidelson had ended their book with the 1940s, with the existentialism of Sartre and Camus; Bradbury and McFarlane declared their terminal date of 1930 in their title. The consensus revealed in these academic developments is straightforward. Whether we regard modernism as having begun in the 1850s with Baudelaire, or later, with the French Symbolists, or, for Anglophone writing, by the end of the first decade of the twentieth century, most literary surveys agree that it peaked around the period 1914–24. As events in Europe became more turbulent and politicised, the modernist impulse faded into the background, even though many of the major modernists continued to live and publish for decades after the end of World War II, and modernist impulses in the visual arts, such as abstract expressionism, continued into the 1940s.

The plural approach

Discussions of social modernity have been more forthcoming in their recognition of the efficacy of a plural approach to how institutions and individuals become 'modern'. In cultural practices outside Europe, becoming 'modern' tended to take one of two alternative paths. Both paths tended to reject old modes and practices. One path was undertaken from a desire to emulate and adapt Western modernist practices to local needs and circumstances, the other to become 'modern' without any interest in Western modernism. This latter variety helps us bracket the specificity of Western European modernisms, and the speciousness of the idea of a monolithic modernism.

The first path is readily illustrated from India, where painters turned to primitivist styles and techniques, under the influence of Western primitivism. They adapted its repertoire of motifs and techniques to three local needs. The first was the rejection of naturalist modes of pictorial representation that had been imbibed through admiration for Western realism during the period of colonial dependency. The second was the recuperation of indigenous modes of stylisation and symbolisation that preceded the realism learnt through colonial dependency. The third was the spirit of nationalist resistance to colonialism, which rejected conventional subjects sanctioned by the hierarchies of empire, and turned instead to the representation of the indigenous poor and the underprivileged.

We can illustrate the second path through a quick reference to the new drama that developed in China (*Hua Ju*) and Japan (*Shingeki*) during the late nineteenth and early twentieth centuries. The 'modern' element in these two transformations had nothing to do with Western modernism, and everything to do with renovating indigenous conventions and styles by importing Western naturalist techniques and canonical authors such as Shakespeare or Ibsen into local drama. To become 'modern' could thus mean very different things, depending on the context. This type of plurality is a function of geography: the logic that animates these modernisms varies from one region to another.

There is another way of resisting the pull towards treating modernism in the singular, and that is through the notion of alternative modernisms. When the category of race plays an explicit role in the discourses of modernism, we get the category of 'black modernism'. It provides an alternative to standard 'white' accounts of modernism. The recognition of plurality based on region, and plurality based on racial difference, are both recent trends, although the writers and practices to which such terms refer have been around for a while. In Western English-language academic writing, the most recent change in climate about literary modernism is symptomatised by the appearance of academic books that make more and more concessions to the argument in support of plurality, a trend illustrated by Peter Nicholls's *Modernisms: A Literary Guide* (1995), where the title declares its desire to canonise plurality by pluralising the canon.

The direction inaugurated by Nicholls and others is followed up, but with a curious feature, in David Bradshaw and Kevin J. H. Dettmar's *A Companion to Modernist Literature and Culture* (2006). The compilation retains many of the features of the Ellmann and Feidelson approach. The new feature is a section called 'Other Modernisms'. Here, readers are given what the current climate of opinion concerning global representation expects more insistently than before: modernisms that are racialised, gendered, queered, postcolonialised and globalised. This is a heartening development, even if some part of such coverage cannot quite shake off the impression of tokenism.

Another recent compilation, *The Oxford Handbook of Modernisms* (2010), edited by Peter Brooker and others, also declares its allegiance to plurality like a badge of honour in its title. By 2010, the 'Other Modernisms' of the 2006 compilation have ballooned vastly to provide chapters on a much larger variety of regional modernisms. Even here, however, and despite the viability of the pluralisation, one generally gets an enumeration of regional names engaged more often with their local variation of social modernity than with anything that might be regarded as substantively modernist in technique or modernist in relation to a critique of local variants of a globalising social modernity. That notwithstanding, henceforth it will be difficult to promote a mono-cultural modernism. More is at stake than fashion, trend, or political correctness. Just as social modernity may have had an origin in Europe, but found its story becoming global, likewise, modernism may have originated in Europe, but its stories do not stop any longer with the US and Europe.

Latin American *modernismo*

If we look briefly at Latin American literary history, it is easier to grasp that 'modernism' was never a singular term. Authors in Latin America had begun using the concept of *modernismo* since the 1890s to articulate an aspiration to a new form of the aesthetic impulse. The trend was established, and the term given currency, by the Nicaraguan poet Rubén Darío (in his volume *Azul . . .*, 1888): 'I seek a form that my style cannot discover, / a bud of thought that wants to be a rose' (Tapscott 1996: 33ii). *Modernismo* soon became popular in Spain and in Hispanic Latin America. In Brazil, a very different kind of modernism followed slightly later, committed less to formalism and elegance than to the liberating effects of free verse forms, as developed in the work of poets such as Oswald de Andrade (1890–1954).[14] The distinctiveness of *modernismo* was rooted in late nineteenth-century romanticism and symbolism. It owed a special debt to the Parnassian element in the French poetry of

Théophile Gautier (1811–1872), a precise and lapidary elegance, which Ezra Pound extolled in the first two decades of the twentieth century.

The scholar Andrew Bush notes in connection with the romantic legacy of *modernismo* that 'one may find in the reaction of *modernista* (modernist) or *vanguardista* (vanguard) poetry the process that Ortega y Gasset referred to as "negative influence" in Hispanic literature' (Bush 1996: 376). In his anthology of Latin American poetry in translation, Tapscott makes the same point. *Modernismo* both challenged and refined Romantic tenets. He also alerts English-language readers to a crucial feature of Latin American poetry. What other societies experienced as the traumatic and alienating aspects repressed by social modernity was engaged with in Latin American modernist writing as a problem and an opportunity about writing itself (Tapscott 1996: 3ii).

What Tapscott has to say about Latin American *modernismo* applies, with small variations, to the seesaw enacted by modernist writers concerning attachment to Romantic habits and the desire to break free of those habits. That is also how we might interpret the postcolonial modernism of Anglophone authors such as Yeats, Pound and Stevens. As with Joyce's protagonist Stephen, from *A Portrait of the Artist as a Young Man* (1914), the *modernistas* chose 'to fly by those nets' (Joyce 2000: 171), the nets of a modernism that would help them avoid being corralled by either colony or postcolony, preferring instead to create a community of writers founded on aesthetic modernism.

Another scholar of Latin American literature, Neil Larsen, draws attention to the lack of congruence between modernism and *modernismo* as concepts. They differed either 'as a consequence of the inherent Eurocentrism or cultural imperialism of the aesthetic or literary category *per se*', or because 'the irreducible difference of the would-be but never-quite modernist texts' can be understood 'as merely the sign of their radically non-European, "Latin American" essence' (Larsen 2001: 115). Larsen argues, plausibly, that it does not suffice to apply European ideas to the Latin American context. What is needed, instead, is a rethinking of how modernism is 'transculturated' within the postcolonial context (122). In conditions that did not lead to the creation of a consciousness similar to that of European bourgeois ideology, the import of European aesthetic forms could not produce comparable effects. In Alejo Carpentier's modernist-historical epic, *El sigo de la luces* (1960, *The Explosion in a Cathedral*), for instance, Larsen argues that 'it is modernism that, dialectically speaking, suffers a negation', and we are left with a paradoxical situation in which 'what has in effect become the "old" still presents itself here in the guise of the "new"' (124).

The general issue at stake is the need for a plural concept of modernism, commensurate to plural experiences of modernity. Here is a recent articulation of this perception from a scholar of Latin American cultures, Walter Mignolo: 'Instead of conceiving alternative or peripheral modernities, what are needed are alternatives to modernity; that is, to the single narrative of modernity by a subject that is not universal and disincorporated' (Mignolo 2008: 20). His sentiments reiterate the timeliness of the need to move away from monologic and Eurocentric accounts of modernist practice towards a fuller appreciation of the transformations undergone by modernist ideas in the writing of all the former colonies, from Latin America and the Caribbean to Africa, Asia and Oceania.

'Otherness' and the Modernist Imagination

All modern art begins to appear comprehensible [. . .] when it is interpreted as an attempt to instil youthfulness into an ancient world.

José Ortega y Gasset

Empire and 'otherness'

As European overseas empires grew in scale between 1580 and 1640, occasions for Western encounters with other societies, cultures and civilisations became more frequent. Economic and territorial power opened up more and more of the world to the acquisitive gaze of Europe (and from the end of the nineteenth century, the equally acquisitive gaze of the US). In the process, new regions were integrated into the expanding economy of the colonising powers. The process created formal empires of territorial control and, especially during the course of the nineteenth century, much larger though less well-defined informal empires of varying degrees and kinds of influence (cf. Gallagher and Robinson 1953), in which materialist motives were 'linked to social and political developments' (Cain and Hopkins 2002: 2).

Corresponding cultural developments were not far behind. They took two forms: the creation of new typologies or the consolidation of existing ones; and the assimilation of new knowledge about Europe's racial 'others' into the kinds of antitheses familiar to Western literature through the pastoral tradition, which set up polarities such as the metropolis versus nature, sophistication versus simplicity, and so on. We see these processes at work in Montaigne's essay 'On Cannibals' (1580), and in Shakespeare's *Othello* (c. 1601–2). By the time we reach Jean

Jacques Rousseau's *Discourse on Inequality* (1754), the idealisation of the natural was already well entrenched.

In the early nineteenth century, the philosopher G. W. F. Hegel gave an abstract account of the encounter between sameness and difference, describing identity formation through the assimilation of difference into a continually self-revising sense of selfhood.[15] Race, and typologies concerning race, became crucial elements in European identity formations. David Theo Goldberg, in *The Threat of Race* (2009), stresses 'the centrality of race to the expansive and extensive global order(ing) of European modernity and the (late) modernity of medieval categories of disposition and dominance, imposition and order once racially conceived' (Goldberg 2009: 2).

In the European nineteenth century, travel and trade expanded hugely as new technologies abridged space and time. The European scholarly enterprise of building knowledge about other societies and civilisations also grew apace. This activity, as Edward Said has argued, was never innocent or objective. The representations of 'otherness' constructed as part of the colonial encounter were significant for what they contributed to European identity formation as well. The modernist segment of this history reveals the importance given to notions of the primitive in the process of cultural (self-) representation.

A conception of 'other' races as primitive was a staple of the Enlightenment. Attitudes to the primitive ranged across the entire spectrum from admiration to disgust, with plenty of room in between for ambivalence, fascination and fear. The primitive was 'discovered' to be everything that Europe was not: technologically undeveloped, culturally unsophisticated and uncouth. The primitive lacked the capacity for sustained reasoning. The primitive confined itself to a life of unreflecting sensory experience. The primitive was brutish, violent, unpractised in ethics and uninhibited. The primitive lacked history and a sense of history. Ironically, it was also always possible to turn these ascriptions of value inside out. Thus, the primitive was endowed with every attribute that Europeans believed they had lost. The primitive possessed simplicity, nobility, an affinity to nature, spontaneity and an uncomplicated acceptance of all natural processes from birth to death. The primitive had the ability to feel intensely and act vigorously without the constraints of repression or social inhibitions. The primitive retained a capacity for wonder, magic and enchantment that was lost to Europeans (cf. Torgovnick 1990: 46).

Though such notions had congealed into stereotypes by the end of the nineteenth century, a new development occurred during the early years of the twentieth century. Specific associations concerning the primitive acquired a fresh hold on the creative imagination, and led to work of great originality. This work showed the impact of cultural productions from Europe's 'others' in a bold, new light. The most prominent example of this new tendency was a painting such as Picasso's *Les Demoiselles d'Avignon* (1907). This was the period when modernist art and writing developed primitivism into a form of self-critique in the service of a mode of imaginative self-renewal for the West. There is some irony in the fact that this self-critique, and its fictions of self-renewal, often drew upon distorted forms of knowledge about Europe's 'others', a process facilitated and abetted by colonialism.

In this process, standard attitudes to 'otherness' – which varied from xenophobia to idealisation – began to function as projections rather than representations. The attitudes were based on needs, fears and desires within the projecting self at least as much as they were based on knowledge of all the 'others'. The process could work, in principle, both ways: the colonised nursed prejudices about colonisers comparable in reverse to those nursed by colonisers about the colonised. However, since the coloniser had more power and control over the colonised and over their capacity to create representations, his projections proved the more dominant.

When artists or artefacts travelled

Artists from colonising nations were more likely to travel to the colonies than the other way round. When the colonised did travel to the West, they ended up as slaves, exhibits, or unwelcome immigrants. It was different, of course, with cultural artefacts from the colonies. They were freely looted, sold and displayed in the museums and emporiums of the US and Europe. Western goods and technologies were much slower to make their way to the colonies. When they did – as in the case of export commodities sold to the colonies at exorbitant prices, or modern innovations such as all-weather roads and railways – these primarily served the needs of empire. If they served the purpose of modernising the colonies, they did so as a secondary service.

What applied to technologies also applied to cultural artefacts, though the fate of Western languages in the colonies differed from colony to colony, depending on the linguistic policies of the colonising nation. English and French, for example, and Portuguese and Spanish before that, spread even more widely than the Christian faith, though not Dutch, or Italian, or German. The Philippines shows the reverse:

Christianity took hold, but the Spaniards restricted access to their language to an elite minority, and it did not survive the dissolution of empire in the same way that English and Portuguese lasted in their respective colonies even after colonialism was over and done with.

When it came to cultural artefacts from Europe reaching other shores, the impact varied. There are several examples of modern art from Europe making a decisive impact overseas. The Armory Show of 1913 in New York revolutionised thinking about art and writing for many American artists and authors. A similar effect was produced on the artists of the Bengal Renaissance in India by an exhibition of works by Paul Klee, Wassily Kandinsky and other Bauhaus artists. Their work was displayed in Calcutta in 1922. This exhibition was organised as a result of a request by Rabindranath Tagore, on a visit to Europe, that his countrymen be given a chance to experience at first-hand the work of the European avant-garde (Mitter 2007: 10, 68).

Authors from the West could move more freely in the colonies once empires became established and access to distant regions became easier than in pre-colonial times. Modern technologies of transportation such as ships, trains and motor cars helped this access. Authors and artists were drawn to the colonies regardless of whether they professed modernist or traditional affiliations. Travel could be real or virtual. The former needed enterprise and initiative; the latter was the easier and the lazier option. The results in the case of modernist writing remain interesting in either case. The impact of colonial travel on writing is illustrated by the novels of Conrad and Lawrence, and works such as André Gide's *Les Nourritures térrestres* (1897), André Malraux's *La Condition Humaine* (1933), and Michel Leiris's *L'Afrique fantôme* (1934).

The scholar Mary Louise Pratt draws attention to a specific kind of writing from the 'neocolony', which involves 'Europeans trapped at the terminus of Empire's reach', in situations characterised by 'the norms of metropolitan modernity' (Pratt 2008: 224). Pratt argues that when writers work through such predicaments, their narratives contribute an 'energising aspect' to Latin American modernism, as in García Márquez's *One Hundred Years of Solitude* (1962) and Ricardo Piglia's *La ciudad ausente* (*The City Away*, 1997). Likewise, in a poet like Gabriela Mistral, 'travel and mobility again articulate the crisis of longing and belonging that is the cultural predicament of the neocolony' (234).

A context for literary Orientalism

The late nineteenth century witnessed the consolidation of capitalism and industrialisation in the West, and in their overseas empires. However, historians such as P. J. Cain and A. G. Hopkins have questioned 'the widespread and long-standing assumption linking the "triumph of industry" to imperialist expansion'; they argue, instead, that it was 'the role of finance and services' that provided powerful incentives 'for territorial expansionism' (Cain and Hopkins 2002: 400). From the seventeenth to the nineteenth century, European constructions of 'otherness' rarely rose above the level of stereotypes, largely because the belief in Western superiority over 'other' peoples and civilisations went hand in hand with the celebration of progress measured along economic lines. The American scholar David Theo Goldberg, for example, notes that while Hegel thought of African and Asian societies as 'irrational or barbaric', 'Marx thought of "Asiatic" states as historically undeveloped' (Goldberg 2002: 51), although we might qualify his claim since late Marx rethought his earlier notion of a simple process that moved from Oriental despotism to European capitalism. To give the benefits of Western modernity, and the progress it signified, to the colonies, in whatever measure, contributed as much to hubris and complacency as to the conviction that Europe and the US shared 'the white man's burden' (Kipling's phrase) of civilising the allegedly more benighted portions of humanity.

During 1875 to 1914 – the period which the British Marxist historian Eric Hobsbawm characterises as 'The Age of Empire'– European economic power ensured that an appreciation of, and interest in, the art of other civilisations was always in alliance with consumerism.[16] Increased awareness of the arts and crafts of non-European civilisations, from the East, from Africa and from Oceania led to a huge increase in art collecting. Several institutions played a significant role in this process: trade in artefacts; regular exhibitions of art; growth in museum holdings in metropolitan centres such as Paris, London, Amsterdam, New York, Boston and other major Western cities; scholarly publications in the form of translations of foreign texts; and historical surveys of non-Western cultures. All this activity contributed to a transformation of Western sensibilities. Meanwhile, modernist authors and artists disgusted or alienated by the social modernity of the West, turned towards various forms of cultural 'otherness', working with the intuition that there they might find an escape from the negative dimension of modernity: urban alienation, boredom, ennui, obsessive materialism and spiritual as well as interpersonal sterility.

Modernist Japonisme

The European appetite for exotic artefacts ranged far and wide. The Far East was especially fascinating, and many regions, such as Japan, were found particularly exotic, as they did not have even the superficial familiarity that colonising a region produced for the West. Klaus Berger, in his survey of *Japonisme in Western Painting from Whistler to Matisse* (1980), notes that Japonisme came to assume a 'liberating, fostering role' among the Western avant-garde of the late nineteenth century (Berger 1992: 1, 3). This phenomenon gained impetus after the opening up of Japan to international markets in the years following the Meiji Revolution of 1868, through the display of Japanese wood-cuts and other artefacts. One of the highlights of the process was the display of works by Katsushika Hokusai (1760–1849) and Utagawa Hiroshige (1797–1858) in a series of hugely popular exhibitions starting with the 'Universal Exhibition' of 1862 in London, and of 1867 in Paris. These exhibitions were preceded, from the 1850s onwards, by Western imports of Japanese art-objects whose popularity among artists and the public grew dramatically in the last three decades of the nineteenth century.

John Walter de Grucy, in his survey of the career of the translator Arthur Waley, notes that 'japonism was no mere passing fad of the period but a movement that was produced by imperialism and in turn supported and served Anglo-Japanese imperialisms' in the period before the start of the First World World War (de Gruchy 2003: 9). The Japanese print on the wall in Manet's *Portrait of Emile Zola* (1867–8), the kimonos worn by the reclining subjects of Whistler's *The Balcony* (1867–8), the colour harmonies of Whistler's *Nocturnes* of the 1870s, his interior decorations for *The Peacock Room* (1876–7), the motifs adapted from the Japanese in Degas's *The Bather* (1890): such examples show that the values of form, composition, colour and stylisation that characterised Japanese prints, textiles and other art-forms were assimilated gratefully into the work of Western modernists.

American Japonisme was mediated by exhibition displays at venues such as the 'World's Fairs' in Philadelphia (1876) and Chicago (1893). The scholar Ernest Fenollosa made a singular contribution to the development of an Oriental Collection at the Boston Museum of Fine Arts from 1890, which was soon followed by many, well-endowed American museums and art galleries. The architect Frank Lloyd Wright's first masterpiece, the Robie House (Chicago, 1909), would not have been conceivable without his 'discovery of Japanese architecture' (Berger 1992: 265). The US-based scholar Zhaoming Qian describes the modernist poetic interest in China and Japan during the early decades of the twentieth century 'not as foils to the West, but as crystallising examples of the Modernists' realising Self' (Zhaoming 1995: 2).

American writers such as Wallace Stevens, Marianne Moore, William Carlos Williams, Ezra Pound and the Imagists (and others who showed the way for the London-based modernists without being modernist themselves, such as Laurence Binyon and Allen Upward) were attracted to Chinese and Japanese art. What drew them to it was that they found there what they aimed for in their own writing: 'intensity, precision, objectivity, visual clarity' (3). W. B. Yeats felt the same about Noh theatre. Even T. S. Eliot, who was drawn more to Buddhist and Hindu texts than to the texts and arts of the Far East, conceded that 'I am willing to believe that Chinese civilisation at its highest has graces and excellences which may make Europe seem crude' (Eliot 1933: 43).

The modernists constructed their East on the basis of very little by way of experience or expertise. Pound knew little Chinese and no Japanese; Yeats, Stevens, Moore and Williams knew nothing of either language. Their access to these cultures was based on museums, books, a few personal contacts (none truly intimate or sustained) and intuitions. The cultural difference posited directly or implicitly in their creative writing between themselves and the 'East' may have been ethnocentric, but the value they discovered or projected onto the East was based on their need for cultural difference rather than a sense of Western cultural superiority. Their type of need covered the entire spectrum from mild curiosity to passionate endorsement. We can approach this spectrum from several directions. The first concerns the complex, often mixed or ambivalent, role played by the colonial experience in the modernist imagination. The second concerns the role played in the modernist imagination by exposure to foreign cultures in cases where the relation was not overtly colonial, but involved a degree of appropriative ethnocentrism. The third concerns the negative values attached to colonial experiences in modernist writing. A fourth variant concerns the reverse: the significance of Western modernism to the colonised imagination. We will survey two examples of that in the last section of Chapter 3.

Modernist Chinoiserie

Modernist Chinoiserie and Japonisme show how certain kinds of sensibility found it possible to move from casual interest or superficial curiosity to an informed awareness of other cultures. The articulation of difference at the level of society and civilisation gave ample scope for self-critique. One version of this is described by Cynthia Stamy as 'subversive orientalism' (Stamy 1999: 25), which is cautionary and quizzical of domestic rather than foreign mores, as in Gertrude Stein's recitation from *The Geographical History of America* (1936): 'In china china is not china it is an earthen ware [. . .] China in America is not an earthen ware [. . .] and all who like china in America do like to have china in china be an earthenware' (1999: 35).

Although a poet like Marianne Moore (1887–1972) makes only a handful of references to Eastern cultural practices or artefacts in her poems, her attraction towards the Far East had a specifically American application: 'Like Franklin and Emerson, Moore's orientalist practices were bound up with an enduring American mandate to articulate America' (Stamy 1999: 7). Moore reveals her fascination with the Far East with reference to Chinese dragons, to the 'Chinese / "passion for the particular"' (Zhaoming 2003: 182), and to a large book on *The Tao of Painting* (1956) by Mai-mai Sze. In an essay titled 'Is the Real the Actual?' (*The Dial*, 1922), Moore refers to what is lost or desired by an author such as herself as 'A reverence for mystery'; and in a 1937 review titled 'Concerning the Marvellous', she extols the 'primitive tendency to depict side by side, the real and the imaginary' (Stamy 1999: 60, 65).

An early play by Wallace Stevens (1879–1955), *Three Travellers Watch a Sunrise* (1916), illustrates a similar fascination with China. His later poems reveal a less superficial interest in states of mind in which human consciousness and awareness of natural processes become seamlessly one, as in the poem 'An Old Man Asleep' (Stevens 1997: 427). The poem represents the drowsiness of old age as a state of consciousness similar to the meditative modes evoked by Taoist Buddhism. We might say, therefore, that the aesthetic impulse celebrated in late nineteenth-century England by Walter Pater (1839–1894) and Oscar Wilde (1854–1900) migrated to writers from the US. This happened at a time when the political and economic hegemony of the West ensured that its artists and intelligentsia had the world's art at hand as commodity and loot.[17] Curiously enough, the appeal of the exotic to authors such as Moore and Stevens was not very different from its appeal to a scholar such as Arthur Waley (1889–1966). He translated from the Chinese and the Japanese without ever feeling the need to travel to the Far East. He preferred, instead, to confine his expertise to what he could access of Japan and China from books in London.

The East served a psychic need. Western interest in authors and artefacts saw whatever they admired through the refractive index of that need. This holds true of Yeats's brief (and Pound's much shorter and more qualified) admiration for a Rabindranath Tagore whose writing they knew only through his stylised English self-translations. They, and others like them, projected onto Tagore and his translations (of the vividly poetic Bengali into rather tame Edwardian English) an aura of exalted mysticism that hardly does justice to why he is admired by those who understand Bengali (which has an evocative power and cultural resonance difficult to capture in translation).

Such projections were the indirect result of a problem analysed by the sociologist Max Weber. In a lecture on 'Science as a Vocation' (1917), he described the problem as 'the disenchantment of the world' (Weber 1958a: 155).[18] In this respect, the modernist authors differ from more conventional authors only in degree. The single difference was that the modernist admiration for Eastern artefacts and modes of life provided the reverse image of the antipathy they showed towards the path taken by the modernity of industrial capitalist societies in the West.

The modernist as colonial traveller: Lawrence in Mexico

Visiting new places and encountering new peoples led writers and artists, including those we recognise now as modernists, to creative outputs that remain significant as cultural symptoms of a desire for new inspiration as well as new values, new techniques corresponding to new materials. This holds true of Paul Gauguin (1848–1903) in Polynesia (1891), John Singer Sargent (1856–1925) in Arabia (1891), Henri Matisse (1869–1954) in Morocco (1912–13), or the more indirect matter of Gustav Klimt (1862–1918) and Korea, or the Japonisme of James McNeill Whistler (1834–1903) and Pierre Bonnard (1867–1947), to name only a few examples. The work they produced was a direct consequence of varying degrees of acquaintance with, and immersion in, places and cultures made more accessible to them by colonialism. The desire to experience difference through travel was in part motivated by their reactions to the tenor of modern life in Europe and North America. Gauguin chose to live in Tahiti because it was not Paris; Vincent Van Gogh (1853–90) never left Europe, but travelled in imagination through the Japanese prints he bought in Antwerp in 1885.[19]

Travel encouraged changes in either theme, or technique, or both. A comparison between conventional and popular novelists like G. A. Henty (1832–1902) or Rider Haggard (1856–1925) and a modernist like Joseph Conrad (1857–1924) is revealing: the former pair fostered a mix of old and new stereotypes, whereas Conrad tried to break out of stereotyped thinking (as we shall see in Chapter 2).

Here we are interested only in the latter kind of writer. In their work, more was at stake, in the encounter with the racial 'other', than the frisson of novelty, or the charm of the exotic. The history of Oriental motifs in Western classical music from Nicolai Rimsky-Korsakov (1844–1908) to Béla Bartok (1881–1945) is also an account of music becoming modern through assimilation of cultural difference. Likewise, the history of the Odalisque motif from Jean Ingres (1780–1867) to Matisse measures the changing fortunes of gendered representation under the shadow of the ocular consumption of the feminine exotic. The entire history of Eastern motifs in intellectual history from European Romanticism and German idealism to Nietzsche (1844–1900) on to Herman Hesse (1877–1962) is revelatory of a crisis within the history of European attitudes towards the spiritual dimension of life.

Consider the case of D. H. Lawrence (1885–1930). After some traumatic war years in England, he became increasingly disgusted with the quality of life in an industrialised environment. That propelled him into self-exile for the rest of his life. He travelled first to several places in the Mediterranean region, then to Sri Lanka (five weeks sufficed for him to reject a tropical climate and the Buddhist alternative to Western attitudes and values), Australia (a few months, first in Darlington, then in New South Wales) and then New Mexico. Chapter 18 of *Kangaroo* (1923) dramatises his reaction to Australia: 'It is said that man is the chief environment of man. That, for Richard, was not true in Australia [. . .] But it felt like a clock that was running down. It had been wound up in Europe, and was running down, running right down, here in Australia' (Lawrence 2002: 345).

Wherever he went, he carried the same set of preoccupations and habits with him. He oscillated between enthusiasm and dejection about every new place and society he encountered. Each reaction was based on a contrast with what he had left behind in England. In *Kangaroo*, for example, he writes: 'the heavy established European way of life. Like their huge ponderous cathedrals and factories and cities, enormous encumbrances of stone and steel and brick, weighing on the surface of the earth' (346). The work also reflected the ups and downs of his turbulent married life with Frieda. On the one hand, there was his disgust at 'the mess of industrial chaos and industrial revolt' (1968: 552), and on the other hand, his hope that every new place he tried would turn out to be what he was looking for. Consider the role of Australia in this quest: 'It is the land that as yet has made no great mistake, humanly. The horrible human mistakes of Europe. And, probably, the even worse human mistakes of America' (2002: 347).

There are many occasions in his work where the negative impetus towards alternative utopias can be seen through as a self-reflexive fiction: 'It is all a form of running away from oneself and the great problems' (1932: 561–2). On the other hand, the motive for travel could take on a much more eager and hopeful aspect, and become part of a desire to 'make a great swerve in our onward-going life-course now, to gather up again the savage mysteries' (1966: 137–8). Whenever that fiction of desire could be sustained, it seemed possible for him to affirm, at least for a while, as in New Mexico, that it 'was the greatest experience from the outside world that I ever had [. . .] [it] liberated me from the present era of civilisation, the great era of material and mechanical development' (1970: 203). But the problem had more to do with a loss that could not be recovered from than with a finding what would suffice. The loss emanated from a powerful feeling that 'we are cut off from the great sources of our inward nourishment and renewal, sources which flow externally in the universe' (1959: 107).

Lawrence evolved a type of narrative in which the spiritual or psychic sterility and enervation of the West could be rejuvenated in fictions of desire. This was accomplished by a cultural transfusion of what Europe lacked. The transfusion came from a civilisation that had not lost touch with the vital energies and mysteries of a life lived in greater harmony with nature than possible to Western civilisation ever since it had chosen to follow the path opened up by the Enlightenment and the industrial revolution. From the dichotomous sexual pairings of *Women in Love* (1920) – one member of each pair redeemable, the other not – to the ritualised merger of sexual and religious impulses in *The Plumed Serpent* (1926), to the sexual fantasies of *The Woman Who Rode Away* (1928) and *Lady Chatterley's Lover* (1928), Lawrence reworked the same fable over and over again. *Mornings in Mexico* (1927) is particularly eloquent about the underlying idea:

> The consciousness of one branch of humanity is the annihilation of the consciousness of another branch. That is, the life of the Indian [in Mexico], his stream of consciousness of being, is just death to the white man. And we can understand the consciousness of the Indian only in terms of the death of our consciousness. (1960: 55)

The fable reworked a motif as old as the European and English preoccupation with what a character in the English poet John Dryden's play *The Conquest of Granada* (1672) refers to as the 'Noble Savage'.

The 'other' as an alternative to the West

Lawrence's increasingly feverish writing shows how 'other' civilisations could present themselves to the modernist author or artist as modes of life that had remained at a stage of evolution in the history of civilisations that Europe or the West had left behind, to its disadvantage. In such cases, the cultural productions of another civilisation exercised the appeal of something stronger, purer. We see this in the enthusiasm for Balinese theatre, as expressed in *The Theatre and Its Double* (1938) by the French playwright Antonin Artaud (1896–1948). His argument focuses on the use of conventions and mime, as refined over centuries, to evoke through the power of rhythm, 'the musical quality of physical movement', 'the most impulsive correlations' between sight and sound, and intellect and sensibility, for which there are no equivalents in 'our European sense of stage freedom and spontaneous inspiration' (Artaud 1989: 89). Artaud was attracted to Balinese theatre for the difference it provided from Western theatre, which appeared to him as an extension of the genre of literature, because of its reliance on language in the overall economy of the theatrical. In contrast, as he writes in 'Oriental and Western Theatre', 'The Balinese theatre was not a revelation of a verbal but a physical idea of theatre where drama is encompassed within the limits of everything that can happen on stage, independently of a written script' (121).

Fascination with 'otherness' is as old as travel. How then does the modernist interest in 'other' cultures tell us something specific about the relation between modernism and colonialism? Chris Bongie has a persuasive answer. The modern predilection for exoticism is 'a discursive practice intent on recovering "elsewhere" values "lost" with the modernisation of European society' (Bongie 1991: 5). This entails that 'at some point in the future, what has been lost will be attained "elsewhere"' (15). Western exoticism is a process in which 'modernity has taken the place of tradition; a writing and colonising society has devastated a primitive oral culture' (6). It is intended as a solution to a problem, but it is bound to fail because it proffers a fiction of fulfilment for a need that cannot be fulfilled through a fiction. This need is produced by the damage done to individualism by 'the supposed threat of homogenisation that mass society poses – a threat that for the exotic imaginary proves indissociable from the specifically modern form of territorial expansion' which characterises colonialism (11).

The supposed threat cannot be satisfactorily resolved because the individual living in the shadow of social modernity is 'from the beginning, a posthumous figure of and in crisis, an afterimage in search of what is itself no more than an afterimage' (10), 'always alienated from experience and tradition' (13). In the 1920s, Walter Benjamin developed an analogy between the baroque and the modern eras based on allegory as the mode suited peculiarly to the representation of the processes of ruin and fragmentation (we will read more about it in Chapter 3). Bongie adapts the Benjaminian idea to his exposition of the problem: he describes the exoticisms of authors such as Victor Segalen and Joseph Conrad as ideologies which 'by means of the duplicitous strategy of allegory' conserve the exotic rhetorically, 'engaging in a renewed, and strategic, dreaming of what they know to be no more (but no less) than a dream' (23).

Literary modernism and 'the decline of the West'

The concept of civilisation differs from the concept of culture, and this difference plays a crucial role in a postcolonial perspective on modernist writing and art.[20] The sociologist R. M. MacIver noted, as far back as 1926, that 'our culture is what we are, our civilisation is what we use'. This proposition leads to the distinction that 'one people can borrow civilisation from another people in a way in which culture cannot be borrowed' (MacIver 2003: 94, 95). The issue of borrowing comes up in the case of modern writing and art, as part of a process that began with Europe's colonising encounters with other races. The process became a distinctive motif in the writings of a handful of eighteenth-century individuals. It acquired more prominence with the European Romantics, and became a continuous thread of preoccupations among European writers, scholars and artists throughout the nineteenth century.

The process involved the habit of working with a binarism that presented the West in a relatively negative light, as suffering lack or decline, in comparison to some positive quality discovered in (or projected onto) another civilisation. Let us call this the self-denigratory binary, which must never be read separately from its reverse, the self-congratulatory binary, in which Europeans confirm their own superiority by finding reasons for denigrating all other races and civilisations. The self-congratulatory element of the binary came into its own with the work of scholars and policy-makers who compared Eastern (and other civilisations) with European civilisation to Europe's advantage. The most notorious example, among many, would be the British historian Thomas Babington Macaulay (1800–59), the author of the *Minute on Indian Education* (1835). In that document, he dismissed Asian civilisations as having less to offer than a single shelf of books from Europe, because they did not show him evidence of the kind of modernity achieved by Europe.

Other Westerners, however, were open to a different realisation. The self-denigratory element came into its own when European Orientalism professed to find values enshrined in Oriental civilisations which it was believed Europe had either lost in the modern period, or lacked all along. Consider, for example, the reason given by the German philologist and Orientalist Max Muller (1823–1900), in a Gifford lecture delivered at Glasgow in 1890, for his commitment to the study and translation of ancient texts from India. It echoed sentiments expressed by the philologist Sir William Jones (1746–94) as far back as 1792. Muller writes of the European 'discovery of a literature in India [. . .] more ancient than Homer, of a language less changed than Latin, of a religion more primitive than that of the Germans, as described by Tacitus' (Ballantyne 2002: 42). The dualities concealed in such praise are particularly clear in the tradition of German Orientalism.[21]

Modernist writing plays a significant role in perpetuating this line of self-reflection. Lawrence was eloquent about what he professed to discover in New Mexico: it 'liberated me from the present era of civilisation, the great era of material and mechanical development [. . .] In the magnificent fierce morning of New Mexico one sprang awake, a new part of the soul woke up suddenly, and the old world gave way to the new' (Lawrence 1961: 142). From a different angle, a text such as T. S. Eliot's *The Waste Land* (1922) alludes to several Buddhist and Sanskrit texts to shore up its sense of the fragmentation of modern European civilisation.

Africa and modernist primitivism

Racial difference and its assimilation into art were decisive factors in constituting modernist primitivism, at least as far as its more aggressive dimension was concerned. This dimension was revealed in acts of appropriation and projection. Modern artists and authors professed to discover violence inherent to the expressions and implied values in tribal masks from various parts of Africa, but this violence had more to do with their own preoccupations than with the nature and tradition of African representations. T. S. Eliot's poems illustrate a related tendency of releasing violence in oneself (of language and attitude) in the act of ascribing it to 'other' races.

Recent scholarship has cast a disquieting light on this aspect of his work, especially his interest in scatological verse. This obsession was contemporaneous to his role in laying the foundations of Anglophone modernism in *Prufrock and Other Observations* (1917).[22] Eliot's obscene verses have a direct and unusual bearing on the interface between modernism and colonialism. They focus on a caricatured Columbus, Queen Isabella, King Ferdinand, and a fictive pair, King Bolo and his queen ('King Bolo's big black kukquheen', Eliot 1988: 206):

Now while Columbo and his men
Were drinking ice cream soda
In burst King Bolo's big black queen
That famous old breech l(oader).
Just then they rang the bell for lunch
And served up – Fried Hyenas;
And Columbo said "Will you take tail?
Or just a bit of p(enis)?" (42)

No one is likely to promote such 'Priapism' (86) as good modernism, or even as tolerable doggerel. It remains surprising that Eliot (before the success of *The Waste Land*, 1922) should have nursed the hope that such work could be published under his own name by the same Sylvia Beach who had published Joyce's *Ulysses*. It is disconcerting to realise that Eliot thought his smut as original and interesting as the Vorticist desire to 'blast' custom and hypocrisy (455). The promoter of Vorticism, Wyndham Lewis, would have none of it (Eliot 1988: 66–7). He dismissed Eliot's doggerel as trivia, which were part-and-parcel of the subculture of male bonding. Eliot's inclination towards such scribbling was not a youthful fad. He circulated similar verses among fellow modernists such as Pound and Conrad Aiken throughout his life.

Defenders of Eliot will argue that the ribaldry is light and satirical in intent, steam let off by a repressed, puritanical sensibility overburdened by a genteel breeding, and a general sense of displacement and unbelonging. Regardless, the modernist, in this case, was hardly any better than the most prejudiced of colonialists or sexists. More to the point, the case reveals the degree of ambivalence attached by a male modernist to the repressions nursed within his own sensibility, and the use made of women and other races in tackling those repressions. There is more (and less) to modernist primitivism than asking people to shake themselves out of their complacence.

Notes

1. Michael Levenson distinguishes between current uses of 'modernisation', 'modernity' and 'modernism' as follows: 'modernisation as the condition of social, economic, and technological change; modernity as the lived social experience of these transforming conditions; and modernism as the cultural activity situated within and alongside these other dimensions' (2005: 1465ii).

2. Renaissance humanism established the triad of classical, medieval and modern (Kosselleck 2004: 17), while 'modernity', 'modernise' and 'modernisation' came into use soon after, in the eighteenth century. The latter two terms were used initially with reference to buildings, and various changes brought about by new technologies, and they continue to have a more specific range of meanings. The word 'modernism' too came into use in the eighteenth century, but its early usage had unfavourable connotations, which acquired the sense of tendencies specific to the arts later, from the middle of the nineteenth century (Williams 1989: 208; also Childs 2000: 13).

3. *OED* (2009): 'Modern: Of or pertaining to the present and recent times, as distinguished from the remote past; pertaining to or originating in the current age or period. (A.2.a); Modern: Characteristic of the present and recent times; new-fashioned; not antiquated or obsolete. (A.3.a).' *Merriam-Webster's 11th Collegiate Dictionary* (2003): '1a: of, relating to, or characteristic of the present or the immediate past: CONTEMPORARY: 1b: of, relating to, or characteristic of a period extending from a relevant remote past to the present time; 2: involving recent techniques, methods, or ideas: UP-TO-DATE: 3: capitalised: of, relating to, or having the characteristics of the present or most recent period of development of a language; 4: of or relating to modernism: MODERNIST.'

4. J. Hillis Miller cites Arthur Rimbaud's 'It must be absolutely modern' (*A Season in Hell*, 1873), as the basis for the assertion that 'The "modern" is [. . .] the imminence, the almost about-to-be, of any period whatsoever. Whatever is now is the almost-modern' (Miller 1996: 198).

5. In anthropology, for instance, Cro-Magnon man is called 'Modern Man' (Everdell 1997: 7). In narratives of Western philosophy, 'modern' can mean from Descartes onwards, or from Kant onwards. In political science, modernity is inaugurated in terms of the emergence of the citizen-subject after the French Revolution. In Eastern history, a term like 'modern China' can begin its narrative with the onset of the Qing (Manchu) dynasty (1644); in the context of South Asia, a term like 'modern India' can refer either to its first colonial encounters (in the late fifteenth century) or to political independence (in 1947), and so on. However, there is also a sense in which 'modern' is timelessly significant: thus Chaucer is more modern than Spenser, Donne more modern than Ben Jonson. Tagore remarked of this sense that 'It is a thousand years since the Chinese poet Li Po wrote his verses. He was modern; his eyes had freshly viewed the world' (Tagore 2001: 288).

6. 'Only ascetic Protestantism completely eliminated magic and the supernatural quest for salvation' (Weber 1968: 630).

7. Graham MacPhee's *Postwar British Literature and Postcolonial Studies* (2011: 70–115) provides a wide-ranging account of postcolonial studies as an intellectual and institutional phenomenon with specific reference to its role in British literary and academic culture.

8. The American anthropologist Clifford Geertz is insightful: 'When the colonial system in its classical form, wealth-collecting metropoles carrying off products from wealth-yielding possessions, began to break down during and after the Second World War, the relation between countries in which industrialism,

science, and the like had settled [. . .] and those in which they had not, had to be phrased in a more forward-looking way [. . .] The whole pattern of global connections was reformulated [. . .] as an effort to "close the gap", bring the world up to speed' (Geertz 1995: 137).

9. The Indian social scientist, Ashis Nandy, provides an overview of the resistance to social modernity from Western authors: a distrust of modernity (as in D. H. Lawrence, the primitivism of Picasso and the defiance of science and rationality by the Surrealists); and a rejection of Enlightenment values, as in the work of Blake, Carlyle, Emerson, Thoreau, Ruskin and Tolstoy (Nandy 2004: 18–19).

10. Edward Said remarks: 'One of the critical distinctions of modern literature is the importance given by the writer to his own paratexts – writings that explore his working problems in making a text. James's *Notebooks* come immediately to mind, as also do Gide's *Journals*, Rilke's *Letters*, Valéry's *Cahiers* and Hopkins's letters to Bridges' (Said 1975: 251).

11. The art historian T. J. Clark comments on the role of French painting in the inauguration of modern art in Europe: 'Something decisive happened in the history of art around Manet which set painting and the other arts upon a new course. Perhaps the change can be described as a kind of scepticism, or at least unsureness, as to the nature of representation in art' (Clark 1985: 10). The result was an art that 'seeks out the edges of things, of understanding; therefore its favourite modes are irony, negation, deadpan, the pretence of ignorance or innocence' (1985: 12).

12. Edward Said notes: 'The attention paid to narrative technique by James, Conrad, and Ford is evidence of the way in which the novel abandons its quasi-paternal role in favour of an almost total supplementarity' (Said 1975: 151).

13. In an essay, 'On the Teaching of Modern Literature' (1961), the American cultural critic Lionel Trilling expressed misgivings about his own role as a teacher in assimilating modernism to an educational function. He warned about the danger of going too far in domesticating and canonising the radically disturbing dimension of modern literature, and advised against 'the socialisation of the anti-social, or the acculturation of the anti-cultural, or the legitimisation of the subversive' (Trilling 1965: 26).

14. Tapscott contrasts Spanish and Portuguese modernisms neatly for Latin American writing: 'what Spanish America called "Modernism", Brazil had experienced as "Symbolism". What Brazil experienced as "Modernism", post-Darío Spanish America would work through under the name of post-Modernism' (1996: 11ii).

15. 'I cannot be aware of me as myself in another individual, so long as I see in that other an other and an immediate existence: and I am consequently bent upon the suppression of this immediacy of his' (Hegel 1971: 171).

16. Eric Hobsbawn writes: 'so much of what is still characteristic of the late twentieth century has its origins in the last thirty years before the First World War' (Hobsbawm 1989: 7).

17. Graham Huggan describes the triple-mechanism of commodity fetishism underlying the exoticisation: 'mystification (or levelling-out) of historical experience; imagined access to the cultural other through the process of consumption; reification of people and places into exchangeable aesthetic objects (Huggan 2001: 19).

18. In *The Protestant Ethic and the Spirit of Capitalism* (1904), Weber makes the tendentious claim that scientific rationality and the scientific method are unique to the West (Weber 1958b: 13). Kwame Anthony Appiah (1992: 144–7) points out that Weber's claims concerning secularisation, charisma, disenchantment, rationality and rationalisation need qualification when applied globally.

19. Japanese artefacts became very popular in Europe after the Paris Exposition Universelle of 1867, which followed shortly after the US had ended over two hundred years of self-imposed Japanese isolation from Western incursions in 1858.
20. Tzvetan Todorov notes that 'for over two centuries, "culture" has assumed a broader meaning than as a synonym of "civilisation". Ethnologists have largely been responsible for this change. They realised that the societies studied by them, often lacking writing and monuments and works of art of the kind we habitually associate with culture, nonetheless possessed practices and artefacts that played an analogous role within them; they called these, in turn, "cultures". This "ethnological" meaning has now gained ascendancy' (Todorov 2010: 26).
21. The peculiar complicity between excessive praise/dispraise of the 'other', and an implied self-gratification/self-abnegation, is evident in the long tradition of Germans extolling Sanskrit for its foundational role in the antiquity of the Indo-Aryan family of languages. For example, August Wilhelm Schlegel: 'if the Orient is the region from where the regeneration of mankind is to come, then Germany must be seen as the Orient of Europe' (Murti 2001: 16).
22. Gabrielle McIntire reports: 'the body of work these poems represent is incredibly vast, totalling at least seventy-five stanzas in all. So far, twenty-nine of these have been published – including nearly ten in Valerie Eliot's 1988 *The Letters of T. S. Eliot: Volume One, 1898–1922*, seventeen in Christopher Rick's 1996 *Inventions of the March Hare*, two in *The Faber Book of Blue Verse* – and many more sit unpublished in archives' (McIntire 2008: 14).

Chapter 2

Three Debates

Modernist Literature and the Left

The nexus between colonialism and modernist literature has always been matter for intense critical scrutiny from the intellectual Left. This tradition is characterised by an emphasis on the materiality of culture, and the transformation of social classes by changes in modes of production.[1] Marx's 1853 dispatches to the *New York Daily Tribune* on British rule in India reveal a keen interest in the impact of colonialism on feudal societies, though subsequent scholarship does not always agree with his interpretations.[2] Meanwhile, the orientation and analysis of Lenin's *Imperialism, the Highest Stage of Capitalism* (1916) continues to receive attention for its relevance to our times.[3]

Marxian approaches to colonialism retain the merit of linking modern empires to the global search for raw materials and markets, and of recognising the element of exploitation in the selective modernisation of the colonies. They also divert preoccupations concerning the category of nation towards an emphasis on the role of class in colonial and postcolonial societies. Twentieth-century Marxian critique has continued to focus on the complicated ways in which capitalism exploits and modernises societies and nations in its own image. Subsequent contributions from the Left have taken a special interest in the impact of capital on culture and the arts. The contemporary value of the Left to the study of cultures has not diminished despite the seeming global triumph of capitalism, the collapse of the Soviet Union and the rapid if guarded entry of China into the transnational flux of capital and commodities.

Lukács and Brecht

We begin our survey with a disagreement concerning the role of realism in art. This takes the form of a reaction to the position on modernism articulated by the Hungarian Marxist Georg Lukács (1885–1971) from the German playwright Bertolt Brecht (1898–1956). Brecht's reaction constitutes one of the most significant – but implicit, since he never published his views in his lifetime – disagreements about the nature of modernism in Europe between the two World Wars. It was a turbulent time: the consolidation of communism in post-1917 Russia, the struggle between communism and fascism in 1930s Germany, and the rapid and feverish avant-gardism of Expressionism, Surrealism and Dada in Western Europe. Brecht, the maverick radical playwright, opposes Lukács, the party member whose own 'cultural or theoretical work runs implicitly against the grain of the political establishment' (Eagleton 1996: 10). It may be ironic that the uneasiness expressed by the ever-cautious Brecht in 1938 to the increasing dominance of Lukács (Soviet-based since 1933) in Germany was to remain unpublished until 1968. Brecht's reluctance to publish his response does not diminish the import of the issues in question.

The position developed by Lukács against Expressionism in the 1930s remained relatively unchanged throughout his career, expanding to its fullest in 'The Ideology of Modernism' and the other essays contained in *The Meaning of Contemporary Realism* (1958), including a comparison between Kafka and Mann which is developed in favour of the latter. Lukács treated the series of developments from Naturalism to Expressionism to Surrealism as the reaction of bourgeois creativity to the impact on consciousness of the crises created by capitalism. The result in art was 'a vivid evocation of the disintegration, the discontinuities, the ruptures and the "crevices" which Bloch very rightly thinks typical of the state of mind of many people living in the age of imperialism' (Adorno et al. 1977: 34).

Styles and techniques based on Surrealist montage are interpreted (in agreement with its defender, Ernst Bloch, and using Bloch's words) as 'an account of the chaos of reality as actually experienced, with all its caesuras and dismantled structures of the past' (35). The difference between Bloch (or Brecht) and Lukács becomes evident in their attitude to what is thus accomplished. To Lukács, there is more to the task of the writer than representing the disturbed surfaces of contemporary reality. Mann's fictional character of Tonio Kröger, for instance, may have been presented by his creator as a 'bourgeois who has lost his way', but

Mann also shows his readers 'how and why he still is bourgeois, for all his hostility to the bourgeoisie' (36). Mann may represent a state of consciousness in chaos, but he also contextualises it within a larger totality, which provides a more satisfactory sense of an underlying reality that is not mere surface. The kind of realism recommended by Lukács accomplishes this by 'transcending the limits of immediacy, by scrutinising all subjective experiences and measuring them against social reality' (37).

The 'formalism' condemned by Lukács as the helpless mirroring of trauma raises important questions which are as pertinent to our reading of modernism today as in the 1930s. Is it sufficient for art in a time of disorientating fragmentation to represent the process and experience of fragmentation as an end in itself? Is the type of realism Lukács recommends, based on his admiration for writers such as Balzac or Tolstoy, apt for later times? Were the terms in which he couched the response to modernity by novelists apt: subjectivism and formalism on the one hand, and realism on the other?

Brecht's response to the position laid out by Lukács was a firm 'No'. He rejected the idea that emulating past types of realism was an apt strategy for the twentieth century. For him realism was an artistic goal that could be approached through several formal means. He also rejected the bases on which Lukács set up his antithesis between realism and formalism: 'the so-called sensuous mode of writing – where one can smell, taste and feel everything – is not automatically to be identified with a realist mode of writing [. . .] Realism is not a mere question of form' (82). As playwright, poet and novelist, he also rejected the bias shown by Lukács towards the genre of prose fiction. That was in 1938. A similar view was developed from a different direction, three decades later, and voiced with a good deal of mandarin rudeness, by Theodor Adorno (1903–69), whose position within the intellectual Left differed considerably from that of Lukács.

Lukács and Adorno

As in the 1930s, so in the 1950s, for Lukács modern experience is marked by solitariness and fragmentation: 'man is constitutionally unable to establish relationships with things or persons outside himself' (Lukács 1963: 20–1). In this situation, he finds that the modernist writer exalts subjectivity, as in Joyce's stream of consciousness, Musil's 'active passivity', or Gide's 'action gratuite'. For Lukács, the inner disintegration of consciousness evoked by modernist fiction is matched at the level of technique and form by 'the negation of outward reality' (25).

Modernist writing is obsessed with the pathological. It lacks a concept of the normal against which to contextualise its morbid fascination with the distorted. It is unable to distinguish between naturalism and realism, a distinction that 'depends on the presence or absence in a work of art of a "hierarchy of significance" in the situations and characters presented' (34). Kafka, as an example of modernist writing, presents 'this vision of a world dominated by angst and of man at the mercy of incomprehensible terrors' (36).

Against all this, Lukács reaffirms his conviction that the task of writing is to provide 'a truthful reflection of reality', which can 'demonstrate both the concrete and abstract potentialities of human beings in extreme situations' in such a way as to balance the representation of abstract potentiality with concrete potentiality. For him, this is the key distinction between modernism and realism: 'Abstract potentiality belongs wholly to the realm of subjectivity; whereas concrete potentiality is concerned with the dialectic between an individual's subjectivity and objective reality' (23–4). There is more to his essay, which we will come back to later. But first, we take note of Adorno's response, which offers numerous objections along the lines articulated thirty years before him by Brecht.

In 'Reconciliation Under Duress' (1961), Adorno, like Brecht, rejects the antithesis between realist and formalist, and dismisses the desire for a reflection of objective reality in art as a 'vulgar-materialist shibboleth' (Adorno et al. 1977: 153). He argues that Lukács is guilty of reintroducing organic metaphors to describe social phenomena; that he lumps modernists indiscriminately together, disregarding their mutual differences. Adorno argues that Hegel's idea has been misapplied in using the distinction between abstract and concrete potentiality merely to defend the traditional against the avant-garde. The distinction is inadequate to recognise what the modernists accomplish by way of 'the unity of pragmatic fidelity', as in Proust, where 'we find the most intimate fusion of an extremely "realistic" observation of detail with an aesthetic form based on the principle of involuntary recollection' (157–8).

According to Adorno, Lukács fails to distinguish between art and life. The view promoted by Adorno is anchored to the axiom that 'In art knowledge is aesthetically mediated through and through' (160). Modernists like Kafka, or Beckett, or Proust demonstrate as much: 'Proust decomposes the unity of the subjective mind by dint of its own introspection: the mind ends by transforming itself into a stage on which objective realities are made visible' (160). That brings Adorno to the affirmation that 'The great works of modernist literature shatter this appearance of subjectivity by setting the individual in his frailty into context, and by grasping that totality in him of which the individual is but a moment and of which he must needs remain ignorant' (160–1). He would prefer to drop the notion of realism. In its place, he proposes the idea that art is autonomous, and creates a world different from the real world. He thinks that Lukács underestimates the role of technique, style and form as mere formalism. For him they are essential in making art autonomous: 'Art does not provide knowledge of reality by reflecting it photographically [. . .] but by revealing whatever is veiled by the empirical form assumed by reality, and this is possible only by virtue of art's own autonomous status' (162).

Lukács had characterised modern art as representing human beings isolated in their individualism. To Adorno, this is not an ontological but a historically conditioned predicament. Modern art shows how that alleged solipsism is transcended in art as art: 'the solitary consciousness potentially destroys and transcends itself by revealing itself in works of art as the hidden truth common to all men' (166). If art gives knowledge, it does so through mediation. This type of knowledge is not usefully comparable with scientific knowledge because 'in art nothing empirical survives unchanged' (163). The trouble with Lukács, according to Adorno, is that he reads 'for content and for the message of a work of literature, which he confuses with its nature as an artistic object' (172). Given the vehemence of Adorno's objection, it is worth noting that there have been several recent attempts at presenting Lukács in a more nuanced light, as in the essays collected by Timothy Hall and Timothy Bewes in *Georg Lukács: The Fundamental Dissonance of Existence. Aesthetics, Politics, Literature* (2011), and in the special issue of the *Modern Language Quarterly* on 'Peripheral Realisms' (Sept. 2012).[4] In the latter, for example, Yoon Sun Lee argues that Lukács's aspiration to totality finds a method of broadening the significance of what is ordinarily understood as the merely particular or the purely contingent aspect of life that realism captures. This, she argues, is accomplished through the device of 'typicality', which she illustrates with reference to Asian American literature. Its contexts – in authors such as Jade Snow Wong and Maxine Hong Kingston – sometimes resemble, and at other times differ from, those of postcolonial writing.

The disagreements between Lukács and Brecht, and between Lukács and Adorno, show that differing premises lead to divergent expectations and value judgements. Terms become slippery when exchanged between combatants who, in any case, do not always speak to one another as much as they talk to themselves. Lukács evokes a past whose modes of representation he would like to restore. His moral and intellectual disapproval of modernist literature stems from a worry at what he fears might be irrationalism. Brecht is impatient with theory and sustained argument, but strong on intuition, especially when it comes to what he wants to do in his writing. His reservations against Lukács recognise the threat presented to his kind of exploratory and free-wheeling creativity by the scepticism of Lukács. What he seeks to defend is neither modern art nor this or that author, but his own stake in his own future as producer. He may be curt and sharp, but he is is primarily defensive.

In contrast, Adorno's polemical manner betrays a degree of intellectual pride in his own capacity to mount and demolish arguments. Ironically, he is even more elaborately aggressive about Lukács than the latter had been in the 1920s about Rabindranath Tagore and the German endorsement of Tagore.[5] Adorno's aggression need not distract us from recognising that his Marxism is at the service of the value he placed on modernism. The authors that he puts in its canon (Proust, Kafka, Joyce and Beckett), and the importance he attaches to the ideas of mediation and autonomy in art combine in an effort to make of modernism what Robert Frost said about poetry, that it is 'a momentary stay against confusion' (Frost 1995: 776).

The issues argued over by these three writers might seem to belong to the archive of history, but to treat them as dated would be a mistake. Brecht had the intimation that there were viable alternatives to realism in narrative. Adorno made the notion more nuanced and complex. The debates raise several interrelated questions. Is realism a conviction about what in life art should represent, or does realism concern techniques of representation? Has the term become redundant or pernicious, or does it keep us alert to what an author aims to accomplish?

Fredric Jameson surveyed these debates in the late 1970s, and raised another pertinent question: is realism primarily cognitive or referential? He noted that just as the debate between realism and modernism created a binary opposition, modernism created another binary for itself. It sought to erase history; or to pretend that such erasure could be accomplished. However, this claim to have erased history itself had a place in history. It was the contingent need of a specific time to pretend that it was outside or at the end of history. This he called the paradox or self-dividedness of the historically determinate nature of the erasure of history attempted by modernism.[6] That was in the late 1970s. More recently, in 2012, Jameson redefines realism as having more to do with 'the revelation of tendencies rather than with the portrayal of a state of affairs' (Jameson 2012: 479), and concludes, even-handedly, that while in some situations a modernist stance might be progressive, in other situations, realist fiction might prove more progressive.

What is the relevance of these debates today? The antinomy created by Lukács and berated by Adorno and Brecht between realist and non-realist modes might look too simple and clichéd to conjure with. Nevertheless, it serves to distinguish the more experimental type of writing associated with modernism from the more conventional type that links the twentieth-century writers admired by Lukács to writers such as Balzac and Tolstoy. The experimental tradition, as we might call it, extends from Laurence Sterne (1713–68), the author of the astonishingly self-reflexive and 'proto-modernist' novel *Tristram Shandy* (1761–7) to Salman Rushdie. A collateral branch of this genealogy can be identified in writers such as Nikolai Gogol (1809–52), Franz Kafka (1883–1924) and J. M. Coetzee (1940–), while William Faulkner (1897–1962) and Latin American magical realism exemplify another branch of the same experimental family.

A rival genealogy gathers around the realist camp, from Elizabeth Gaskell (1810–65) to Margaret Drabble (b. 1939); from Anthony Trollope (1815–82) to Arnold Bennett (1867–1937) to Vikram Seth (b. 1952); from Jane Austen (1775–1817) to V. S. Naipaul (b. 1932). These authors aim at different goals, and adopt techniques very different from those used by the experimental camp. Both camps (experimental and realist) are linked internally by a set of resemblances and affinities, even when the social and psychological materials they deal with are very different.

To point the contrast in simple terms, the Sterne-to-Rushdie tradition prioritises manner over matter, style and form over content; it foregrounds modes of representation and narration over whatever is being narrated as a 'story'. Modernist fiction and postcolonial fiction find themselves close to one another in this tradition, making common cause in their resistance to the colonising power of realism. The other tradition aspires to a kind of transparent narrative technique that is well reconciled to realism and intent on giving this or that domain of lived experience a continued lease on life through narrative. We need not exaggerate the split between realist and non-realist writers, but it does seem to continue all the way through the late nineteenth century, past the heyday of the conjunction between empire and modernism, to the era of post-war decolonisation, and into the era variously described currently as neo-realist, postmodern, or postcolonial. It does so regardless of the social background, race and gender of the author. Nor is the applicability of this genealogical commonalty confined to fictional prose, as in the discussion launched by Lukács. The ways in which this speculative hypothesis might be extended to include poetry and drama hinges on what we make of non-realist modes in the specific sense in which the modernist element in writing is associated by Lukács with allegory: this is a topic to which we will return in Chapter 3.

Jameson and Ahmad on the 'third world'

Our final debate has a lively and an ironic side to it. Writing from an American Marxist perspective, Fredric Jameson (b. 1934) offered a hypothesis in the 1980s, but made it sound more assertive than proved apt for a hypothesis. Aijaz Ahmad (b. 1946) responded (from India, as a fellow Marxist) with a good deal of force, which though justified by the issues at stake, felt as if a heavy gun had been brought to bear on a target of moderate proportions. Not that Jameson was ever inconsiderable; on the contrary, as Ahmad acknowledges, Jameson has been something of a hero for the contemporary Left. His speculative hypothesis was secondary to his chief preoccupation, the nature of late modernity and the role occupied by postmodernism (rather than colonialism) in it. His career has been influential, provocative and prolific, with a series of books from *Sartre* (1961) and *Marxism and Form* (1971), to *Representing Capital: A Reading of Volume One* (2011). His essay 'Third-World Literature in the Era of Multinational Capitalism' (1986) remains significant, and proved controversial in light of the debate that followed the response from Ahmad (1987) and a brief, rather subdued, rejoinder from Jameson (1987).

The aspirational category of 'nation' provides a utopian quality to most forms of anticolonial resistance, which does not always find adequate realisations in new nationhood. Although Frantz Fanon voiced his apprehensions in relation to Pan-Africanism and the role of intellectuals in decolonising societies during the 1960s,[7] few could have predicted the traumatic history of the postcolonial nation in most parts of Latin America, the Caribbean, Africa and Asia. Pre-independence optimism about the dream of autonomous nationhood had little or no intimation of the mistakes and betrayals that would frustrate the path to autonomy, once self-government was at hand, and independence led – far too often – to various kinds of misrule. Jameson addressed the issue of how literary production might be affected by such circumstances with the conjecture that a commitment to the idea of imagined nation – as articulated in *Imagined Communities* (1983) by the Anglo-Irish and US based academic Benedict Anderson (b. 1936) – might be the characteristic or defining trait of 'third-world' predicaments. Jameson surmised that writing from within such conditions might be political and allegorical in orientation, in a manner quite unlike its Western counterparts: 'All third-world texts are necessarily, I want to argue, allegorical, and in a very specific way: they are to be read as what I will call *national allegories*, even when, or perhaps I should say, particularly when their forms develop out of predominantly western machineries of representation, such as the novel' (Jameson 1986: 69).

Jameson had two objectives in mind. The first was to help revise the notion of a Western literary canon in the direction of a truly global canon. The second was to urge his Western audience to be more mindful of how texts from regions outside their comfort zone might be salutary in grounding consciousness in contemporary realities very different from any with which they might be familiar. His thesis was based on the alleged difference between Western and non-Western cultures, and this binary mode of thinking was victim to the irony that he reinscribed the very difference he sought to bridge. Regardless, he characterised the West as sharing 'a deep cultural conviction that the lived experience of our private existences is somehow incommensurable with the abstractions of economic science and political dynamics' (69). He then proceeded to give a reading of a Chinese text in translation, 'Diary of a Madman' (1918) by Lu Xun (1881–1936), and the Senegalese novel *Xala* (1973) by Ousname Sembène (1923–2007). His analysis was meant to support the claim, on behalf of peoples who had undergone recent colonisation, that in consequence they could be expected to have a more troubled grasp of the idea of nation. In such predicaments, 'the story of the private individual destiny is always an allegory of the embattled situation of the public third-world culture and society' (69).

Jameson based his argument on the premise of radical difference, and resorted to a distinction about which he had misgivings. He overcame them with the claim that there was nothing better at hand to make the point that contemporary reality was divided between first, second and third worlds. His use of this distinction between three worlds proved unwise. It was roundly criticised by Aijaz Ahmad for its alleged consistency. Moreover, the controversy about the so-called three worlds deflected attention from the far more significant claim concerning allegory and postcolonial modernity in situations entailing the use of Western modes of representation.

The trouble with the terms used by Jameson was that they were vague, politically loaded and polemical rather than descriptive. In the alleged division between worlds, while first and second are contrasted on the basis of capitalist versus socialist systems of production, the notion of a third world is no more than a hold-all category for all those who have suffered recent colonisation. That is not all. The division implies that while the first world is modern, progressive and affluent, the second is only selectively progressive, whereas the third world has yet to arrive at a stage of development where it can claim either modernity, progress, or affluence. This is both complacent and disparaging. It remains unclear whether the nations grouped under the category of the third world are in a process of change in which socialist and capitalist modes of production might both be at work, in different degrees of adaptation and modification. Ahmad dismisses the division as a gross simplification whose polemical properties ensure that its use for the construction of knowledge becomes little more than a form of 'positivist reductionism' (Ahmad 1987: 4).

Ahmad went on to complain that a well-meaning intellectual such as Jameson had based his generalisations on the little he had read from non-Western cultures, which was generally from works in English, or works translated into a metropolitan language. Such texts, he argued, were not necessarily typical or representative, nor did they justify the generalised claims essayed on their behalf from the outside. Worse, the vast and flourishing literatures in non-Western languages from formerly colonised societies were elided by such essays in theorising. Jameson surmised that writing from former colonies was necessarily preoccupied with nation as a category that is embattled and in doubt. But he made the claim without adequate awareness of the other preoccupations, themes, topics and agendas that might be at stake in regions which were, in any case, far too diverse in history and predicament to merit the singular appellation of a third world.

Jameson and Ahmad on 'national allegory'

Ahmad objected to Jameson's focus on nationalist ideology as the dominant preoccupation for postcolonial writing. He argued that the plan to focus on that as the primary theme seemed inevitable only because Jameson chose to define the so-called third world as united through the fact that different peoples were all at one point or the other colonised by Western nations. In his view, it was an oversimplification to think of the world's future as a binary choice between nationalism and American postmodernism. He opposed the totalising meta-narrative that Jameson conjured up in his thesis.

He insisted that literary production was an activity that could be split between first and third worlds because many writers from the alleged third world were first world in sensibility and life style. As far as Ahmad's first language, Urdu, was concerned, he noted that the topics that dominated Urdu writing were not colonialism, or nation, but the nature of feudal societies, the rise of the bourgeoisie and the changing status of women in society. Class and gender were likely to be as prominent postcolonial preoccupations as the idea of nation. British novelists like E. M. Forster (1879–1970) and Paul Scott (1920–78) revealed more fraught anxieties about the colonial encounter than two hundred years of Urdu prose.

Ahmad used a specific language and its literary culture to make his point. One could come up with different examples from other linguistic cultures, and the debate would remain open. It might also be the case that whether the category of nation dominates writing might vary as an emphasis from language to language, and society to society. Writers using a metropolitan language might be more prone to certain anxieties than those who work within languages secure in long traditions of their own, which have conventions at hand capable of handling (and inducing authors to handle) much else by way of thematic material besides the experience of colonisation. The situation was likely to be different with the metropolitan languages, whose very dissemination in the colonies produced new authorial identities, identifications, affiliations and aspirations as well as anxieties.

Subsequent commentators have tended to defer to Ahmad's objections or to try and do some repair work on Jameson's claims. The critic Neil Lazarus, for example, in material first published in 2004 and reprinted in *The Postcolonial Unconscious* (Lazarus 2011: 89–113), looks for plausible explanations for why Jameson's use of the term 'third world' is not exactly what Ahmad said it was. He points out that Jameson does have access to the languages of the Caribbean and Latin America. Likewise, a large part of the writing from Africa does take place in the metropolitan languages introduced to the continent by colonialism from Europe. To that degree Ahmad's stricture against Jameson about generalisations based on metropolitan languages, without access to the non-Western languages of the third world, needs modification. He also argues that Ahmad attributes to Jameson a simplification that Jameson is not guilty of: the supposition that the third world has no choice except between American postmodernity and barbarism. All this shows that the debate is by no means concluded.

It is my belief, however, that a discussion of the terms 'first' and 'third' world is a red herring. Their use by Jameson may have been a matter of contingency. Perhaps it even betrayed an involuntary prejudice, and put his liberalism-from-the-Left in question. However, none of that need deflect attention from the question of whether his thesis is tenable. Some parts of the world did colonise, and other parts of the world did remain colonised for long periods. Therefore, and regardless of terms, there came about a kind of division that is worth looking into, even if we concede that the nature of that division was neither simple nor fixed. Does writing from the once colonised parts of the world reveal the preoccupations he claims they do? If so, how dominant or consistent do they prove to be, in relation to the other issues, topics and themes to which writers from newly independent nations might be drawn? Any resolution to this debate must remain necessarily contingent and subjective. A lot depends on the texts one adduces, the languages one knows and on whether one makes a sweeping or a qualified claim.

I am inclined to support Jameson's conjecture, but in a qualified form. Before I proffer my reasons for supporting the Jameson hypothesis, it is useful to refer to a distinction given currency by the Russian linguist Roman Jakobson (1896–1982) in his discussion of the difference between metonymic and metaphoric modes of writing (Jakobson 1956). Jakobson demonstrates that the metonymic mode leads to forms such as realism and naturalism in fiction, whereas the metaphorical mode leads to forms that seek alternatives to realism. We can see that the field of postcolonial writing shows examples of both kinds. There are far more novelists from India, for instance, who write like Amitav Ghosh (b. 1956) or Vikram Seth (b. 1952) than novelists who write like Salman Rushdie (b. 1947), or William Faulkner (1897–1962), or the novelists associated with Latin American magical realism.

The point of drawing attention to the distinction between metaphoric and metonymic modes is to suggest that whenever and wherever novelists are drawn to modernist influences or adaptations, they are much more likely to be drawn towards the metaphorical mode of writing than to the metonymic. That is to say, postcolonial modernism, if it extends the life of modernism in writing, does so along the metaphorical axis (which corresponds, not as an exact mechanism of language, but in terms of its referential function, to the allegorical mode Lukács associated with modernist writing). In contrast, fiction written along the metonymic axis continues to adapt pre-modernist modes to the realities of specific times and places and human encounters.

Some of these claims will be illustrated and developed further in Chapter 3. Here we conclude with a modified formulation in defence of Jameson's hypothesis, which makes sufficient concessions to what

Ahmad points out. To begin with, I would stress that whatever is claimed is subject to the texts and languages in hand, and subject to the historical frame of reference invoked by the works themselves. Having said that, it is possible to claim that a preoccupation with nation as a dominant theme, and the use of a symbolic-allegorical mode of writing, reveal themselves to be part of a recurrent habit with a sufficiently sizeable sampling of authors to merit recognition as a characteristic, but not necessarily a defining, trait of writing in postcolonial predicaments.

My claim is based on the kind of imaginative writing discussed in the final section of Chapter 3: the postmodernist writing of the Filipino author Nick Joaquin (writing in English) and the Indian poet Arun Kolatkar (writing in English and Marathi). Both combine metonymic and metaphorical modes, and are deeply personal or private in their references and sources of inspiration, yet their work always also takes up positions in an on-going conversation that is part of the cultural politics of the world at large as much as of their respective regions and societies. Joaquin's entire oeuvre lends support to the Jameson hypothesis. His stories and novels, the powerful play *A Portrait of the Artist as Filipino* (1966) and the verse as well as the non-fictional prose, all betray a preoccupation that is at once both allegorical and nation-centred. A good deal of Philippine writing, in all the genres, and especially in English (which is a staple element of Filipino multilingualism) confirms that impression, as does writing in English from Malaysia and Singapore.

Ahmad's criticism of Jameson retains cautionary value. It is necessary to move away from the habit of talking about the world as divided into first, second and third. It is more useful to engage instead with a debate about whether and why allegory has a special application that is both modern and postcolonial. In his response to Ahmad, Jameson emphasised allegory as a mode that may have lost its edge in American writing. Its 'constitutive presence' (Jameson 1987: 26) gives writing from the former colonies a new way in which to conceive of the relation between experience and writing, events and reflection. This way is closer to what Walter Benjamin articulated as the 'the antinomies of the allegorical' (Benjamin 1977: 174). That refers, for our purposes, to the link between the condition to which we give the name 'modern' and the mode of thinking we call 'allegory'. The fictional space created by allegory is a place in-between; it is a profane world, with intimations of a sacred world to which access seems now lost.

The Jameson–Ahmad debate was based on thinking of economic and social splits between the private and the public realms. Ahmad pointed out that when Jameson shifted his discourse from the category of 'nation' to that of 'collectivity', the process of allegory then referred to something broader and more flexible in its potential embodiments than the more specific political idea of 'nation'. Our literary examples in Chapter 3 will show us that the splits are – as often as not – between the sacred and the profane, between modernity as reason and pre-modernity as faith. A preoccupation with the idea of 'nation', as Jameson charac- terised it, can also pertain to the capacity to engage with one's unbelief in souls. If a nation is a fiction difficult to envisage, so is the notion of a self for whom the profane can suffice without need of the sacred. The direction in which one might take Jameson's hypothesis would lead us out of the premises of Marxism and a discourse based on ideas such as forces of material production towards a new horizon defined by the forces conducive or inimical to the production of spiritual values.

As a contemporary footnote to this on-going debate, it is worth adding that Jed Esty and Colleen Lye have argued recently that the diversity of twentieth-century non-Euro-American literatures is masked by the crea- tion of a literary narrative that partitions 'a liberal modernism from a socialist realism', 'thus inclining post-colonial critics based in metropoli- tan institutions toward modernist criteria', whereas, the 'political nona- lignment for the Third World writer in fact entailed an agnostic stance, with both modernist and realist forms usable for anticolonial expression' (Esty and Lye 2012: 269). I agree with them on this, but I remain mindful of the objections raised by Ahmad to the notion of 'the third world', and I am less concerned with 'the possible transcendence of the realism/ modernism antinomy' (269) than with showing how one half of that antinomy contributes significantly to the afterlife of literary modernism.

Modernist Literature and the Right

> You were silly like us; your gift survived it all.
>
> W. H. Auden

Modernists like W. B. Yeats (1865–1939), Ezra Pound (1885–1972) and T. S. Eliot (1888–1965) present us with a seeming paradox: their writing is radical, experimental and revolutionary; but their views on society, politics, race and gender were extremely conservative and reactionary. Their nostalgia for the past matched their apprehensive disgust at the future. Yeats declared that if 'he could be given a month of Antiquity and leave to spend it where I chose, I would spend it in Byzantium a little before Justinian opened St Sophia and closed the Academy of Plato' (Yeats 2008: 158). In Pound's case, he would have chosen the twelfth-century Provençe of the Troubadour poets. In Eliot's case, it would have been Dante's Italy. The three manifestations of nostalgia have one feature in common: attachment to an epoch utterly unlike the twentieth century, one in which artistic culture had a special place in a hierarchically ordered society remote from any kind of egalitarianism. In terms of social prejudice, their views were racist; in terms of literary practice, their views were progressive. Of course, racial prejudice of the anti-Semitic kind has been commonplace in the West, and is by no means unique to these modernists. How can we reconcile an experimental aesthetics with a politics of the extreme right? More pertinently, what does this disjunction tell us about their kind of literary modernism?

The radical aesthetics of Anglophone modernism

We approach the matter of prejudice obliquely, through their formal radicalism. Yeats, Pound and Eliot approached metropolitan culture as outsiders infiltrating a system whose values they revised. Our stage is set in London in the first decade of the twentieth century; a period when all looked rosy in Edwardian England (at least superficially) and Kipling had recently encouraged the US to take on 'the white man's burden' of colonialism in the Philippines (Kipling 1982: 602). The radical aspect of their modernism resembles a postcolonial orientation, since it approached the imperial centre from the margins of their respective countries of birth. The relegation of the British tradition to the margins by these expatriate insurgents did not last long. The British reaction set in from the 1960s. Eliot and Pound remained active for several decades after World War II. Poets like Hugh MacDiarmid (1892–1978) in Scotland and David Jones (1895–1974) in England and Wales retained their modernist sympathies longer than most of their contemporaries. However, subsequent trends in literary historiography took the line that literary modernism in English was a creation of foreigners, as argued in *Exiles and Emigrés* (1970), by Terry Eagleton.

Anglophone literary modernism centred on London during the first two or three decades of the twentieth century, but it had something un-English about it. Henry James may have acquired British citizenship late in life, but he lived in England for many years as an expatriate American. Yeats was Irish. Eliot and Pound were American. Katherine Mansfield (1888–1923) moved to England from New Zealand; H. D. (1886–1961) moved from the US to London and Paris. Wyndham Lewis (1882–1957) was born in Canada.[8] Virginia Woolf (1882–1941) was very English; but James Joyce (1882–1941) kept clear of England. Though Yeats spent a large part of his adult life in London, he always identified with the life and politics of Ireland. Eliot came to England in 1915, became a naturalised citizen in 1927, lived in London for half a century, but remained in some ways as American as Hardy was English. Pound lived in England from 1908 to 1920, but left in disgust, making Europe his home thereafter. It is evident that the writers at the core of Anglophone high modernism lived a diasporic and interstitial existence. If we look briefly at modern art and music, the margin-to-centre movement within Europe is evident in several major figures such as Pablo Picasso, Igor Stravinsky, Wassily Kandinsky, Marc Chagall, Chaim Soutine and others.[9]

When T. S. Eliot, in 'A Preface to Modern Literature' (*The Dial*, 1923), enumerated the names of Anglophone authors who were to be treated as part of a *dead* tradition, because they were *not* modern, his list included many of the most prominent British (and Irish) authors of the day: 'Wells, Bennett, Chesterton, Shaw, Kipling' (Longenbach 1988: 170). A leading modernist, sketching the contours of a new literary history, was leaving out the British. The implication was clear: others – immigrants and self-exiles – were now the preservers of the vital energy that would keep the literary tradition alive in English, and take it in a new direction. That is how Pound put it in his valediction to London, *Hugh Selwyn Mauberley* (1920). Its *Envoi* (1919) alludes to a seventeenth-century poem by the English poet Edmund Waller (1606–1687) to underline the claim that the English were no longer the best custodians of their own literary heritage:

> *Tell her that goes*
> *With song upon her lips*
> *But sings not out the song, nor knows*
> *The maker of it, some other mouth,*
> *May be as fair as hers,*
> *Might, in new ages, gain her worshippers,*
> *When our two dusts with Waller's shall be laid,*
> *Sifting on siftings in oblivion,*
> *Till change hath broken down*
> *All things save Beauty alone.*

(Pound 2003: 557)

That was shortly after the end of World War I. Pound reiterated the point more bluntly in *How to Read* (1931):

The decline of England began on the day when Landor packed his trunks and departed for Tuscany [. . .] Henry James led, or rather preceded, the novelists, and then the Britons resigned en bloc; the language is now in the keeping of the Irish (Yeats and Joyce); apart from Yeats, since the death of Hardy, poetry is being written by Americans. All the developments in English verse since 1910 are due almost wholly to Americans. (1931: 40, 41–2)

The reaction to modernism from British writers

The English themselves, one generation later, did not think differently.[10] In 1960, on becoming the Johore Professor of English at the University of Malaya in Singapore, the poet-critic D. J. Enright (1920–2002) delivered an inaugural lecture titled 'Robert Graves and the Decline of Modernism'. In it, he declared 'that the British were returning to their native element: a sort of eternal Georgianism' (Enright 1960: 8). Literary modernism was over; it had hardly been properly British to begin with, though admirable in its way, and canonised to the point that saying anything critical of it – he felt – was like spitting in church. Others in England felt the same. The poet Robert Graves (1895–1985) alluded dismissively to 'the foul tidal basin of modernism' (Graves 1962: 5). An English poet from a later generation, Philip Larkin (1922–85), reviewing John Press's *The Chequer'd Shade* (1958) suggested that modernism should be set aside as 'fun no more' (Press 1969: 4). In 1962, introducing the anthology *The New Poetry*, the English critic A. Alvarez narrated a series of what he called 'negative feedbacks', which had undone the capacity of the modernist example to take root in Britain.[11]

By 1973, Donald Davie (1922–95), an English poet by no means averse to the modernist example, would declare roundly that 'in British poetry of the last fifty years (as not in American) the most far-reaching influence, for good and ill, has been not Yeats, still less Eliot or Pound, not Lawrence, but Hardy' (Davie 1973: 3). His narrative reinforced the point made by Graves, Enright and Eagleton before him: literary modernism was a phenomenon perpetrated by Americans and other foreigners, while the English poetic tradition continued its way unhurriedly along a path that led from John Clare to Hardy, to the Georgians, to Edward Thomas, to Philip Larkin. As far as poetry in English was concerned, modernism was like a rumour stirring in the metropolis for no more than two decades or so. It may have dazzled the critics, revolutionised the academic curriculum and distracted a few writers from their calling for a while, but the aberration did not last long. Modernism fell back to the status of an episode whose fire had once shone bright, leaving a lot of academic smoke behind, while poets in England could go about their task in a less agonistic and a more humdrum manner. The reaction to modernism was strong and lasting, and when a British poet like Geoffrey Hill (b. 1932) harks back to the modernist oeuvre from the early twenty-first century, it is with a full sense that his post-modernity is atypical for Britain now.

We turn next to fiction. In the first two decades of the twentieth century, in London, it is evident that a number of English novelists did contribute significantly to the establishment of modernist fiction in English: Ford Madox Ford (Ford Hermann Hueffer before 1919), Dorothy Richardson, Virginia Woolf, Wyndham Lewis and D. H. Lawrence (to name some of the most prominent). However, it is equally significant that the other major novelists associated with literary modernism in English came from outside Britain: James (resident in England since 1863), Conrad (settled in England from 1896) and Joyce (for whom settling in England was inconceivable, given the long and turbulent history of relations between Ireland and England). As for early twentieth-century drama, Shaw and Beckett were Irish, and Ibsen, Strindberg, Chekov, Pirandello and Brecht were deeply embedded in their respective national cultures. If their work partook of a variegated modernism of the theatre, it did so from a commonalty that was European, but with few correspondences to drama from England.

Yeats's modernism

The work of Yeats, Joyce and Beckett after them gives some credence to the belief that modernism in English had two branches, of which one was Irish, the other American. If the Irish kind of modernism has something embattled about it (as did the writing of the Haarlem Renaissance), white American modernisms – as befitting a nation that was rapidly coming into its own as the dominant economic power of the century – showed themselves eager to shed the burden of the European and the British traditions. The modernisms of Yeats, Pound and Eliot were more fraught with tensions than those of William Carlos Williams (1883–1963), Wallace Stevens (1879–1955), or Marianne Moore (1887–1972).

Yeats's modernism was embedded in a uniquely modulated struggle for political autonomy and cultural significance for Ireland. His example shows how a modernist could use English as a first language (often while living in London), and yet bring to the metropolis a form of literary and cultural capital foreign, and even hostile, to England. Yeats admired

Mussolini. The novelist and political commentator George Orwell remarked, in a review of a book on Yeats, that

> Throughout most of his life, and long before Fascism was ever heard of, he had had the outlook of those who reach Fascism by the aristocratic route. He is a great hater of democracy, of the modern world, science, machinery, the concept of progress – above all, of the idea of human equality. Much of the imagery of his work is feudal, and it is clear that he was not altogether free from ordinary snobbishness.

The debate over whether to blame or exonerate Yeats for his reactionary views continues to this day.[12]

In purely literary terms, the latter part of his career, from *The Green Helmet and Other Poems* (1910) and *Responsibilities* (1914) to his death in 1939, showed a remarkable capacity for stylistic self-renovation. The significance of his achievement in relation to postcolonial discourse continues to be fought over by rival camps. Critics such as Edward Said and David Lloyd have argued that Yeats's work exemplifies a postcolonial predicament in terms of the troubled and often violent domination of Ireland by England. Others, such as Edna Longley, argue that the desire to co-opt Irish culture into postcolonial discourse ignores the many ways in which life in Ireland has been closer to life in England and Europe than to life in England's colonies.[13] Regardless of how one evaluates the matter, it is undeniable that Yeats's position was burdened by several kinds of irony.

His early work promoted a form of cultural nationalism that proved problematic. It was out of touch with the political realities on the ground. It derived from a world of myth and symbolism whose only basis in mundane social reality was the Catholic peasantry, a class and community with whom the Anglo-Protestant Yeats had very little affinity. Yeats promoted cultural nationalism without the support of an indigenous language. His friend and contemporary George Moore (1852–1933) had argued in a lecture on 'Literature and the Irish Language' (1900) that 'a nation should express itself in the language fashioned by the instinct of the race out of its ideas and spiritual aspirations' (Storey 1988: 158). With no Gaelic to draw upon, Yeats was in no position to provide this kind of consistency to his nationalism.

Edward Said described Yeats as 'an exacerbated example of the *nativist* phenomenon which flourished elsewhere (e.g. *négritude*) as a result of the colonial encounter' (Said 1990: 81). Both kinds of nativism show themselves trapped in a polar opposition that they inverted but did not escape. In the same vein, the Irish critic Declan Kiberd declares that Yeats's relation to late English romanticism was re-enacted in Césaire's relation to surrealism (Kiberd 1996: 21). Meanwhile, since the 1970s, nativists like Ngugi wa'Thiongo from Kenya and the Marathi novelist Bhalchandra Nemade from India have continued to promote the argument typified by George Moore: a national culture cannot be founded on the language of the former coloniser, whose alien modes displace the native into a position of permanently mimetic secondariness.

Yeats pursued Celtic revivalism in a verse idiom derived from the British Romantics. The choice may have been virtually unavoidable for an Anglo-Protestant writer of his generation and social position, but it weakened the case for cultural nationalism, a position he gradually abandoned after 1909. Nevertheless, Yeats never saw himself as a colonised sensibility in relation to the English language. He insisted without any sense of irony that colonised individuals such as Indians should not aspire to write poetry in a language whose cadences were not their own (Yeats 1961: 520). The English language was his, as indubitably as it was not Tagore's, though they were both born in societies that were colonised by the British. On this issue, Yeats stood by the first part of his Anglo-Irish heritage. The subsequent history of postcolonial creativity shows that he was mistaken about at least one thing. People could master English without having to be British or Anglo-Irish. Rhythms could be acquired once writers had naturalised themselves to a colonial language, and naturalised the English language to their cultures. We may not see this in the stilted idiom Tagore used for rendering his work into English; but it is the promise of the future augured in the now famous preface to the novel *Kanthapura* (1938) by the Indian-born, Europe and US based novelist, Raja Rao (1908–2006):

> The telling has not been easy. One has to convey in a language that is not one's own the spirit that is one's own. One has to convey the various shades and omissions of a certain thought-movement that looks maltreated in an alien language. I use the word 'alien', yet English is not really an alien language to us. It is the language of our intellectual make-up – like Sanskrit or Persian was before – but not of our emotional make-up. We are all instinctively bilingual, many of us writing in our own language and in English. We cannot write like the English. We should not. We cannot write only as Indians. We have grown to look at the large world as part of us. Our method of expression therefore has to be a dialect which will some day prove to be as distinctive and colourful as the Irish or the American. Time alone will justify it. (Rao 1970: 5)

Time has proved him right.

Pound's modernism

The young Pound was always clear about shaking the dust of America from his heels. Europe appealed as strongly to him as it did to James before him, and to Eliot shortly after him. Nevertheless, his first volumes of poetry were scarcely more than a pastiche of nineteenth-century models such as Browning and Swinburne. Pound arrived at his modernity quite suddenly. In his 1939 obituary on Ford Madox Ford, he recollected with much self-deprecation that in 1911 Ford had rolled in laughter on the floor upon hearing for the first time Pound reading from his volume *Canzoni* (1911). The ridicule proved salutary because, as Pound confessed, 'my third volume displayed me trapped, fly-papered, gummed and strapped down in a jejune provincial effort to learn, *mer-hecule* [by Hercules! Assuredly; indeed], the stilted language that then passed for "good English" in the arthritic milieu that held control of the respected British critical styles' (Pound 1973: 431–2). No surprise then that one of his biographers suggests that 'If one were to seek a date to mark the beginning of modernism, August 7, 1911, would not be a bad nomination' (Wilhelm 1990: 75).

Pound the critic was keen to slough off derivativeness, though his verse style did not shed late Victorian habits of phrasing until he had assimilated the minimalist influence of the shorter Japanese verse forms, and until he began 'translating' from the Chinese. During 1910–14, he was a catalyst for some of the self-modernising under way with Yeats. During the same period, without Pound's desire to help H. D. and Richard Aldington, there would have been no Imagist movement. Although the Symbolist mode that suited Yeats was very different from the lean and spare styles preferred by the younger poets, Pound the intermediary held on firmly to the central ideas of the modernising process.

He preached its message to Harriet Monroe, the editor of *Poetry* magazine, in 1915: 'Poetry must be *as well written as prose*. Its language must be a fine language, departing in no way from speech save by a heightened intensity (i.e. simplicity). There must be no book words, no periphrases, no inversions. It must be as simple as De Maupassant's best prose, and as hard as Stendhal's' (Pound 1971: 91). Wordsworth and Coleridge may have professed a similar intention in their preface to the *Lyrical Ballads* (1798),[14] but they did not succeed in returning poetry to a heightened selection from the language actually spoken in ordinary life. Wherever Pound recognised others on the same path to literary modernity (as with Yeats, or Eliot, who accepted his help in revising *The Waste Land*), he was unstinting in praise and support. He had a propensity for promoting causes and talents. He accomplished his ends by means of a unique combination of brashness and sensitivity, a capacity to use and abuse friendships and acquaintances for the greater good of the values enshrined in his notion of civilisation. It is no exaggeration to say that without Pound there would have been individually distinctive modernist practices, but no articulated poetics of literary modernism in English.

Pound began to inject directness, simplicity and intensity of visualised emotional content into his poetry with economy and precision from 1914 onwards. His success can be illustrated by contrasting part of a poem in Chinese by Liu Ch'e, as given in one of Pound's early guides to Chinese poetry, Herbert Allen Giles's *A History of Chinese Literature* (1901), with Pound's version.

> Giles:
> Fallen leaves in heaps block up the floor.
> For she, my pride, my lovely one, is lost,
> And I am left, in hopeless anguish tossed.

> Pound:
>   and the leaves
> Scurry into heaps and lie still,
> And she the rejoicer of the heart is beneath them.

> A wet leaf that clings to the threshold.

> (Zhaoming 1995: 40, 41)

Pound had no knowledge of Chinese in 1914 when he 'translated' the poems from the notes of the American art historian and scholar Ernest Fenollosa (1853–1908). He had no Japanese either when he 'translated' the Noh plays from the same material. He relied on cribs, translations, Fenollosa's notes and his own gumption. The English scholar Arthur Waley (1889–1966), who knew Japanese and Chinese, fared much less well as a translator from either language. Fenollosa (and Pound) believed – mistakenly – that the Chinese written character was inherently pictorial. Pound also extolled Confucianism from that period onwards through the rest of his life. One of his reasons: the Chinese 'sought precise verbal definitions of their inarticulate thoughts'.[15] He imbibed from Fenollosa a life-long enthusiasm for the 'concrete colours' of Chinese poetry.[16] However, he neglected the auditory dimension of Chinese poetry until much later in life. His belief in the pictorial nature of the Chinese writing system has not been endorsed by more recent scholarship.[17] Regardless, and ironically, Pound's (mis-)conceptions concerning the pictorial element in

Chinese writing proved fruitful for his own verse, and for the history of modernist writing influenced by his precepts.

His most recent biographer, A. David Moody, notes that even though Pound 'didn't much care for theorising, and would throw out a remark here and a statement there without concerning himself with constructing a full account of it. Yet a coherent and cogent theory can be put together from those occasional remarks' (Moody 2007: 225). What Pound looked for and found in Chinese poetry (and in his private canon of Provençal poets of the twelfth century, Tuscan poets of the thirteenth century, Dante, Gautier and a few other favourites was linguistic precision. In *ABC of Reading* (1934), he claimed that Fenollosa's essay 'gets [. . .] to the root of the difference between what is valid in Chinese thinking and invalid or misleading in a great deal of European thinking and language' (Pound 1951: 19). This difference, according to Pound, was that European thinking remained committed 'to the method of abstraction, or of defining things in more and still more general terms' (20), whereas this was avoided by the residually pictorial elements in written Chinese.

In 1928 Eliot praised Pound's translations as 'translucencies', inventions which provided a version of Chinese poetry, but having to do more with their own time and place in the West as with 'a Chinese poetry-in-itself' (Eliot 1987: 13–14). The trick was to sound contemporary while reinforcing the 'otherness' of the foreign culture. In terms of fidelity to the original, Pound's success, when it occurred, was as much a matter of intuition as of scholarship. Materials and ideas borrowed from cultural systems outside the West proved useful for what they could enable him to accomplish in English as a writer. Eliot tried to have it both ways on behalf of Pound when he remarked of *Cathay*, that it was not Chinese poetry, but great in itself for its time. Eliot's dual claim (that the translations were not Chinese, but that they were as Chinese as the West needed for its time) brings us to the central problem raised by Pound's translations. The scholar Eric Hayot identifies this as 'the question of representation itself, or more specifically, the ability of representations to seem real while being unreal, or to be unreal while seeming real' (Hayot 2003: 12). There is some irony to the fact that one of the major paths to poetic modernity was (mis)translation. Ironic, too, that Pound should introduce one of his short Imagist poems in 'How I Began' (1913), as if it had been a translation:

it struck me that in Japan, where a work of art is not estimated by its acreage and where sixteen syllables [Pound gets that wrong] are counted enough for a poem if you arrange and punctuate them properly, one might make a very little poem which would be translated about as follows:–

The apparition of these faces in the crowd;
Petals on a wet, black bough.

(Pound 1991: 147)

We see how Pound's modernism grew from the process and experience of translation. It confirmed what he wrote of the literary history of England in *How to Read* (1931): 'some of the best books in English are translations [. . .] every new exuberance, every new heave is stimulated by translation, every allegedly great age is an age of translations' (Pound 1931: 43, 44).

The importance of Pound to Anglophone modernism, and of translation to Pound, when placed in the context of postcolonial studies, provides us with a neat inversion of the central claim in what the American critic Eric Cheyfitz has called 'the poetics of imperialism', in which 'translation was the central act of European colonisation and imperialism in the Americas' (Cheyfitz 1997: 104). Pound represents a reversal of the British imperial template. He colonised the English poetic idiom of the early twentieth century with the modernising Orientalism of his Chinese idiom in English. What Pound does with the Chinese is thus secondary to what he does to English. Eliot claimed as much when he described Pound's *Cathay* as a 'Windsor translation' (Pound 1948: 15).

Pound's later career, especially after he left England, led to a medley of eclecticisms, a preoccupation with economics as a political ideology, and a kind of detour from the modernist fervour of his English years (1908–21). Pound as poet never quite recovered from this rupture, though it led him to many fascinating translations and the interminable ad-libbing of *The Cantos*. Although he continued to support and foster the modernism of others, his own stylistic problem remained unsolved. The poetics he worked with remained a matter of eclecticism. While Eliot settled in England and learned to educate his British (and then his international) reading public to the revolutionary element in his writing, Pound cast himself on the waters of self-exile, eccentricity and energetic self-dissipation in extra-literary obsessions.

Modernism and anti-Semitism

Pound and Eliot expressed views on race and gender that many have found provocative and disturbing. Must we engage with their prejudices when we read their work? Or can they be set aside, or explained away? This debate induces awareness of the precariousness and risk of the modernist venture. Yeats, Pound and Eliot were forward-looking when it came to writing But they were also extremely backward-looking when it came to class hierarchies, modes of political governance and the struggle for racial and gender equality that runs as a continuous thread of progressive social, political and ethical thinking right through the twentieth century into our own times. Their kind of aesthetic modernity was ill-adjusted to most forms of social modernity. They disparaged democracy; they were free and frequent in declaring their racial and gender prejudices. Their regressive attitude towards society and culture was inextricably bound up with how they wrote. One way out of the problem is to set aside the most extreme instances of prejudice as caprice or misguided error. The alternative is to insist that the convictions from which prejudice arose must be taken seriously, and can affect how we react to an author.

It bothered a critic such as George Steiner that Eliot's best or most characteristic poetry could be racist. He found it less troubling in the case of Pound because the latter voiced his objectionable opinions in poems that Steiner did not find interesting as poems. For someone not persuaded by Steiner's argument, prejudice is equally suspect, regardless of how well the poem succeeds or fails as art. In fact, we might wonder if any piece of writing can succeed as art whose views are hurtful and unjust in relation to sizeable parts of humanity.[18] Can the willing suspension of prejudice come into play and allow us to react to works of art without having to agree or evaluate the author's beliefs against one's own? Consider part of the evocative beginning of Eliot's 'Gerontion' (1920):

My house is a decayed house,
And the Jew squats on the window sill, the owner,
Spawned in some estaminet of Antwerp,
Blistered in Brussels, patched and peeled in London.

(1996: 349)

Consider a typical stanza from 'Burbank with a Baedeker: Bleistein with a Cigar' (1920):

But this or such was Bleistein's way:
    A saggy bending of the knees
And elbows, with the palms turned out,
    Chicago Semite Viennese.

And lines like these, from the same poem:

> The rats are underneath the piles.
> The Jew is underneath the lot.

(1996: 353)

Such writing is habitual in its anti-Semitism. Eliot's prose in *After Strange Gods* (1934) makes the issues at stake for him explicit through his insistence on certain 'dogmatic beliefs' that he thinks are essential to preserve 'tradition':

> The population should be homogeneous; where two or more cultures exist in the same place they are unlikely to be fiercely self-conscious or both to become adulterate. What is still more important is unity of religious background: and reasons of race and religion combine to make any large number of free-thinking Jews undesirable [. . .] (1934: 19–20, quoted in Ricks 1988: 40–1)

Astonishing sentiments, uttered baldly in *After Strange Gods* (1934). One can cite other such examples from his work, but this should suffice to underline the seriousness with which a particular kind of conservation preoccupied Eliot in the 1930s.

Meanwhile, Pound supplies his own set of offensive utterances. Eliot never republished *After Strange Gods*; but Pound kept making anti-Semitic remarks throughout his prose and throughout *The Cantos*. The critic Robert Casillo (Casillo 1988: 3) notes for instance that while Canto 94 speaks of maintaining 'antisepsis' in probable relation to Jews, Canto 97 speaks of the Jews in terms of the need for 'clearing fungus' (Pound 1972: 635, 676). The published work provides countless other examples of anti-Semitism. To begin with, it was a form of distaste and suspicion of Judaism as a religion, and of Jews as a people associated with the Near East and the Middle East (that is, not European in origin). During the 1930s, these opinions became strident and obsessive. From the 1940s, until a very late recantation, they became virulent.

Pound blamed Judaism for its monotheism: he believed it led to repressive practices. He also blamed it for its alleged tendency to abstraction (which led to what he believed were culturally sterile practices such as allegorical or metaphysical thinking). Above all, he blamed it for its support of usury (despite his awareness that Judaism was clear on the kinds of lending that were not to be used for gain). He also believed that it had a debilitating and castrating effect on thought and culture. From the 1930s, Pound's emphasis shifted towards the economic field as central to societies and cultures. 'Jewish rationalism and commercialism', Robert Casillo notes (1988: 71), became 'the primary forms of modernity', and Pound grew insistent in his conviction that they 'corrupted Western agriculture and the sacred homestead', notions that formed the bedrock of his cherished nostalgia for a Europe of the mind.

The racism of writers like Eliot and Pound raises a persistent question. How can art and literature be judged solely on aesthetic grounds (whatever those grounds may be in specific terms), when a reader is likely to be provoked into outrage by some of their more extreme declarations? The notion of the autonomy of art can break down when writers address issues on which readers might have strong convictions of their own. Consider a less blatant example. Eliot, in a 1962 booklet on George Herbert, wrote: 'I regard it [Herbert's *The Temple*] as a more important document than all of Donne's religious poems taken together.' His reason: in Donne he finds 'dominance of intellect over sensibility', whereas he prefers what he discovers in Herbert, 'the dominance of sensibility over intellect' (Eliot 1962: 36). Clearly, value judgements are the outcome of specific systems of belief, and there is the risk in Eliot's preference for Herbert over Donne that he values a particular type of religious practice over another as the main reason for preferring one poet to another.

Eliot asserts that readers who are not Christian and readers who do not subscribe to Herbert's Church can respond equally favourably to the poetry as poetry. It seems, however, that how he values or devalues Herbert is linked to how he thinks Herbert relates to a specific religious practice. The example raises a more general point of debate. When is a writer's belief or prejudice irrelevant or marginal to how a reader might respond to the writing, given that we can hardly expect consensus on all beliefs and prejudices between authors and readers, nor expect odious prejudices to be simply ignored when they occur in literary writing? More to the point, how does this general situation come to focus in the interaction between literary modernism and postcolonial discourses?

Our survey of modernism and the Right casts some light on two related but distinct terrains. The first covers the relation of modernist writing to metropolitan literary traditions in Britain. The second covers the ground that links modernism to modernity. The anti-establishment nature of the rhetoric deployed by writers such as Pound and Eliot has a postcolonial dimension. In its time, it overthrew metropolitan norms of good writing to create an audience amenable to an alternative view of writing. As we have noted, the effects of this rebellion did not last long (on writers, as distinguished from academics and teachers). Authorial sensibilities and tastes within Britain reverted to a modified form of the indigenous tradition. Poets such as W. H. Auden and Louis MacNeice may have admired Yeats and Eliot, but they did so with mixed feelings, and their own writing adopted a more conventional and colloquial tone. Even though the modernist canon in English was ingested into the academy, most writers in Britain had moved away from the spirit of radical experiment that characterised the first quarter of the twentieth century.

Our second terrain covers the two traits shared by Pound and Eliot: their vehement prejudices, and their almost desperate desire to find solutions to the problems of the West in other civilisations. Without exonerating such authors from responsibility for their views, it is possible to interpret their attitudes as symptoms of distress in the face of social modernity. The Eliot who wrote anti-Semitic verse and prose was desperately uneasy and scared that the world he cherished was disappearing rapidly, and what lay ahead filled his conservative temperament with foreboding. This hypothesis does not excuse his type of view. It suggests that modernist experiments with language and form were no mere adventures of the mind; they were symptoms of strain, frustration and apprehension. If Yeats voiced admiration for Mussolini, and Pound too praised the Italian dictator for the wrong reasons, or Eliot declared himself a Royalist in politics, they took those positions at least in part because of their unease about the modern tide of events. The strategies and formal experiments that we associate with their literary modernism had less to do with mastery than with looking for a coping mechanism.

Modernist Literature and Race

We have seen that authors like Eliot or Pound were anti-Semitic. With Joseph Conrad (1857–1924), we encounter an issue that is related to anti-Semitism, but takes a more diffuse form: less extreme than xenophobia, but more than mere Eurocentrism. Fear, incomprehension, suspicion, shock and revulsion may well be some of the involuntary ways in which most people react to other races. Does it matter when it comes to issues of race whether a writer is modernist or not? Was Conrad a racist despite himself, as the Nigerian novelist Chinua Achebe (b. 1930) suggests? Or is that impression neutralised by the basic sympathy his works reveal for the plight of the colonised?

Achebe claimed to find evidence of involuntary ethnocentrism in *Heart of Darkness* (1899). We can look at the evidence, and then at a question. Conrad was well aware of the depredations to which Europe's colonies were subjected in the decades following the abolition of slavery in Britain (during the 1830s). He was also aware of the rush for profit that characterised the parcelling out of African territories among European nations after the Berlin Conference of 1884–5. Does the evidence for how this awareness is reflected in the novella offset the alleged involuntary racism?[19] Patrick Brantlinger reminds us that when Conrad went to the Congo in 1890 as an employee of King Leopold of Belgium, 'he was appalled by what he saw. In both his "Congo Diary" and *Heart of Darkness*, Conrad bears witness to the atrocities that, starting in the late 1880s, grew into an international scandal' (Brantlinger 2009: 143). Achebe would have us set aside such evidence and judge the novella as compromised.[20]

We have seen how many European writers and artists looked to other races and their cultures for a symbolic rejuvenation of their own society and culture. D. H. Lawrence, as we saw in the previous chapter, diagnosed the malaise of the West as a form of psychic enervation, and it sent him on a quest for religions modelled on what he thought were vital rituals of blood and violence from Aztec civilisation. In such contexts, it would appear that the racial 'other' is 'seen' only insofar as a particular need is concerned. That makes the interest in the racial 'other' liable to distortion. When Eliot turned to figures like Sweeney, it was to find or place in this fiction a form of brutishness that appeared to repel as well as fascinate him. Achebe suggests that something similar might have been the case with Conrad. The kind of life Conrad had led up the point of writing stories such as *Youth* (1898) and *Heart of Darkness* (1899) had given him more experience in dealing with other races than Pound and Eliot ever had with Jews in Europe. If anyone was likely to be aware of the interface between the colonial and the modern as fraught with complex overtones, it was Conrad. Therefore, to accede to Achebe's allegation would show up one of the founding texts of that interface as canonised despite its problematic nature, and concede a troubling limitation to the imaginative range and sympathies of the modernist achievement.

Achebe on Conrad

Heart of Darkness (1899) is a widely read, admired and studied text. Work such as André Gide's *Voyage au Congo* (1927), or a movie such as Francis Ford Coppola's *Apocalypse Now* (1975), are testimony to the symbolic power and cultural resonance of Conrad's tale. Its fame might have been part of the reason why Achebe chose to attack it in a lecture delivered at the University of Massachusetts in 1975. That was just over three quarters of a century after the publication of Conrad's novella. For Achebe, the Conrad text exemplifies a general problem: the failure to give Africans and their continent the same consideration as Europeans or Westerners would expect to give one another and their homelands. He picks on Conrad because the novella is by no means simple or crude in its seeming prejudice against Africa and Africans. According to Achebe, Conrad reveals his bias in a manner that is typical of the overt as well as involuntary disparagement Africans receive (along other colonised peoples) in intercultural encounters by Western writers.

These disparagements arise from the common supposition that Africa lacks a history, and that life on the continent, especially in the tropical regions, has barely evolved from the primitive stage of human existence. Related prejudices include the notion that the region is populated by wild beings that are scarcely human, because they have little or nothing by way of culture and civilisation. Such people, it is professed, are violent and brutish. Worse, they seem capable of inducing in Westerners all the savagery that the civilising process has tamed over many centuries of social and cultural evolution: 'Going up that river [the Congo] was like travelling back to the earliest beginnings of the world, when vegetation rioted on the earth and the big trees were kings. An empty stream, a great silence, an impenetrable forest' (Conrad 1999: 66). Conrad indicates that a developmental process similar to that enjoyed by the civilisation centred on the Thames region did not occur – for whatever reasons – around the Congo. We can describe this attitude in Brantlinger's splendidly ironic phrase as 'a self-congratulatory anthropology' (Brantlinger 1985: 184). Conrad, though, is quick to deflate the complacency of that attitude with the cautionary reflection shared by Marlow with his audience aboard the *Nellie*, that 'this also [. . .] has been one of the dark places of the earth' (Conrad 1999: 29).

Contact with Africans, as Achebe interprets Conrad's narrative, is liable to bring out all the savagery and corruption that human beings are capable of, once the civility and civilisation inculcated into them by Western civilisation is tainted by association with Africa. Conrad insulates the question of whether he is implicated in the views and opinions expressed in his tale through two narrators: the unnamed Englishman who provides the framing narrative, and Marlow's recollections of his experience of the Congo, which form the bulk of the novella. For Achebe, the tale is symptomatic of a wider malaise afflicting the West: Africa is denigrated as savage; and the corruption of human ideals to which even the best minds of Europe are susceptible is projected onto Africa. Africa becomes an instigator of brutishness in someone like Kurtz, who began his encounter with Africa in a spirit of utopian idealism. He was once 'a prodigy', 'an emissary of pity, and science, and progress, and devil knows what else', the repository of 'the cause entrusted to us by Europe [. . .] higher intelligence, wide sympathies, a singleness of purpose' (55). Africa changed all that.

Achebe begins with the natural irritation with which any African might regard the Western habit of declaring and assuming that Africa has no history. This habit has a long history. Its most notorious exemplar was the philosopher G. W. H. Hegel, who dismissed Africa out of hand: 'it is no historical part of the World'.[21] Does Conrad share this assumption? In a manner not very different from Hegel, the English historian James Anthony Froude was to recommend 'enlightened despotism' in the British administration of Ireland during the 1870s; and shortly thereafter, in *The English in the West Indies* (1888), he declared that 'there were no people there in the true sense of the [. . .] word' (qtd Chamberlin 1993: 38). His sweeping dismissal of enslaved humanity continues to haunt Caribbean writing to this day. V. S. Naipaul echoed this prejudice in *The Middle Passage* (1975); Derek Walcott attacked it furiously in his Nobel lecture, *The Antilles Fragments of Epic Memory* (1992). Achebe's indignation has a context in how the colonised have been misrepresented. The question is, does the Conrad represented by Achebe seem plausible?

The textual evidence

The first claim made by Achebe is that *Heart of Darkness* exemplifies the need 'in Western psychology to set Africa up as a foil to Europe, as a place of negations', as 'the antithesis of Europe and therefore of civilisation' (Achebe 1988: 3). He argues that the Congo is represented in comparison with the Thames, as its 'primordial relative', as that which could bring about 'an avenging recrudescence of the mindless frenzy of the first beginnings' (4). And indeed, Conrad has such a connection in mind: 'They howled and leaped, and spun, and made horrid faces; but what thrilled you was just the thought of their humanity – like yours – the thought of your remote kinship with this wild and passionate uproar' (1989: 69). The remote kinship is activated across time, once space is crossed; as if Europe's past self, in African guise, was brought face to face with its late nineteenth-century visage. The operative word to describe the feeling dramatised by Conrad in Marlow is 'thrilled'. The word is not directly denigratory; it indicates a sudden and surprising onslaught of ineffable feelings, and provides testimony to the powerful effect produced by the encounter on Marlow. Achebe is unimpressed, though he recognises Conrad's capacity for linguistic complexity as a key element of the narrative.

The second feature that bothers Achebe is the manner in which Conrad represents Africans as types. His comment on the group activities narrated by Marlow is telling despite (or because of) its sarcasm: 'these people must have had other occupations besides merging into the evil forest or materialising out of it simply to plague Marlow and his dispirited band' (15). It will be easy for most readers to concede that Conrad's representation of women is not the most plausible part of his narrative. His account of Kurtz's 'Intended', as contrasted with his stereotyped representation of Kurtz's African mistress ('a wild and gorgeous apparition of a woman',100), drives home for Achebe the significance of Conrad's 'bestowal of human expression to the one and the withholding of it from the other' (Achebe 1988: 8). Even if we grant Achebe the recognition that Conrad favours the European woman with an exaggerated display of courtesy on the part of Marlow, the more general implication of Achebe's criticism is a different matter.

The narrative of *Heart of Darkness* is refracted through the index of two personas, an unnamed speaking voice and the character of Marlow. Despite Marlow's wealth of travel experience, he is represented as someone who is conscious of his limited knowledge of other societies and peoples, more used to sea than land, more familiar with the company of sailors than of women, and rooted in English culture. Should we give Conrad the benefit of the doubt that Marlow's limitations are not shared between novelist and narrator? Could we then accept the difference in treatment between Africans and Europeans as a function of realism in characterisation? Or does the blame apply to both narrator and novelist, since neither Marlow nor Conrad had encountered the continent or its people before, and Africa appears strange and estranging to them both?

Those who argue that Conrad deliberately creates a Marlow unaware of his own limitations emphasise the manner in which Conrad uses that flawed nature to imply a critique of Western colonialism. We are meant to see how even a well-intentioned liberal such as Marlow is limited by his cultural conditioning. This argument interprets Marlow's characterisation as embedded in irony. In this line of argument, Conrad's narrative style is capable of irony and his obliquely subversive manner defuses any simple notion that he took Europe's civilising mission uncritically. Consider the irony he deploys in this example from 'An Outpost of Progress' (1897): 'The Managing Director of the Great Civilising Company (since we know that civilisation follows trade) landed first, and incontinently lost sight of the steamer' (Conrad 1920: 116).

Achebe, however, has little patience with irony. He insists that in the absence of an explicit alternative or corrective to Marlow's simplified and distorted representations of Africa, the reader is left with little but prejudice. He complains that Conrad 'neglects to hint, clearly and adequately, at an alternative frame of reference by which we may judge the actions and opinions of his characters' (Achebe 1988: 10). Conrad may be a liberal, but that does not mean that either Conrad or his narrator accept Africans as equal to Europeans in their humanity: 'The black man lays a claim on the white man which is well-nigh intolerable' [to the white man] (11).

Conrad's defenders shift the emphasis from Africa to the unravelling of a mystery, Marlow's discovery of Kurtz. The narrative, it is argued, has less to do with Africa than with the decline and fall of a former European idealist.[22] This argument does not satisfy Achebe: 'Can nobody see the preposterous and perverse arrogance in thus reducing Africa to the role of props for the break-up of one petty European mind?' (12). He goes on to argue that even after due allowance has been made 'for all the influences of contemporary prejudice' on Conrad's sensibility, 'there remains still in Conrad's attitude a residue of antipathy to black people which his peculiar psychology alone can explain' (13). Achebe broods on the frequency with which Conrad's work alludes to 'niggers'. He finds Conrad full of irrationality in his love of Englishness and his distaste of, and horror at, black people.

It bothers Achebe that Conrad perpetuates 'prejudices and insults' (15) that have brought suffering to Africa for the major part of the history of its encounters with white men. He notes the irony that at about the time that Conrad was busy depicting Africans as savages, tribal art in the form of masks from a region to the north of Conrad's Congo was about to make its impact felt on European sculpture and painting. The works of Derain, Picasso, Matisse and others from the decades after 1905 show more discernment about, and enthusiasm for, African sophistication than Conrad's fearful and fascinated revulsion in *Heart of Darkness*. The traditional masks of the Fang people (like other 'primitive' art) may have played an instrumental role in transforming European modes of representation, but Achebe seems not to be bothered with the likelihood that they too were acts of misappropriation: African materials for European needs. They too – like Conrad – stand accused of turning African encounters into a pretext for Eurocentric concerns. Instead, he uses the contrast to condemn Conrad's prejudice as dated and illiberal even for its times. His conclusion: 'Conrad saw and condemned the evil of imperial exploitation but was strangely unaware of the racism on which it sharpened its iron tooth' (19).

Achebe's attack on Conrad is an attempt at redressal. It uses Conrad as a pretext to condemn a much larger and more diffuse discourse. Whether it is fair to Conrad's text remains a complex question, capable of polarising readers. The interface between 'colonial' and 'modernist' is not easy to assess. Colonialism created the circumstances in which Europe and its many 'others' encountered one another. Regardless of the art-form in hand, and the artistic temperament, the modernist side of the interface remained preoccupied with articulating Europe's unease with itself, with its ways of doing, thinking and being. Colonialism sharpened the sense of unease through the differences it provided for cultural self-reflection. An ethics of the 'other' was so much more difficult to manage, even for someone as liberal and conscientious as Conrad, or Marlow. European civilisation – however worn out or open to criticism from insiders – was not likely to value or respect other peoples, societies and cultures except as a means to its own ends.

For Achebe, Conrad is implicated in the Western set of assumptions and habits about the black races. That compromises his critique of colonialism and limits his sympathy for the racial 'other'. The see-saw between fascination and repulsion in the European attitude towards Africa and Africans is a motif that recurs before and after Conrad. The problem Conrad set himself was the question of how to reverse the pride in European assumptions that they are the true embodiment of civilised values, while constructing an ambiguous subjectivity as his narrative frame. We can see such an example in a postcolonial writer whose admiration for Conrad is mixed with recognition that the values that Conrad both upheld and criticised could do great damage when assimilated by the colonised into their own problematic aspiration for a liberating modernity of outlook. We find this discerning and complex response in Tayeb Salih's Arabic novel from postcolonial Sudan, *Season of Migration to the North* (1966).

Tayeb Salih (1929–2009): modernity inside out

To move from Joseph Conrad to Tayeb Salih allows us to examine the literary interface between 'colonial' and 'modern' from a perspective that is the opposite of the one provided by *Heart of Darkness*. Salih's *Season of Migration to the North* was serialised in a Lebanese magazine in 1966 and published as a book in 1967. It was translated into English in 1969. Salih's novel alludes to both Arabic and Western traditions of narrative.[23] The story is set in a village in northern Sudan, on the banks of the river Nile, at a time when the region had already been under British Home Rule for some years. In most fledgling African nations the end of colonial rule was followed all too swiftly by brutal dictatorships, coups, civil war, pestilence, or simply by sheer mismanagement. Meanwhile, Arab anti-colonial nationalist elites expressed the desire to drive out the European powers and to forge modern nation-states. This desire was premised upon political demands for modernisation on the Western model.

Salih recollected the time of composition and publication of *Season* as a period in which his part of the Arab world experienced 'a great upsurge of intellectual energies, both political and cultural' (Salih 2003: v). The novel recalls this moment. As in Conrad's tale, the narrative moves fluidly between a certain kind of social realism and an impressionistic mode of narration. This flexibility allows Salih to develop a conversation with canonical texts such as Shakespeare's *Othello* as well as *Heart of Darkness*. A young Sudanese, Mustafa Sa'eed, wins the attention of the colonial establishment in Khartoum and Cairo. He shows enormous promise and enters the academic and social world of post-World War I London. There he is brilliantly successful as an economist. He is even more successful in sweeping white women off their feet. Several of these women first believe that he would marry them, only to realise later that he had always meant to dupe them. Many of them ultimately come to a tragic end.

Mustafa's sexual appetite leads him first to the dedicated pursuit of, and then marriage to, a woman named Jean Morris. Marriage is followed by British citizenship for Mustafa. Wild rumours circulate at this time about his involvement 'in the plottings of the English in the Sudan during the late thirties' (Salih 2009: 46). The marriage does not last long, and Jean Morris is killed by Mustafa. The tale becomes one of crime and atonement: Othello gone wrong, as in Shakespeare, but for reasons unrelated to the machinations of an Iago. Mustafa's downfall is brought about by his dual impulse to self-colonisation and self-modernisation. He kills from the perverse desire to extract revenge for empire from the Desdemonas of the English nation. He resents what he has cherished. His hatred of the culture that so thoroughly colonised him induces from him this savage and Kurtz-like overturning of civilisation: 'Everything which happened before my meeting her was a premonition; everything I did after I killed her was an apology' (26). Moreover, unlike Desdemona, Jean almost wants this death, indeed goads Mustafa into killing her.

The narrative structures and ideological underpinnings are as complex as Marlow's narrative within a narrative. *Season* is narrated by a young man who meets Mustafa for the first time after Mustafa's return from England. The narrator is fascinated and intrigued by Mustafa, and an affinity develops between them for which one can find a partial analogy in *Heart of Darkness*, in which the second narrator, Marlow, reports on what he discovers of Kurtz to the reader. The appetites and compunctions that drive Mustafa are no less enigmatic than Kurtz's attraction to corruption, or Marlow's desire to preserve as well as protect the memory of what Kurtz became. The ambiguity surrounding Mustafa is kept in the foreground throughout the recollected narrative of his career in England, and afterwards, in the new life he creates in the Sudanese village of Wad Hamid, with a second marriage and two children. Towards the end of the novel, he disappears, leaving the narrator, to whom he has confided a lot about his life, to handle the mess that results: it is later reported that he is either dead 'by drowning or suicide' (51). What remains is a responsibility that stays with the narrator. The moral dilemmas are now his to solve.

Conrad and Salih: parallels and contrasts

Like *Heart of Darkness*, *Season* adopts the distancing device of two narrators. We read the story at one remove. The first-person narrator is a young man freshly returned to his home village in northern Sudan after seven years of studying literature in Europe. Just as Marlow is a window that opens onto Kurtz, this young man opens onto the mystery that is Mustafa. For his setting, Salih creates the village of Wad Hamid, closely resembling his own childhood home. It provides the setting for all of Salih's fiction: the seven Arabic stories in *Dawmat Wad Hamid: Sabʻ Qisas* (*The Down Tree of Wad Hamid*, 1960), of which two were published in English translation in *The Wedding of Zein* (1962), and two other stories collected in *Bandarshah* (written in the 1970s, published in translation in 1996). It is interesting to note that though Salih spent most of his adult life outside the Sudan, in London and Paris, with English and French as his working languages, all his fiction retained the locale and language of his childhood region.

Heart of Darkness draws upon Conrad's African journey; *Season* draws upon Tayeb Salih's educational career in England, which provides an oblique autobiographical model for the educational careers of his two narrators. For the two characters (as for the novelist), education proves the means towards Westernisation and modernisation; it is also that which takes a young man from the village to the city; and it sets up the dilemma that Salih poses for his framing narrator: should one embrace Western modernity, and the inevitable transformation of the self that it entails? Or should one choose differently? The analogy stops there. Like Conrad, and unlike his two protagonists, Salih never quite went back to Sudan, working first in London, later in Paris, and finally living out his retirement in London. In Conrad's novella, Marlow confronts the decision whether to tell Kurtz's 'Intended' a 'white lie'. Salih's narrator is implicated in the story of Mustafa on the matter of having to make an even more personal decision: whether to tell Mustafa's wife of his growing feelings for her. Eventually, his delay is unable to prevent a tragedy: she kills herself rather than accept physical abuse in marriage to an old man on whom she is forced after it is presumed that Mustafa is dead, leaving her a widow. Salih's narrator, unlike Marlow, is not given the luxury of mere anecdotes exchanged among friends in the comfort of a security that faces no hard decisions. He suffers bitter self-recrimination.

In Conrad's tale, the experience narrated both is, and is not, Conrad's own. Likewise, Salih's own life is implied, but not directly reproduced, in the story narrated in *Season*. In *Heart of Darkness*, as we saw earlier, a great river snakes through the Congo, primordial analogue to the now-civilised Thames. Likewise, in *Season*, the river Nile (a great bringer of nourishment, and a breeder and destroyer of civilisations) splits Sudan into east and west, with Europe, England and the Thames a distant north-west. Just as Marlow felt an affinity towards Kurtz, Salih's narrator expresses an affinity towards Mustafa Sa'eed. Marlow is witness to a dark secret: the utter degradation of Kurtz; Mustafa also entrusts the narrator with the story of his sexual exploits in England. In each case, the narrator, who traces the footsteps of the central protagonist, must learn the lesson not to allow that memory to be forgotten; yet he must also protect it.

What does the contrast and parallel between Conrad and Salih suggest of significance for literary modernism? The narrative as a fable or psychic *Bildungsroman* dramatises a process. The process is cognitive and self-reflexive, an act of intertextual mirroring which enjoins recognition of repeatability: what has happened once can happen again. Marlow follows soon upon Kurtz, but even in the small gap that separates their journeys, we infer that enough has changed for Marlow to show us both what Kurtz might have seen, before he went to the Congo, and what Marlow sees in his own moment of the 'now'.

Conrad's modernism is evident at the level of narrative technique in the deliberate giving-up of an omniscient point of view. Truth is relative and subjective to the perceiver. Salih retains this kind of relativism. The unnamed narrator of *Season* walks a path of Westernisation similar to that walked before him by Mustafa. He works in Khartoum (rather than London or some other metropolitan centre), and remains less susceptible to the kinds of seductions and empowerments to which Mustafa succumbed in his time. We also see how Mustafa creates a narrative of his life in retrospect for the benefit of his younger friend, and what the younger man makes of that narration. In no sense is the doubling merely repetitive.

Instead, the doubling shows how the one who follows might (or might not) learn from the one who went first: the repetition need not be complete and exact. Since the end of the first fable in each instance is tragic, there is a drive for the narrative to avert tragedy the second time round – the one that follows must recognise a crisis as an occasion that demands a decision and a moral choice. In any doubling, the second has certain advantages. He can learn from the first, whereas the first has no precedent to guide him. Moreover, the doubling introduces a deliberate blur. Whose story are we reading? Kurtz's or Marlow's? Or Marlow's refraction of what it meant to have discovered something about Kurtz, and thence about many other things besides Kurtz? The same applies to Mustafa Sa'eed and the unnamed narrator. The 'story' is about an interstitial element; the first seen through the gradually awakening awareness of the second. This cognitive process, in all its impressionistic subjectivity, constitutes the centre of each narrative. It is mirrored again in the eyes of the reader. The modernist element arises in how room is made for ambiguity to play a central role in determining or obscuring whatever we might choose to call the 'truth' of the matter. Salih's text also enables us to ask if we might think of his relation to Conrad as a specific instance of the more general relation of modernist to postcolonial, or of modernist to postmodern discourses.[24]

In Conrad, as Achebe complained, the racial 'other' is relatively opaque to scrutiny, often read, or misread, through stereotypes. The entire problem of stereotyped perceptions is turned on its head in Salih. The character of Mustafa uses stereotypes to pander to the appetite for the Oriental exotic amongst his English female victims. He is like a debased and self-deconstructive Othello, happily acceding to the use of distorted stereotypes for the sake of pursuing his sexual quarry:

There came a moment when I felt I had been transformed in her eyes into a naked, primitive creature, a spear in one hand and arrows in the other, hunting elephants and lions in the jungles. This was fine. Curiosity had changed to gaiety, and gaiety to sympathy, and when I stir the still pool in its depths the sympathy will be transformed into a desire upon whose taut strings I shall play as I wish. 'What race are you?' she asked me. 'Are you African or Asian?'

'I'm like Othello – Arab-African,' I said to her. (Salih 2009: 33)

Achebe worried that Africans were misrepresented by the well-meaning but purblind Conrads of the colonial world. In Salih's hands, the pressure exerted on identity by ethnicity and by racial stereotypes is dramatised in earnest and in parody. The Sudanese Mustafa does not question but rather acts out the racial stereotypes of black men, but for his own ends. It is not how he is seen, or represented, that concerns him; it is what he can get from representations that matters. Mustafa is indeed a hunter, but one whose bow is bent by the white woman's stereotype. It is male hubris taken to an almost comical (or insufferable) extreme that speaks such lines as these 'There is a still pool in the depths of every woman that I knew how to stir' (27).

What does Salih achieve through such inversions? The character of Mustafa enjoyed playing to stereotypes when in England; later, in Sudan, when he narrates his exploits to the unnamed narrator of *Season*, he is contrite about the enjoyment he derived in England in practising his predatory skills. Salih is thus able to have his protagonist condemn what he also enjoyed once. Neither side in the hunt is allowed exemption from implied critique. The woman-victim is parodied, but so is the colonised-hunter. Each falls prey to her and his respective desires. Stereotypes are thus the means to foolhardy ends. If Mustafa uses stereotypes, the unnamed narrator has a different perspective to reveal. We may even find it a more sanely questioning alternative: 'How strange! How ironic! Just because a man has been created on the Equator some mad people regard him as a slave, others as a god! Where lies the mean?' (89).

Before we are done with stereotypes, it is worth noting that the most obvious way in which a postcolonial/postmodern Salih 'improves' upon his modernist predecessor is in the matter of how women are represented in his fiction. Achebe accused Conrad of letting his Marlow depict women through stereotypes. We have seen Salih's protagonist use stereotypes about the exotic Oriental male against his victims. There is another aspect to Salih's social realism that raises a question about the relation between characterisation and stereotypes: his representation of Arab women. Consider the relatively minor female character, Bint Majzoub. A woman who is frank and humorous about sexual matters; drinks, smokes and swears freely among men; and is shown always at ease and full of swagger. Do we find the characterisation plausible? Does it succeed in avoiding Western as well as Islamic, and Arab-African clichés? Do we see her as a 'round' character in E. M. Forster's sense of a 'round' character (Forster 1956: 78)? Or do we find the representation strained and implausible? Is the characterisation more robust than either of Conrad's female characterisations?

A similar set of questions could be asked about Bint Mahmoud, Mustafa's widow, who wishes to remain loyal to the memory of her dead husband, refuses remarriage (except to the narrator, who cannot deal with his own reactions to her physicality), kills the old man she is forced to marry, and then kills herself. Does the characterisation topple over into hysterical bathos? Or does it persuade us into believing that while Salih's male characters negotiate a complicated relation with stereotypes, his characterisation of women steers clear of gender stereotypes?

The novelist keeps a surprise ready in waiting for the reader towards the end of the novel. When Hosna Bint Mahmoud is dead, the narrator opens the locked chamber that Mustafa had maintained in his village home. It reveals the *mise-en-scène* of an English study preserved intact in this village of the Sudan. The startling revelation brings the narrator to two realisations: that he loved Bint Mahmoud, but to no avail; that he now hates Mustafa for having brought such degradation to all the women he touched. What Mustafa thought of the English world he had left behind, and why he carried it with him, in metonymy, to his Sudanese village remains a mystery. We could say of this enigma what Marlow said of Kurtz's Africa, that it is part of 'an inscrutable intention' (Conrad 1999: 66).

Modernity, colonisation and race

In reading *Season*, the critic Mike Velez, like other readers, is bothered by the steadiness of Salih's ambiguities: 'Why did he refuse to settle for a simplistic denunciation of colonialism and why does everything remain uncomfortably ambiguous in his world?' (Velez 2010: 191). The question answers itself. Why be simplistic when you are aware of the complexity of the situation? Another commentator, Musa al-Halool, in contrast, is convinced that the novel is clear in its focus on 'a conceptualisation of colonialism as rape and of anti-colonial struggle as sexual revenge' (al-Halool 2008: online). While there is some evidence for this reading, the analogies can appear restrictive. Instead, I would venture to suggest that the centre of attention for the reader is constituted at the intersection of (or in the interconnections between) several claims that tug at the two protagonists. The novel captures the tug of those tensions effectively.

One is the idea of home, which makes the narrator feel 'like that palm tree, a being with a background, with roots, with a purpose' (Salih 2009: 4). A similar claim is echoed, though not without some retrospective irony (or is it a touch of the disingenuous?) by Mustafa when he explains that he gave up business in Khartoum in order to withdraw to farming in a village: 'All my life I've longed to settle down in this part of the country, for some unknown reason' (11). Conrad, even more than Marlow, was looking for some such attachment, and discovered it, or made it up, tenuously, through his admiration for England, and his exaggerated attempts at reminding readers of what Englishness meant to his narrator and to the other English characters in his novella. Salih in his life felt the tug and responded to it by writing his stories in Arabic, and setting each of them in the same ancestral village, though he left Sudan behind him for the major part of his life, and did not visit it after the coup of 1989. If the modern era is one of crossings, diasporas, displacements and relocations, then the idea of home serves as a counterbalance to that state of being neither-here-nor-there-fully.

The second force that tugs at Mustafa and the narrator is the call of the West. The foreign-returned narrator of *Season* muses on his return to the village: 'How many were the hours I had spent in my childhood under that tree, throwing stones into the river and dreaming, my imagination straying to far-off horizons!' (6). The image mirrors in reverse the siren-call that Marlow would have us understand Africa exercised on Kurtz, by providing him with a situation and an opportunity where he could uncover the potential nature held back or undiscovered within him by Europe. The two forces pull in contrary directions. Conrad's fable stops well short of suggesting that Africa might exercise the same fatal attraction for Marlow as it did for Kurtz, but the implication is present subliminally throughout the narrative. It is also underlined by Conrad's autobiographical recollection that one day he would go to where the maps of his childhood showed a blank space yet unexplored by Europeans.[25] It does not appear as if Salih was one to succumb too readily to either force. The narrator reports a conversation with an Englishman long after Mustafa is dead, in which the Englishman voices a sweeping scepticism concerning many cherished postcolonial 'superstitions': 'the superstition of industrialisation, the superstition of nationalisation, the superstition of Arab unity, the superstition of African unity' (49). No less than Fanon, Salih shows a remarkably astute scepticism through his protagonist.

The third force makes itself felt when neither the first nor the second can prevail. It is like a duality that fails to resolve into a third. It is like the tree Mustafa talks about: 'Some of the branches of this tree produce lemons, others oranges' (14). Without the viable possibility of a synthesis or an entirely fresh start, a desire to turn upon either the first or the second force takes hold, and becomes a driving obsession. Mustafa turns upon the West with vengeance, after having first excelled in everything it taught him to cherish and aspire to. Likewise, but in reverse, Kurtz could be said to have turned with vengeance upon every virtue inculcated in him by Europe. Each bites one of the two hands that offer to feed him. In relation to this third force, it is curious to note that the novelist seems to have adopted in his life a course of action that differed from the ones undertaken by his protagonists: as if they did, symbolically, what he did not undertake in real life; and he undertook to lead the kind of life they turned down symbolically. When Mustafa is dead and the narrator comes to talk with his widow, the narrator reports hearing Mustafa's voice speaking aloud as if to an English jury. Part of what he says is explicit about what he thought he did in England: 'Yes, my dear sirs, I came as an invader into your very homes: a drop of the poison which you have injected into the veins of history. "I am no Othello. Othello was a lie"' (79). We are left wondering, in what sense, or why, was Othello a lie?

If Mustafa is one of the damned, is the narrator the one who is saved? He muses: 'I would think that such was life: with a hand it gives, with the other it takes' (6). Should we think of the fable and its creator as having it both ways between them? This duality is more clearly discernible in Salih than in Conrad, except for evidence of Conrad's self-awareness that his hold on equanimity was always a rather precarious one. The modernist way of tackling these multiple tensions is to allow each force some room in which to demonstrate its effects, while a certain negative capability remains at play, and ensures that no reaching out for this or that ethical certainty takes place too obviously. Such predicaments, and their representations, suggest that the sensibilities they portray (and the sensibilities they emanate from) are hardly done justice to when we apply to them words such as intercultural, bicultural, hybrid, or cosmopolitan. They work their power at a different level. Conrad captured that sense in some careful and exact words from 1917. They refer to *Heart of Darkness*, but apply just as well to *Season*: 'Its theme had to be given a *sinister* resonance, a tonality of its own, a continued vibration that I hoped would hang in the air and dwell on the ear after the last note had been struck' (Conrad 2002: 189). Conrad's fable surrounds the sense of horror with its framing and layering of narratives. Salih unravels part of his own weaving when he chooses to end with an act of symbolic assertion. Whether caught brooding on the mystery with Marlow, or choosing to regard his contamination by the Mustafas of colonialism, literary modernism becomes a repertoire of strategies intent on coping with that which divides and corrupts.

Notes

1. Terry Eagleton (1996: 7–13) provides a handy overview by identifying four strands of Marxist criticism: *anthropological* ('How does art relate to myth, ritual, religion and language?'), *political* ('whether avant-garde experiment is a way of figuring the revolutionary future or merely of alienating the unsophisticated masses'), *ideological* ('Is art reflection, displacement, projection, refraction, transformation, reproduction, production? Is it an embodiment of social ideology or a critique of it?') and *economic* (attention to 'that intermediary space which is the material apparatuses of cultural production, all the way from theatres and printing presses to literary coteries and institutions of patronage, from rehearsing and reviewing to the social context of producers and recipients').
2. For example, Marx, 'The Future Results of British Rule in India,' *New-York Daily Tribune*, 5 August 1853, <http://www.marxists.org/archive/marx/works/1853/07/22.htm> (accessed 25 April 2012): 'England has to fulfil a double mission in India: one destructive, the other regenerating the annihilation of old Asiatic society, and the laying the material foundations of Western society in Asia.' Ahmad (1992: 226), in his discussion of Edward Said's treatment of Marx in *Orientalism* (Said 1979: 153–7) notes that 'the status of Marx's writings on the possible consequences of British colonialism in India is not theoretical but conjectural and speculative'.
3. For example, in works such as Slavoj Zizek's *Revolution at the Gates* (2004) and Sebastian Budgen, Stathis Kouvelakis and Slavoj Zizek's *Lenin Re-loaded* (2007).
4. In 'Temporalised Invariance: Lukács and the Work of Form' (Hall and Bewes 2011), Yoon Sun Lee notes that an idea of form that conceives of temporal process 'in a moment or a collection of moments cannot defend itself against the greater and more constant force of life's temporal flow'. She argues that Lukács overcomes this problem after 1930, 'not by turning away from aesthetic form but by incorporating time within his idea of form', so that 'He comes to conceive of form temporally, and of time formally' (18). Such an argument, with its attention to the role of recurrence in narrative realism, provides a corrective to the bias shown by Brecht and Adorno against Lukács. Meanwhile, in his 'Foreword' to the 'Peripheral Realisms' issue of *Modern Language Quarterly* (Sept. 2012), Joe Cleary concedes that the debates between Lukács and his adversaries from the Left 'retain their significance even now', but reads the modernism versus realism polarisation as a narrative 'warped by the subsequent history of the Cold War' (262), that is, as a simplification, which hindsight reveals to have been a more complex realignment of strategies further complicated by post-World War II decolonisation, and the emergence of several kinds of writing from the former colonies of Europe, some beholden to modernist models, others to realist models.

5. 'Tagore himself is – as imaginative writer and as thinker – a wholly insignificant figure. His creative powers are non-existent; his characters pale stereotypes; his stories threadbare and uninteresting; and his sensibility is meagre, insubstantial' (Lukács 1983: 8). It must added that this rare instance of a Western Marxist writing critically about a non-Western writer has less to do with modernism than with what Lukács saw as Tagore's failure in the novel *The Home and the World* (1916) to express unambiguous support for Indian's anti-colonial struggle. Lukács attacks what he sees as Tagore's philosophy of acquiescence, and is suspicious of Tagore's popularity and acclaim among the British colonial classes.

6. Jameson draws attention to the argument developed by Paul de Man through a reading of Nietzsche's *On the Use and Abuse of History for Life* (1874): 'Modernity exists in the form of a desire to wipe out whatever came earlier in the hope of reaching at last a point that could be called a true present, a point of origin that marks a new departure. This combined interplay of a deliberate forgetting with an action that is also a new origin reaches the full power of the idea of modernity' (de Man 1970: 388–9). However, 'Considered as a principle of life, modernity becomes a principle of origination and turns at once into a generative power that is itself historical. It becomes impossible to overcome history in the name of life or to forget the past in the name of modernity, because both are linked by a temporal chain that gives them a common destiny.' (390–1).

7. A single illustration will have to suffice here. The moving spirit of the Indian Subaltern Historians group – Ranajit Guha – confessed in an anthology of the group's work that one of the motivating factors behind their historiography was disenchantment with successive nationalist governments in India after political independence: 'What had glowed once as an immense possibility turned to ashes' (Guha 1997: xii).

8. Though counted among the modernists by virtue of his role as a Vorticist, Wyndham Lewis stood apart from much of what Pound or Eliot stood for, in the decade before and after World War I, and does not fit comfortably with them as a fellow modernist.

9. Cf. Reed Way Dasenbrock: 'Modernism was from its beginnings a response of the essentially colonised margins to Western culture' (Dasenbrock 2001: 114).

10. Both Pound and Eliot were astute, each in his own way, about self-promotion. Their consummate 'self-canonising' proved influential, though there are alternative ways of narrating developments in literary history, as was shown later by the poet Donald Davie in *Thomas Hardy and British Poetry* (1973).

11. Alan Sinfield notes that 'the political impetus of British anti-Modernism in the 1950s may be sketched [. . .] in terms of three frames of reference: literary institutions, class and nation [. . .] Modernism was out of key with the welfare state, its claim to make "good" culture accessible to everyone [. . .] Finally, an element of national consciousness, a preoccupation with Englishness, fuelled hostility to Modernism' (Sinfield 1989: 184).

12. Orwell 1968: 274–5. Commentators are divided between condemning or defending Yeats. Orwell and Conor Cruise O'Brien (1965) illustrate the negative view, while Elizabeth Cullingford (1981) illustrates a more positive view. The entire spectrum of opinions on this aspect of Yeats is surveyed in Allison (1996).

13. The debate can be sampled from Edward Said (1993: 220–39), Declan Kiberd (1996, 1997), David Lloyd (1993) and Edna Longley (1994).

14. 'Wordsworth got rid of a lot of trimmings, but there are vast stretches of deadness in his writing [. . .] and he was not conscious of the full problem of writing' (Pound 1951: 73).

15. Pound's translation (Confucius 1951: 31; Pound 2003: 619), which continues:

'the inarticulate thoughts were defined with precision [the sun's lance coming to rest on the precise spot verbally]. Having attained this precise verbal defini- tion [*aliter*, this sincerity], they then stabilised their hearts, they disciplined themselves; having attained self-discipline, they set their own house in order; having order in their own homes, they brought good government to their own states; and when their states were well governed, the empire was brought into equilibrium' (Confucius 1951: 33; Pound 2003: 619).

16. Imagist doctrine as promoted by Pound (with stress on direct, concrete, vivid writing that partakes of the virtues of good prose, and avoids abstractions) was consonant with Fenollosa's claims in 'The Chinese Written Character as a Medium for Poetry', written before 1908 and edited by Pound in 1918: 'Poetry differs from prose in the concrete colours of its diction. It is not enough for it to furnish a meaning to philosophers. It must appeal to emotions with the charm of direct impression, flashing through regions where the intellect may not grope. Poetry must render what is said, not what is merely meant. Abstract meaning gives little vividness, and fullness of imagination gives all' (Fenollosa and Pound 2008: 53).

17. George A. Kennedy's review of Pound's *The Classic Anthology Defined by Confucius* (1958) is blunt about rejecting Fenollosa's claim that in the Chinese written character 'ideographic roots carry in them a verbal idea of action' (Kennedy 1964: 452).

18. The contemporary poet Geoffrey Hill provides an instance of the claim that poetic and ethical discernment should go together (an idea that is at least as old, in English literature, as Ben Jonson's dedicatory epistle to the play *Volpone*): 'the shock of semantic recognition must be also a shock of ethical recognition' (Hill 2008: 405).

19. Britain outlawed the slave trade in 1807 and passed The Abolition of Slavery Act in 1833, which discontinued the practice of employing slaves over the next few years. The other European colonising powers abolished slavery in the period from 1811 (Spain) to 1848 (France), although similar legislation was enacted in the different colonial territories subsequently. The US abolished slavery in 1865; Cuba in 1886; Brazil in 1888. The Berlin Conference 'was attended by delegates from Germany, Austria-Hungary, Belgium, Denmark, Spain, the United States, France, Great Britain, Italy, the Netherlands, Portugal, Russia, Sweden and the Ottoman Empire [. . .] in the following years almost the whole of Africa was occupied' (Bührer 2008: 210).

20. One way of defending Conrad against the claim of racism is to contextualise the narrative amidst a wealth of anthropological-cultural detail about treatments of Africa and Africans by Victorian writers, as Griffith does (Griffith 1995: 43). He is as unimpressed by Achebe's rhetoric as Achebe would be by his scholarly detail. For an overview of the African reactions to *Heart of Darkness*, see Rino Zhuwarara (1994).

21. From Hegel's lectures on the philosophy of history (1830–1): 'The peculiarly African character is difficult to comprehend, for the very reason that in refer- ence to it, we must quite give up the principle which naturally accompanies all our ideas – the category of Universality. In Negro life the characteristic point is the fact that consciousness has not yet attained to the realisation of any substan- tial objective existence – as for example, God, or Law – in which the interest of man's volition is involved and in which he realises his own being' (Hegel 2001: 110–11). He goes on to add that 'At this point we leave Africa, not to mention it again. For it is no historical part of the World; it has no movement or develop- ment to exhibit. Historical movements in it that is in its northern part belong to the Asiatic or European World' (117).

22. D. C. R. A. Goonetilleke notes of Achebe that 'It was only in and after the 1980s and 1990s that the impact of his attack was strongly felt. Hawkins entered the fray in 1982 and 2005 and Watt in 1989. So did Wilson Harris (1981), Cedric Watts (1983), Patrick Brantlinger (1985, 1988), Mark Kinkead-Weekes (1990), Robert Burden (1992), and R. Zhuwarara (1994) among others' (Goonetilleke 2007: 60). Harris will have to suffice as typical of those who conceded that they sympathise with Achebe but still argue that his position 'is a profoundly mistaken one' (Harris 1981: 87).

23. Waïl S. Hassan notes that allusions prominent in *Season of Migration to the North* include Shakespeare's *Othello*, Gérard de Nerval's *Voyage en orient* (1851), Conrad's *Heart of Darkness* (1899), Tawfiq al-Hakim's *Usfur min al-sharq* (*A Bird from the East*, 1938), Yahya Haqqi's *Qindil Umm Hashim* (*The Lamp of Umm Hashim*, 1944), and Suhayl Idris's *Al-hayy al-latini* (*The Latin Quarter*, 1954) (Hassan 2003: 83). Unlike the Arabic writers of what became known as the 'Nahda' movement, who envisaged optimistic resolutions to the conflict between indigenous Arabic traditions and the influence of Westernisation and modernity, Salih adopts a tone of deliberate ambivalence towards the effects of colonial modernisation upon traditional ways of life.

24. Reed Way Dasenbrock (2001), for instance, takes up the question raised by Anthony Appiah Kwame in 'Is the "Post" in "Postcolonial" the "Post" in "Postmodern"?' (1991), and answers it with an emphatic No: 'the aesthetics of post-modernism may have in general "triumphed" over the aesthetics of Modernism [. . .] among the European population [. . . in Europe and the US], but the dominant aesthetic of post-colonial literature is modernist, not postmodernist'.

25. 'It was in 1868, when nine years old or thereabouts, that while looking at a map of Africa of the time and putting my finger on the blank space then representing the unsolved mystery of that continent, I said to myself, with absolute assurance and an amazing audacity which are no longer in my character now: "When I grow up I shall go THERE."' (Conrad 2008: 26).

Chapter 3
Case Studies

1. Modernism and Gender

> She seemed such a poor ghost, I thought I'd like to write her life.
>
> Jean Rhys

Each of the three sections in this chapter provides a reading of authors separated by time and cultural difference but related in terms of the issues that preoccupy them, and the strategies they adopt in dealing with those issues: gender, allegory and the role of religion in modern societies respectively. The broader aim is to survey the evidence for three specific kinds of achievement. How do women modernist writers react to the historical fact and lived experience of empire and colonisation? How does allegory as a literary mode connect modernist and postcolonial writing? How do the energies of Western modernist practices get adapted to different needs and circumstances by writers from various parts of the once-colonised world, giving modernism an afterlife with uniquely postcolonial inflections?

Virginia Woolf (1882–1941) and Jean Rhys (1890–1979)

In this section, we read Virginia Woolf's *The Voyage Out* (1915) alongside Jean Rhys's *Wide Sargasso Sea* (1966). Two women born just under a decade apart; two novels separated by half a century; and linking them, the enormous challenge and difficulty of becoming a modern woman in the shadow of empire. By the time Woolf began drafting her first novel, around 1906, the Boer War had been over for four years in South Africa: her career as a writer began at a time when the British Empire was in its heyday.

Woolf had been writing fiction for almost two decades by the time Rhys began her career as a writer, under vastly different circumstances:

born in Dominica of a Welsh father and a third-generation Creole mother, she had been sent to England for her schooling in 1904, at the age of sixteen (Angier 1991: 11). She found herself ridiculed for her accent and was often called a 'coon' in boarding school. Six years of misery came to an end with a stop to the schooling (brought about by the death of her father in 1910). After that, she drifted into various jobs and misadventures in Europe and England, until encouraged in her attempts to write fiction by Ford Madox Ford in the early 1920s.

In *The Voyage Out*, we encounter Woolf at the beginning of a literary career; in *Wide Sargasso Sea*, we approach Rhys at the end of her career. Each author works out a narrative whose logic drives its protagonist to that which many people would regard as madness. Each novel ends in a death. Each in her time and place struggles against specific ideas of role, function and code of conduct as foisted upon women. Each fights through her writing for the rights associated with European modernity, specifically full social, political and economic equality with European men.

In her first novel, Woolf voices the frustration of middle-class women who struggle to create an independent space for themselves, wanting to avoid depending on men and the institution of marriage for security or identity. In her personal life, however, she had little sympathy for the plight of working-class women. Her relations with female domestic workers in her household repeatedly demonstrated an equal amount of dependency and dislike on both sides, as chronicled meticulously by Alison Light in *Mrs Woolf and the Servants* (2007).

For Rhys, the problem was the combined dominance of racist and patriarchal modes of thought and action as they victimised those who happened to be both women and racial hybrids, like herself and her protagonist. Woolf gestured towards colony as a fact of history, but her text (and her life) lacked the lived experience to realise the historical reality of empire in a plausible fictional context. Nevertheless, as noted by Jed Esty, 'The uncivilised South American landscape (however inauthentically rendered) serves as both figure and context for Rachel's ego dissolution' (Esty 2012: 134). In contrast, Rhys evokes with power and precision a context imbued with the violence of racial and patriarchal colonisation at a personal as well as generic level. The modernity refracted by Woolf refers primarily to the desperate need to renovate the social and cultural attitudes of a specific type of British middle-class, genteel, impoverished and hidebound male culture. The modernity evoked or implied by Rhys has to do with a need to reject both racism and patriarchy as insidious forms of double colonisation.

The Voyage Out was a first novel for Virginia Woolf. It is one of the earliest fictional texts of significance in the canon of English modernism. The process of writing proved slow and stressful: a process of revision that continued from 1906 to 1915, with another set of revisions preceding an American edition of 1920 (DeSalvo 1980: 31; Haule 1996: 319). The motif holding the revisions together was the idea of narrating a rite of passage for a young woman presented to the reader as on a literal as well as figurative journey, like 'a ship passing in the night – an emblem of the loneliness of human life' (Woolf 2001: 94).

The struggle for female autonomy represented in the novel parallels the political struggle for women's rights in Britain. The National Union of Women's Suffrage in Britain was founded by Millicent Fawcett in 1897, when Woolf was a teenager. It was followed in 1903 by the Women's Social and Political Union, which was founded by Emmeline Pankhurst and her daughters. Fawcett's organisation hoped to gain better recognition for the plight of women through peaceful means. Mrs Pankhurst and her followers were militant in orientation. Their struggles parallel those of Woolf's heroine, although the muted defeatism of the plot constructed by Woolf for her heroine contrasts sharply with the willingness of the Suffragettes led by Mrs Pankhurst to engage in acts of violence, to suffer imprisonment and to use hunger strikes in order to highlight their demand that women be given the right to vote.[1]

The Voyage Out (1915) is both a personal and an exemplary text. The sense of frustration and despair projected by the novelist onto her character has drawn much attention from Woolf's biographers, who underline the traumatic aspects of her life as signalled by frequent mental break-downs.[2] One of the earliest episodes followed upon her mother's death in 1895; another may have been related to the death of a mentally disabled elder half-sister in 1897; another followed upon her father's death in 1904. Work on the novel was interrupted several times by more breakdowns, some lasting days, others lasting months. The death of her father left Virginia and her elder sister Vanessa dependent in psychological, economic and social terms on their elder half-siblings from their mother's previous marriage: George, Stella and Gerald Duckworth (the last of whom published *The Voyage Out*). The death of family members was not the only problem.

According to a succession of biographers, starting with her husband Leonard Woolf and leading up to the more recent biography by Hermione Lee (1997), we are told that Woolf retained throughout her life a troubled attitude towards the body, towards eating and towards sexuality. She ate poorly, was repulsed by manifestations of physical desire or love-making and frequently suffered a set of symptoms inconclusively diagnosed during her lifetime (and subsequently). She attempted suicide several times from her teenage years, and did eventually drown herself in 1941. The only kiss that occurs in her entire literary output, as narrated in Chapter 5 of *The Voyage Out* (80), is attended by a strange mixture of arousal, guilt, revulsion and shock. There is 'strange exultation' and a conviction that 'something wonderful had happened' (80); but, on the other hand, at a distance from the initial excitement, the protagonist is reported as 'merely uncomfortable' (81).

Jean Rhys (Ella Gwendolen Rees Williams)

Jean Rhys was the author of five works of fiction, beginning with *The Left Bank and Other Stories* (1927). All but the last are set in Europe. In the 1920s, she may have received some degree of encouragement and guidance from the literary 'impressionism' promoted by the then well-established novelist and editor Ford Madox Ford (1873–1939). Ford claimed later that he brought both Joseph Conrad and Jean Rhys to their first realisations of modernism in the craft of writing.[3] Her career ended, and also reached its apogee, with *Wide Sargasso Sea* (1966). It too, like *The Voyage Out*, went through a process of extensive revision, testifying to the difficulty of the undertaking, and the care taken by the author in bringing the work to completion. This novel was published more than twenty-seven years after her previous one, *Good Morning, Midnight* (1939). The gap gives *Wide Sargasso Sea* a somewhat belated air, since Rhys had virtually disappeared for her readers since the 1940s. The book was well-received, and has since acquired a large readership. It has also been recognised that many of its narrative manoeuvres and techniques, as well as its perceptions and diagnoses, anticipate literary postmodernism and literary postcolonialism, though neither term was in currency when Rhys wrote her novel.

Racial discrimination, experienced at first hand from an early age, taught Rhys what it meant to be doubly colonised: as a woman, and as a racial 'other' (despite her blue-grey eyes, blonde hair and relatively light complexion). She avoided going back to her birthplace for twenty-nine years (until 1936), making England and Europe a kind of distraction, escape and picaresque playground for a life of experimental living that was a mix of the adventurous, the reckless and the sordid: from chorus girl to artist's model to mistress, lover, wife, neglectful mother and an inveterate solitary.

For the daughter of a woman who was a third-generation white

Creole, to become modern meant to be preoccupied with many, often self-conflicted, aspirations and needs. First, there was the duality between the impulse to reject those who rejected or demeaned her, and the desire to gain acceptance from those who derided her. Second was the need to make room within literary writing for the zones of experience she knew as her own, rather than to accept passively the narrative conventions and stereotypes of the Western literary canon. A woman who had had her full measure of hurt and humiliation was yet able to put clarity of perception and style into a novel that transmutes the mess of experience into a carefully crafted and provocative work of art.

Wide Sargasso Sea stands in a dual relation of allusive dependency on, and subversive questioning of, Charlotte Brönte's *Jane Eyre* (1844). Rhys makes it appear as if Brönte had narrated only part of the truth of what happened, while she, in her novel, supplements and challenges that narrative by showing how Brönte marginalised the Creole woman whose money sets up her male protagonist Rochester in Thornton Hall. The afflatus of empire was built on the same principle writ large: looting and depriving others as a way of aggrandising oneself. Rhys remarked in a letter that she had always felt that the character of Mrs Rochester, who is mostly elided in *Jane Eyre*, 'must be right *on stage*' (Rhys 1984: 156) in her novel. Marginalisation was something Rhys understood, having suffered it in her life. But tapping painful autobiographical material proved a slow and difficult process. In all her novels Rhys continually tackled the same problem of making art out of experience. In her final novel, she was able to address her troubled past and bring her quarrel with the feminine stereotype of the English mid-nineteenth-century imagination into sharp focus.

Symbolic narrative in *The Voyage Out*

The Voyage Out narrates a symbolic journey that ends in death. The young protagonist sets sail on board a ship captained by her father for a trading destination in remote South America (a region imagined and invented by Woolf from travels no farther from London than Spain, Italy and Turkey): 'dry goods to the Amazon, and rubber home again' (Woolf 2001: 38). An English couple – Richard and Clarissa Dalloway – comes on board for part of the trip, bringing to Rachel the first set of encounters that constitute her rite of passage. Once she arrives in South America, a hotel inhabited by a miscellaneous crowd of English denizens provides the setting for her second rite of passage: getting to know a young man. They agree to an engagement, although both remain uncertain of their love for one another, and of their commitment to the idea of marriage.

Before matters can develop any further, she falls prey to a fever from which she fails to recover. The novel ends with a seemingly needless death. The reader is left to ponder over why the novelist has chosen to bring its symbolic journey to this puzzling end. Woolf uses an impressionistic style of narration mixed with reflection. The narrative is conducted from the point of view of an omniscient narrator whose adoption of Rachel's point of view is sometimes varied with shifts in focalisation that present thoughts and events from the perspective of other characters in the novel. We might interpret this technique as Woolf's attempt to establish a plurality of consciousness and viewpoint. More specifically, as noted by Jed Esty, 'Rachel's character yields (to) a narrative perspective from which Woolf''s key writerly innovations emerge in the temporal vacuum left behind by the suspended coming of age plot' (Esty 2012: 136).

Narrative technique in *Wide Sargasso Sea*

Rhys is more adventurous in her narrative strategy. She uses two narrative personas, each speaking in the first person. To begin with, we inhabit the consciousness of a girl who narrates her life as a Creole in Jamaica at the time of the Emancipation Act of 1833, which gave freedom to slaves in Britain's colonies (implemented by 1838). The second part of the narrative takes the point of view of a young Englishman, a second son who has come to Jamaica in order to make his fortune. That is to be done by marrying money, even though the plan entails accepting a Creole woman as his bride: the girl who narrates the preceding part of the novel, to whom he is not particularly attracted. He declares to his father (in a letter) that 'I have sold my soul or you have it, and after all is it such a bad bargain?' (Rhys 1982: 70). The novel returns, towards the end, to the first-person narrative of the female protagonist, introduced briefly by a third voice.

The choice of several first-person narratives gives readers access to different kinds of first-hand experience. First, we learn through the voice of the female narrator (later identified as Antoinette Mason) what it means to be derided as a 'white cockroach' (23). She is resented by the black inhabitants of the Caribbean islands for the privileges enjoyed by a Creole (through liaison with a white man, or through marriage or birth into a family with a white man as father or husband). She is also looked down upon by whites, for not being of their race and social standing, in a context in which, as the girl's black maid Christophine ('a Martinique obeah woman', 30) remarks, 'Old time white people nothing but nigger now, and black nigger better than white nigger' (24).[4]

By inhabiting Antoinette's point of view for part of the narrative, the reader gains first-hand acquaintance with the social and political tensions experienced by the reasonably well-off but marginalised Creole minorities of the Caribbean nineteenth century, and the troubled family history of the female protagonist. The robust presence of a character like Christophine also adds a dimension missing in Antoinette: the capacity to stand her ground unabashed by masculinity, whiteness, social hierarchy, or the linguistic authority of standard English: 'She is Creole girl, and she have the sun in her' (158); 'You want her money but you don't want her. It is in your mind to pretend she is mad' (160).[5]

Having heard part of Antoinette's story, we learn what it feels like for her young English groom to feel discomfort in the tropics, and alienation from everything his bride stands for. He is cold towards her, regardless of what he gains from marrying her: 'She never blinks at all it seems to me. Long, sad, dark alien eyes. Creole of pure English descent she may be, but they are not English or European either' (67). The narrative voice is handled by Rhys in such a way that no sense of authorial judgement ever enters the reading experience. The two voices present their versions, each attempting to predispose the reader towards this or that attitude and evaluation of circumstance and character, motive and intention. We go through two such alternations of voice through Parts One and Two of the novel. Part Three is more unusual. The marriage fails to work and the two grow apart; she resorts to a form of black magic (obeah) in the desperate hope of gaining love and sexual desire from her husband. The attempt proves disastrous. The husband beds a servant instead; then the young bride is dragged to an England that she finds as alienating as he had found her homeland.

Finally, in Part Three, two italicised pages give us a third voice. We infer that the locale has now shifted for the final part of the novel. It is England. A house-maid (Grace Poole) speaks to another servant named Leah of having to look after a woman neither young nor old: '*She sits shivering and she is so thin*' (177). This must be the mistress of the house, we suppose, or rather, the Antoinette who was married by the young man we met in Jamaica, a man who is never named in the novel, though he, for his part, exercises the utmost pressure to have Antoinette accept 'Bertha' as the name to which he insists she must answer.[6]

The couple is now in England, in his home, three servants looking after a household comprising the man and a wife who '*hasn't lost her spirit. She's still fierce*' (178). The final pages of the novel shift back to the voice with which we began the novel, that of the girl, now an older woman – the madwoman in the attic – of exemplary feminist nomination, who hates the 'cardboard' world (180) of England that she has lost her way in. There she discovers what she regards as her final purpose in the last paragraph of the novel. That purpose, it would appear, is to nourish a flame that could set fire to the house. The intimation of that fire, never narrated in the novel, ties the narrative to the 'mad woman' in *Jane Eyre* who burnt down the house in which she was imprisoned by the man who had married her. That man, for his part, ended up blind in the fire that killed his first wife, clearing the way for Jane Eyre to look after him. The economy of means with which Rhys creates a sense of an inevitable outcome is at once deeply tragic and amazingly precise in its symbolic aptness.

The parental or sisterly authority of the English text both overshadows and provokes the Rhys text to its act of subversive supplementarity. A story that is marginalised to the point of repression in *Jane Eyre* is here given a position of centrality. Ironically, the narrative centrality only serves to dramatise a form of displacement from which there is no recovery. Death thus becomes not a solution but the recognition of an impasse. It is not the husband who is indicted as much as the processes of history, of which colonialism and patriarchy are the most obvious culprits: one despising the racial (and cultural) hybrid, the other constraining the scope for self-fulfilment by women.

The double-colonisation of the protagonist bespeaks a modernity of outlook, not in the fate to which it consigns the female protagonist, but in the mode of narration that foregrounds oppression, domination, racialisation and essentialism as the forces that deny individuals a chance to live their lives without being oppressed by the prejudices of others. Rhys is 'modern' in her outlook in the specific sense that she enforces recognition of colonisation as an evil. This is not the distressed modernity of a Western writer torn between Enlightenment utopianism and its reversion to dystopia. It is an apprehensive and subjunctive modernity; a wish half-fearful that what it hopes for may have to wait much longer than it can bear.

Englishness, colonialism and narrative technique in *The Voyage Out*

Reading Rhys enables us to approach Woolf from a specific perspective. In *The Voyage Out*, the novelist makes a determined bid to break free of England and Englishness. For Rhys there is no choice: her fictional world and real world both partake of the same condition of being in-between two systems. She can belong to neither with any kind of comfort. Woolf exercises a choice and takes her protagonist away from England, the better to look from a fictional distance at the system in which she and her heroine are confined. England feels like 'a shrinking island in which people were imprisoned' (Woolf 2001: 29). Woolf uses a distancing technique that works out a pattern, rather like the embroidery created by one of the minor characters, Mrs Ambrose, who works 'at a great design of a tropical river running through a tropical forest' (30). We hear in this a remote echo of the two journeys up the Congo river narrated in Conrad's *Heart of Darkness*; Marlow's journey echoed Kurtz's journey. The trip undertaken by Rachel and five other English visitors entails going up a river deep into a dense interior, from which people return not with profit but discomforting self-knowledge.

England's position at the helm of European imperialism allows the novelist to reflect on the experience of growing up as a young woman in a confined English environment. She needs an act of self-liberation. Any such act has many political ramifications.[7] While Woolf wrote and revised, George V visited India – the first time a British monarch had visited the site of his wealthiest colony – to inaugurate what became known as the 'Delhi Durbar' of 1911, providing the occasion for one of the earliest feature films on a public event. However, the seeds of resistance to empire were already being sown. M. K. Gandhi (1869–1948) was to make his political debut in India in 1917. He soon launched the 'Satyagraha' movement (a mode of resistance based on non-violent civil disobedience explicitly alluding to and different from the violent resistance offered by the British Suffragettes of the same period). The novel belongs to an epoch in which the assumptions about empire that Woolf satirised were to meet their match in the strategy initiated by Gandhi. It would eventually break the back of the British Empire by 1947.

The idea of Britain as a self-satisfied and righteous coloniser is satirised through the politician Richard Dalloway who goes on and on about how 'One thinks of all we've done, and our navies, and the people in India and Africa and how we've gone on century after century, sending out boys from little country villages' (51). When asked to put the British claim in a nutshell, he describes it as 'Unity of aim, of dominion, of progress. The dispersion of the best ideas over the greatest area' (67). Such assertions echo and distort well-known utterances from Mathew Arnold. More to the point, the novelist treats imperial complacence and pride with an irony that stops just short of caricature, since Richard is ready to admit that he also knows of the 'unmentionable things done in our very midst' (67).

The novel takes Britain's role in global colonialism seriously enough to articulate a historical overview voiced through the musings of an old friend of Rachel's father, Mr William Pepper, who is on board the *Euphrosyne*, along with Rachel's uncle and her aunt Mrs Helen Ambrose (modelled, critics suggest, at least in part on the novelist's elder sister Vanessa). The 'hardy British' are compared favourably to the Spaniards 'bloated with fine living' (96). The motives for colonisation are given an origin not merely in trade but in a 'movement in search of something new' (97). The natives of the Amazon region are depicted through familiar stereotypes: 'strangely beautiful, very big in stature, dark, passionate, and quick to seize the knife' (97). The novelist's satirical vision contrasts such fine feelings with the ramshackle nature of the establishment that constitutes the 'colony'. When it comes to describing the native women, no particular irony is attached to the description.

> The young women, with their hair magnificently swept in coils, a red flower behind the ear, sat on the doorsteps, or issued out on balconies, while the young men ranged up and down beneath, shouting up a greeting from time to time and stopping here and there to enter into amorous talk. (107)

At other times, British expressions of the desire to 'conquer a territory,' in an era when 'they're all conquered already', become little more than the idle fantasy of people conscious that they lead 'such tame lives' (152).

The Voyage Out: to be a woman here and now

The need to make connections between humans is treated as central to the narrative. Not only is Rachel often alone and lonely, she is shown as recognising herself to be undeveloped in terms of knowledge and awareness of many aspects of life: 'there was no subject in the world which she knew accurately', and 'the most elementary idea of a system of modern life – none of this had been imparted to her' (31). Moreover, as Rachel's aunt Helen speculates, 'From the little she knew of her [Rachel's] upbringing she supposed that she had been kept entirely ignorant as to the relations between men and women' (85). The aunt registers protest at such an upbringing: 'It seems to me not merely foolish but criminal to bring people up like that' (105). The act of writing becomes a means of articulating Woolf's sense of the limitations from which she suffered as a result of family, custom and social inhibitions. The act of writing also expresses a specifically feminine and conventional apprehension: if love and compatibility could lead to a lasting heterosexual relation, might she be able to join the ranks of the married women, and thus 'escape the long solitude of an old maid's life' (155)?

Once off the ship and away from the parental presence of the father, Rachel begins her interpersonal voyage through a growing acquaintance with two relatively young Englishmen, Terence Hewet (modelled in some respects on Vanessa's husband Clive Bell) and St John Hirst (modelled on the writer Lytton Strachey). Their conversations allow the novelist to articulate a number of feminine concerns. Chief among them is the double-preoccupation with building a meaningful relationship with a man of comparable age and compatible disposition, while also recognising, in some measure, that she (Rachel, but, by implication, also the novelist) might want to explore a form of solitariness that avoids interpersonal closeness and intimacy. At one point, the novelist speculates through Hirst if a paradox might be resolved – that 'one never is alone, and one never is in company' – by claiming that 'You can't see my bubble; I can't see yours' (119).

This view is undercut when one of the English people at the colony, Venning, remarks of Hirst that 'although he had such an air of being clever he wasn't as clever as Arthur, in the ways that really matter' (134). A conversation between Hirst and Hewet brings the latter to a formulation that might be closer to what Rachel (and the novelist) seem to wonder about: 'do we really love each other or do we, on the other hand, live in a state of perpetual uncertainty, knowing nothing, leaping from moment to moment, as from world to world?' (141). In circumstances that differ vastly, we yet discover a problem that links the protagonists of *Wide Sargasso Sea* and *The Voyage Out*: the frailty of the desire for interpersonal connection, the fear of the likelihood that the hope is more likely to be disappointed than to be realised.

Out walking together, Hewet and Rachel come upon 'a man and a woman lying on the ground [. . .] rolling slightly this way and that as the embrace tightened and slackened' (155). The sight leaves Rachel affected, not their accidental prying upon others, but at the thought of the embrace, and whether the girl 'was happy, or had suffered something' (156). The episode provided occasion for reflections from both Hewet and Rachel. While Hewet merely thinks that 'Love's an odd thing,' she thinks that the intimacy changes things forever for the two, and 'makes one sorry for them too'. Hewet agrees that 'there's something horribly pathetic about it' (156). Her reaction acts as a prelude to the reluctance and uncertainty she shows thereafter about the prospect of an engagement and marriage to Hewet. He too, at a later point, dismisses domesticity: 'the idea of marriage irritated him. It immediately suggested the picture of two people sitting alone over the fire: the man was reading, the woman sewing' (280). Hewet thus persuades himself that marriage might not be the best thing for him and Rachel, while for her part, Rachel cannot quite comprehend: 'What is it to be in love?' There is no immediate answer, but a tangent opens up in an enigmatic manner: 'a great yellow butterfly, which was opening and closing its wings very slowly on a little flat stone'. The wings hypnotise her, and as the butterfly flutters away, she is 'awed by the discovery of a terrible possibility in life' (197).

Fictions of tragic necessity

The situation between Rachel and Hewet does not develop either simply or smoothly: 'If Rachel was ignorant of her own feelings, she was even more completely ignorant of his' (259). With seeming inevitability, events lead to an impasse between them. On the one hand, they appear to be mutually compatible. They even agree to an engagement. However, the novelist does not want a conventional ending that brings the woman round to the kind of adjustment in which solitariness is relinquished with relief at the prospect of marriage, because society trains young women to expect that for themselves. Rachel does not relish the thought of spinsterhood, but neither does she find the closeness of marriage desirable. The novel is elaborate about her sense of unease: 'She had now reached one of those eminences, the result of some crisis, from which the world is finally displayed in its true proportions' (300). She rejects most of what passes for normality in bourgeois terms, because her bodily 'sense of life in the world was repressed now by Mr Bax, now by Evelyn, now by the imposition of ponderous stupidity, the weight of the entire world' (300). Daily life makes it seem to her that 'We're asleep and dreaming' (301).

Woolf abrogates the situation through a contrivance of plot: a fever intervenes; Rachel dies; and while well-meaning strangers muse on the conventional sense in which that early death is a tragedy, the novelist has managed to register a protest that will tolerate no compromise: an affirmation through negation. The death Woolf chose successfully for herself a quarter-century later was always at hand, as Rachel's death indicates. Should we see it as a solution to a problem? A way out of an irreconcilable dilemma? An act of evasive capitulation? Perhaps none of these. Well before the fever and the sudden death, Rachel meditates on her new grasp of reality. It entails two steps.

The first involves awareness of life's radical uncertainty: 'That was the strangest thing that one did not know where one was going, or what one wanted, and followed blindly, suffering so much in secret, always unprepared and amazed and knowing nothing' (366). The voyage outwards into life must accept 'not knowing', and 'knowing nothing'. The second step, a more difficult one, is to find in oneself the capacity to face uncertainty with calmness: 'one thing led to another and by degrees something had formed itself out of nothing, and so one reached at last this calm, this quiet, this certainty' (366).

For the final stages of the narrative, the novelist chooses to show us events from the outside. We are no longer companions to Rachel's stream of consciousness. A headache turns to fever, delirium and hallucinations. The experiences attributed to the protagonist might have had a basis in Virginia's personal experience of hallucinations during her periods of mental illness. The death, when it arrives, is narrated from Hewet's viewpoint. The novelist attributes to him an acceptance that has a willed quality: 'this was death. It was nothing; it was to cease to breathe. It was happiness, it was perfect happiness. They had now what they had always wanted to have, the union which had been impossible while they lived' (412). With this peculiar twist, Rachel's voyage is at an end. While a storm breaks outside in the night, all the British folk gather indoors. The room is full of 'the indescribable stir of life'. 'Every now and then the moth, which was now grey of wing and shiny of thorax, whizzed over their heads, and hit the lamps with a thud' (431). A young woman thinks it would be kinder to kill it.

Woolf and Rhys fitted their heroines for death as the preferred alternative when each in her world faced the prospect of a life not worth living. The moth that hits its head against the light has its counterpart in the creatures that die by fire in *Wide Sargasso Sea*. When the young protagonist Antoinette's family house is set on fire by drunken blacks, the victims include her mother and baby brother, Pierre, and the family parrot, Coco, who has become bad tempered since his wings were clipped. He cannot fly to freedom (like the moth in *The Voyage Out*) and falls to the ground, 'his feathers alight' (Rhys 1982: 43). The last two sentences of the novel return to the motif of fire: Antoinette shields the flame against the draught, and the flame that will swallow her up and blind her husband is described as having 'burned up again to light me along the dark passage' (190).

Modernist technique in *The Voyage Out*

What makes such fictions modernist? Consider, first, the image of the moth. It is similar to, but different from, the butterfly Rachel noticed in Chapter XII (Woolf 2001: 197), which later seemed to suggest a wordless answer to her question in Chapter XIII (264). The fable-like role assigned to the alternation between butterfly and moth practises its own poetic economy. One belongs outdoors and is encountered in daylight. The other is attracted to the light indoors, at night, and finds itself trapped: 'The only disturbance in the placid room was caused by a large moth which shot from light to light, whizzing over elaborate heads of hair, and causing several young women to raise their heads nervously and exclaim, "Someone ought to kill it!"' (205). The oblique quality of this evocation is as bold as any critique, and far more devastating in its suggestiveness. The motif reappears in Chapter XV, this time as an anecdote from Mrs Flushing, who speaks of a window that became the focus of disagreement during a regular reading aloud of the historian Gibbons: '"Then there were the moths – tiger moths, yellow moths, and horrid cockchafers. Louisa, my sister, would have the window open. I wanted it shut. We fought every night of our lives over that window. Have you ever seen a moth dyin' in a night-light?" she enquired' (225). The fabulist properties of butterfly and moth combine the virtues or principles of imagist and symbolist doctrine. Woolf inscribes through the images of the butterfly and moth her own sense of the fraught aspirations for 'the modern woman'. And she does this while also underlining the hubris of two empires: the Roman Empire surveyed by Gibbon, and the British Empire that provides the narrative its backdrop.

A second way of looking at what it means to be 'modern' for Rachel in her time and place concerns issues of social reality. She is character-ised as an involuntary Christian, whereas Woolf in her time declared religion to be something she had little or no interest in. That was one sense in which a woman could be modern. In an essay on 'Modernism and Religion', Pericles Lewis draws attention to the scorn heaped by Woolf on her friend T. S. Eliot (in a letter dated 11 February 1928 to her sister Vanessa) upon hearing of Eliot's conversion to Anglo-Catholicism: 'I was really shocked. A corpse would seem to me more credible than he is. I mean, there's something obscene in a living person sitting by the fire and believing in God.' Lewis observes,

> Woolf's revulsion against Eliot's religious beliefs may seem part and parcel
> of her rejection of patriarchal authority: what better representative of patri-

archy than God the Father? Yet, Woolf's putative atheism is complicated by her relation to her own father, Leslie Stephen, the most famous agnostic in Victorian England, against whom much of her work rebels. (Lewis 2011: 178)[8]

Woolf reflects some part of her complex attitude to religion in what the novel shows us. Hirst and Hewet declare themselves to have no interest in religion (161); that is their sense of being modern. However, when it comes to women getting the right to vote, Hewet is sceptical: 'Do you think that the vote will do you any good?' (240). Here it is Rachel who is modern. The men, for all their fashionable air of being up-to-date, nurse old prejudices. Hewet succumbs to a common stereotype: 'You've no respect for facts, Rachel; you're essentially feminine' (344). Yet, it is through him that the novelist voices her sense of the silenced condition of women deprived of the modernity of equal rights and opportunities:

> It's the beginning of the twentieth century, and until a few years ago no woman had ever come out by herself and said things at all. There it was going on in the background, for all those thousands of years, this curious silent unrepresented life. Of course we're always writing about women – abusing them, or jeering at them, or worshipping them; but it's never come from women themselves. I believe we still don't know how they live, or what they feel, or what they do precisely. (245)

By attributing this recognition to a man who concedes his own blindness to the plight of women, the novelist makes the case against silence and repression much stronger than if she had made her women protest stridently on their own account. The rage he attributes to Rachel comes to focus on the figure of the father. The attitude to women attributed in the novel to Rachel's father might have had its origin in the personal relationship of Virginia and Vanessa with their father, Leslie Stephen: 'He was good-humoured towards them but contemptuous' (246). Rachel directs her pent-up rage at her aunts: 'it was their world with its four meals, its punctuality, and servants on the stairs at half-past ten, that she examined so closely and wanted so vehemently to smash to atoms' (246). The elder women of the family reinforce patriarchy and become its willing vassals. That is how Rachel's expresses her bitterness at being colonised by patriarchy.

Woolf and Rhys read together

Reading Woolf and Rhys in conjunction drives home several points. For women to be forced to play roles dictated by conventions governing gender (and in the case of Rhys, race) circumscribed understanding and suffocated feminine potential experience. The two novels bear witness to the intensity of that repression. The extremity of the rebellion is more obvious in *Wide Sargasso Sea*: the protagonist chooses to die, unlike Woolf's protagonist, in whose case death is an accident of fate. And racial contempt of the hybrid is perhaps even harder to bear than male bullying. The triumph of patriarchy was constituted as much in uncritical feminine assimilation to its mores as through the prejudices perpetuated by men. These authors would rather kill off their heroines than allow that betrayal of an aspiring will-to-modernity-as-emancipation go unchallenged. Their resources of narrative strategy combine the process of self-discovery with the formal and aesthetic distance needed to objectify the linguistic flow of multiple individual consciousnesses. Each offered a form of subaltern resistance to the dominative and repressive forces in their lives. The failure of their heroines implies the need for a world very different from the ones they are trapped in, in which such tragic fates would be averted.

2. Modernist Allegory

Kafka and empire

Franz Kafka (1884–1923) provides an unusual but interesting angle from which to explore a connection between modernist and postcolonial writing. His fictional world is characterised by profound unease at a human condition seemingly devoid of coherence and justice, where human fate is subject to caprice and human destiny seems inscrutable. Characters and predicaments appear as concrete particulars of a fundamentally skewed world, with the universal never far behind the particular. It is a world presented to us, as remarked by Theodor Adorno, like 'a parabolic system the key to which has been stolen' (Adorno 1981: 246). Kafka and postcolonial writing share a concern for the underdog, the outcast, the exile and the victims of fate or chance. Kafka's unique power in sustaining a creative tension between narrative realism, fantasy and allegory has striking affinities with the kinds of postcolonial writing that resist the realism associated with European fiction of the nineteenth century.

Writing in German from Prague, Kafka's experience might seem to have little to do with colonial history. Germany was not among the most prominent of colonisers. Its imperial ambitions began well after the establishment of overseas colonies by Britain and the other sea-faring nations of Europe. The few German overseas colonies and protectorates of which Kafka would have known – in Africa, in the Pacific (German New Guinea and the Samoan islands) and in China (the Jiaozhou Bay concession) – were short-lived ventures soon swallowed up in the German defeat that ended World War I. However, behind the imperialist aspirations of Germany there remained the presence of the once powerful Austro-Hungarian Empire, now in decay. Kafka developed as a writer from 1908 to 1924 in the shadow of that empire. His stories retain an oblique sense of what it meant for a people to become a nation through sustained domination over many different peoples and cultures.

We will touch upon three ways in which to read postcolonial studies and Kafka together in such a way as to cast a useful light on both sides. The first approach attends closely to the allusions made by Kafka to the historical and cultural facts of empire, colony and the Orient. It also shows that his way of engaging with the historical fact of empires was to step back from contingent details to a general or abstract level. At that level, story-material apparently concerned with secular dispensations of power translates into searching questions concerning the nature of divine providence. The second approach derives from Gilles Deleuze and Félix Guattari (1975), who read Kafka as an example of 'minor literature', and use the term in the sense of literature written by a minority working within and against the dominance of a major tradition (and not as something secondary or insignificant). The third approach highlights the role of allegory in modernist and postcolonial writing, as a form of resistance to the dominance of realism in fictional narrative. In this respect, there are significant resemblances between Kafka, magical realism, the South African fictions of J. M. Coetzee (b. 1940) and the semi-fantastical aspect of the novels of Salman Rushdie (b. 1947). In each, allegory translates the impulse to verisimilitude that is characteristic of realism into complex fables about the nature of human existence in history.

Kafka on mimicry

Kafka's narratives combine elements of the realist and the expressionist, the commonplace and the fantastical, in their evocation of a variety of settings: wilderness, desert, village, city, empire and colony. Without making a direct allusion to colonialism, the narrative of 'A Report to an Academy' (1917) subverts the idea of the civilising mission of Europe. Its first-person narrator is a 'civilised' ape. He narrates his capture by humans and his success in imitating them in captivity. He reminds his human auditors that they too were apes once, and remarks that he has made at least as much progress in one lifetime as humans in the lifetime of their species.

Once captured, he had no immediate hope of escape, and therefore worked out an alternative strategy to find a 'way out', which differs from the human idea of freedom: 'I do not deliberately use the word "freedom"' (Kafka 1983: 253). The reason for avoiding the word 'freedom' casts an ironic light on the kind of postcolonial history that placed a high value on freedom only to find when decolonisation arrived at new nationhood that freedom was a letdown: 'In passing I may say that all too often men are betrayed by the word freedom. And as freedom is counted among the most sublime feelings, so the corresponding disillusionment can also be sublime' (253). Unlike colonised people, the ape chooses mimicry not because he thinks the way of men superior, but merely because it is so easy to appear human: 'It was easy to imitate these people. I learned to spit in the very first days' (255).

Kafka's sardonic treatment of mimicry anticipates a number of postcolonial writers and critics such as Frantz Fanon, V. S. Naipaul and Homi Bhabha. Fanon writes in *The Wretched of the Earth* that postcolonial peoples should not 'lose time in useless laments or sickening mimicry' (Fanon 2005: 235). Naipaul is bitter in *The Mimic Men* (1967) in his description of the colonised as 'mimic men' who 'pretended to be real, to be learning, to be preparing ourselves for life [. . .] with all its reminders of the corruption that came so quickly to the new' (Naipaul 1967: 146). Bhabha stresses the ambivalence that attends colonial mimicry: 'it is from this area between mimicry and mockery, where the reforming mission is threatened by the displacing gaze of its disciplinary double, that my instances of colonial imitation come' (Bhabha 1994: 123). Kafka's ape practises his civility and his mimicry with exactly this kind of ambivalence, echoing the colonial predicament and anticipating later theoretical analysis.

The story of a humanised ape draws attention to the Western tendency to treat the colonised as savages. The English poet and civil servant Edmund Spenser (1552–99) was bluntly contemptuous of the Irish, England's first target for colonisation, in his pamphlet *A View of the Present State of Ireland* (1598). European colonisers have been vindicating imperialism ever since then as the spread of sweetness and light to savages bereft of both. Kafka, writing in 1914–17, turns that dissembling fable on its head. He reverses roles between apes and humans: 'My ape nature fled out of me, head over heels and away, so that my first teacher was almost himself turned into an ape by it, had soon to give up teaching and was taken away to a mental hospital. Fortunately he was soon let out again' (Kafka 1983: 289–90). We might add that the same manoeuvre occurs in the hugely successful movie series that began with *Planet of the Apes* (1968), of which the most recent sequel is *Rise of the Planet of the Apes* (2011). The salutary irony of such amusement is summed up in the words of Deleuze and Guattari as 'a nonparallel and asymmetrical evolution where the man no less becomes an ape than the ape becomes a man' (Deleuze and Guattari 1986: 13).

Benjamin on Kafka and allegory

Unlike ordinary parables, whose semblance of concealment opens up a significance which, when grasped, can be said to complete a circuit of meaning from author to reader, Kafka's fictions hint and imply significations that are rarely made explicit. His method of telling a story is to quickly sketch out a scene or situation, and then bring in fantastical or unexpected elements as matter-of-factly as possible. Despite the semblance of specificity that marks his narratives, they have more to do with evoking unique zones of experience than with providing material for arguments.[9]

We noted in the first section of Chapter 2 that the Hungarian Marxist Lukács arrived at a discussion of allegory in 'The Ideology of Modernism' (1958) as a way of contrasting modernism and realism, because allegory can function as a trope for the alienation, estrangement and reification that some see as characteristic of the 'modern' condition. His delineation of allegory drew upon ideas developed by Walter Benjamin (in a dissertation published as a book in 1928): *The Origins of German Tragic Drama* (1977). Benjamin imputed the characteristics of the German mourning drama of the seventeenth century to the onset of modernity in the West. He argues that allegory helps distinguish between the literary genres of tragedy and mourning plays, and between historical time and the transcendence of historical time by what he calls 'messianic time'. The Christian origins of allegory give it a characteristic duality replicating the dual nature of Christ as part god and part man. In allegory, we view history in a theological perspective, even in a secular world. That brings Benjamin to one of his more significant claims: historical time is empty and unfulfilled, while 'messianic time' is time fulfilled.

The mourning that gives baroque plays their collective identity is of this peculiar kind that what is mourned is the loss of transcendence, that is, the state of being trapped within (and as one of) the things of the world. The critic Samuel Weber glosses the significance of mourning in Benjamin as follows: 'The Baroque mourns the loss of a notion of death that entails the promise of a New Order, that of self-identical subjectivity: the One God, the universality of Man, determining itself as a People, and gathering itself into the totality of a Community' (Weber 1991: 474). It is obvious where this takes us as Benjamin's later writings, including his essays on Kafka, transpose from the ethos of the baroque and the urban *flânêrie* of Baudelaire in the nineteenth century to the world of early twentieth-century disenchantment. In the kind of allegory he describes, of which Kafka provides prominent examples, the nature of the allegorical reference often remains elusive. It can point, ambiguously, and ambivalently, in more than one direction:

> Any person, any object, any relationship can mean absolutely anything else. With this possibility a destructive, but just verdict is passed on the profane world: it is characterised as a world in which the detail is of no importance [. . .] all of the things which are used to signify derive from the very fact of their pointing to something else [. . .] the profane world is both elevated and devalued. (Benjamin 1977: 175)

This leads Benjamin to one of his most suggestive formulations: 'Allegories are, in the realm of thoughts, what ruins are in the realm of things' (178). The analogy works well with the baroque quality in a novelist like Kafka as he walks us through a landscape peopled with questions but empty of explanations. It works equally well in relation to the kind of visionary chaos into which we are plunged in Rushdie's *Midnight's Children* (1981) and its account of the partition of British India, or *Shame* (1983) and its thinly-veiled allegory of the political power struggle in postcolonial Pakistan between military rule and democracy. In each case, melancholy prevails. For Benjamin it is the result of the loss of transcendence. In Kafka, it leads to riddles that have no clear answers. In a postcolonial postmodernist like Rushdie, it leads, in *Midnight's Children*, to a tragi-comic vision of political miscegenation. In *Shame*, it leads the widowed Rani Harappa (a fictional allusion to the fate suffered in history by Zulfikar Bhutto's second wife, Begum Nusrat Ispahani) to the weaving of eighteen ekphrastic shawls – as in Ovid's tale of Arachne – to represent in concealed allegory the tragedy of assassination and military misrule that is the history of the Bhutto family, and also of modern Pakistan (cf. Ziogas, online).

Kafka's Orientalism

The condition of not being German, while writing in German, provided Kafka distance from the sense of belonging to, or being part of a German or a European norm. Another kind of distance resulted from his prematurely deteriorating health. It reinforced the feeling of being marked out for a fate different from that reserved for others. Furthermore, to be a Jew made it easy to adopt the guise of a wanderer suffering exile. A diary entry for 28 January 1922 says, 'I am now a citizen of this other world, whose relationship to the ordinary one is the relationship of the wilderness to cultivated land' (Kafka 1972: 407). Thus we see that Kafka approaches the German tradition of constructing a 'cultural other in European discourse' (Goebel 1997: 15) in a sceptical spirit.

Several of his shorter works show this tendency, from 'Description of a Struggle' (1904–7) to 'The Great Wall of China' (1917), 'An Old Manuscript' (1917) and 'In the Penal Colony', a text that Kafka drafted in 1914, but held back from publication until 1919 because he felt that its final pages were 'botched' (Kafka 1977: 136). 'Description of a Struggle' shows the impact of translations of Chinese poetry on Kafka. His access to such materials was at second-hand, as with other Western writers handling Eastern cultural motifs, and he used such materials eclectically. His need for them had more to do with adopting a quizzical attitude towards European preoccupations than with trying to understand the motifs in their cultural contexts.

Scholars have suggested several possible sources in Eastern art for the image of 'The Fat Man' in 'Description of a Struggle'. Kafka describes this bald, yellow figure as seated in a litter that some skinny men are trying to carry across turbulent waters. They prove inadequate to the task and he drowns. We are told that he would have accepted this fate as 'the water's and the wind's revenge' (Kafka 1983: 28), since he had imposed his will on nature by naming it in human terms without 'being properly satisfied with the real names of things'. He had named the poplar in the fields the 'Tower of Babel' or 'Noah in his cups' (33). Kafka's seemingly odd preoccupation stems from a particular kind of modernist anxiety, which has a tradition of its own. Kafka's immediate predecessor in this tradition of anxiety was the Austrian writer Hugo von Hofmannsthal (1874–1929). His meditation on this theme, *The Lord Chandos Letter* (1902), articulates the motif at length: the inadequacy of language in relation to that which we call 'truth', 'reality', or 'life'.

Hofmannsthal 'wanted to show that the fables and mythic tales which the ancients have handed down to us and in which painters and sculptors never cease to find mindless pleasure are the hieroglyphs of a secret, inexhaustible wisdom. I sometimes thought I felt its breath, as though coming from behind a veil' (Hoffmansthal 2005: 119). His predicament has since received widespread recognition as a recurrent modernist mis-giving. He has lost faith in language: 'I felt an inexplicable uneasiness in even pronouncing the words "spirit", "soul", or "body" [. . .] Rather, the abstract words which the tongue must enlist as a matter of course in order to bring out an opinion disintegrated in my mouth like rotten mushrooms' (121). There is an inverse relation between loss of faith in language and a new focus on the mundane objects of the everyday world: 'words fail me once again. For what makes its presence felt to me at such times, filling any mundane object around me with a swelling tide of higher life as if it were a vessel, in fact has no name, and is no doubt hardly nameable [. . .] A watering can, a harrow left in a field, a dog in the sun, a shabby churchyard, a cripple, a small farmhouse – any of these can become the vessel of my revelation' (123).

Shortly after Hofmannsthal published his *Letter*, and very shortly after Kafka wrote of poplars misnamed as 'The Tower of Babel', Walter Benjamin articulated a Judaic-mystical account of what he described as the fall from an authentic language into a babble of many tongues. His essay, 'On Language as Such and on the Language of Man' (1916), reworks the Judaic-Christian fable into an allegory that applies equally to the world of Kafka's fictions and the element of melancholy in post-colonial writing. The allegory concerns mourning. In his account, the fall is nothing else but the loss of a 'pure' language adequate to the true essence of the objects of the world. This loss produces guilt at the lack of commensuration between the man-made and the God-given. The mistrust in the capacity of language to correspond to truth leads to a new and necessary compulsion: the habit of treating allegorically whatever cannot be named in unconcealed fashion. Benjamin provides what we might describe as a broad template for how and why allegory acquires a prominence for the modern condition.

'The Great Wall of China' (1917)

The journey through Benjamin can help us appreciate the melancholy dimension to Kafka's or Rushdie's stories, though it cannot account for the elements of quirky humour that animate Kafka's world (or the zany ebullience of Rushdie's language). In Kafka, the geographically specific and the historically contingent always reach out towards the condition of the implied universal. In 'The Great Wall of China', the narrator tells us that the wall will serve the function of 'protection against the people of the north' (Kafka 1983: 235). Now there are many gaps in the wall, which defeat the original purpose. This has led those working at the site to a sense of exhaustion and frustration: the supervisors 'had lost all faith in themselves, the wall, in the world' (237). As the story develops, the reader realises that a narrative about the Great Wall in China might also imply a meditation on writing as an enterprise full of gaps that might lead to frustration and futility.

The orientation of the story changes as the narrator alludes to biblical materials. The Great Wall might seem to have nothing to do with the Tower of Babel. However, they invite comparison. A scholar claims that the Tower of Babel failed because of the weakness of its foundation, but he adds that the Great Wall will provide a basis for a new tower. His speculation leads to a question. How is anybody to build a circle from a meandering line? The narrator hints that these are not merely literal questions. He wonders if they have 'a spiritual sense' (239). We are in the presence of irony. The narrative arrives at a situation familiar to any reader of Kafka: we read of a high command in whose office it might be certain that 'all human thoughts and desires revolved in a circle, and all human aims and fulfilments in a counter-circle' (239–40). The spiritual and the human thus find themselves moving in contrary directions. The inference: the command ruled something that was inexpedient. The narrator declares himself committed to an inquiry that is not satisfied with the official answer for building the wall. He is from the south-east, and does not feel threatened by any invaders from the north.

Given the way the story develops, there are several possible directions in which to develop an interpretation: one could say that the story is specifically about China, and that the author is at pains to engage with issues like governance, polity and the differences between the ideal and the real dimension of imperial rule. Or one can expand the scope to include empires in general, including the Austro-Hungarian Empire nearer home to Kafka, and European imperial policies in the period leading up to World War I. The narrative allows some footholds for this interpretation.

At a more general level, we can also ponder over whether such parables 'present the law as a pure and empty form without content, the object of which remains unknowable' (Deleuze and Guattari 1986: 43). Another way of reading the story would place spiritual issues in the foreground. The parable would then signify how our daily lives are lived in real and symbolic places distant from the empires of the spirit postulated by religious orthodoxy (whether Judaic, or Judaic-Christian, or Chinese). It should be clear without going any further that Kafka's narratives resist closure. It is more useful here to recognise this quality than to argue for the merits of one interpretation over another. It is also possible to recognise that regardless of the meaning we derive from the fable-like narrative, it revises our notion of how we suppose fables and parables to work. Whatever else Kafka had in mind, he did have the construction of meaning in mind.

'In the Penal Colony' (1919)

Kafka's fictional colony resonates to a topical allusion. German-controlled Namibia was the scene of a brutal genocide when the colonial authorities suppressed a revolt during 1904–8: it resulted in the almost total destruction of the Herero and Nama peoples of the region (Adhikari 2008). The realm of public allusion also allows for a personal and professional preoccupation with industrial accidents. The editors of Kafka's *Office Writings* (2009) remind us that his training as a lawyer, and his job in an insurance company in Prague, had a direct bearing on the materials and methods of narratives such as *The Trial* and 'In the Penal Colony'. In his line of work the abstraction that is law and the concrete fact of suffering in the flesh came up against one another repeatedly in the form of 'bodies mutilated in industrial accidents, which he was required to redeem in the form of legal decisions' (Kafka 2009b: xvi). Kafka's job was to deal with the legal ramifications of such accidents 'as the public voice of the comprehensive reforms that Robert Marschner was to initiate as the Institute's new director' (53).

The flow of ideas from workplace to fiction had many features. Machines in industrial places could go out of control and cause damage. Laws were needed to ensure that injured workers would be adequately compensated. The new commandant from 'In the Penal Colony' is like a fictional counterpart to Marschner, Kafka's boss. Kafka had acquired enough expertise at the Institute of Technology in Prague to write a document such as 'Measures for Preventing Accidents from Wood-Planing Machines' (1910). He was thus peculiarly well-equipped to conjure up machines that damaged human flesh not through accident but design. A system of law and bureaucratic procedure that tackled the harsher side effects of the new modernity of industrial processes thus became a kind of ghostly twin to the administration of juridical pain in a tropical colony (the political and geographical alter ego to the modernity of the industrial metropolis in Europe).

In the story, the rendering of place and individuals is generic rather than realist. The principal cast is also minimal: an officer, a condemned man, an old commandant and a person identified in the original German as *Forschungsreisender*. This word is translated as 'explorer' in the Nahum Glatzer collection (Kafka 1983), and as 'traveller' in the OUP selection (Kafka 2009). A note by Ritchie Robertson suggests that the source for Kafka's protagonist could have been a lawyer named Robert Heindl. In 1909–10, Heindl visited penal colonies in New Caledonia, the Andaman Islands and China, and published his findings at the request of the German government (Kafka 2009a: 143).

The traveller is to witness the execution of a soldier 'who had been condemned for disobedience and insulting behaviour towards his superior' (75). The condemned man appears 'dull-witted, wide-mouthed'. The reader is not invited to identify too readily with his plight. Attention is focused instead on 'the apparatus'. The officer describes it to the traveller with pride and pleasure, in French, a language not followed by the condemned man, or by the soldier who guards him. The reference to French might makes one wonder (why French? where is the island in terms of geographical location?), but Kafka's story is written in such a way as to bypass such questions.

The machine is an invention of the old commandant, who is described as a kind of imperial Renaissance man, 'soldier, judge, engineer, chemist, draughtsman all in one' (79). The officer is more keen to describe how the machine works than to explain why it was invented. Admiring machines had become something of a vogue since the Italian Futurist F. T. Marinetti enthused about them in his manifestos and speeches in the years preceding World War I. He announced a desire to embrace the machine, figuratively and literally: 'We went up to the three snorting machines to caress their breasts'.[10] A few years before Kafka began his story, Henry Ford had set up a car factory in Detroit, thus inaugurating the processes of mass production that would become recognised globally as Fordism. Machines were the topical metonymy for a specifically technological manifestation of modernity.

The officer explains that the machine has been built to enact the letter of the law, literally. The phrase or sentence that enshrines the violated command has to be inscribed upon the back of the condemned individual with a Harrow equipped with needles. The officer gives no indication that the punishment might seem gross. The traveller, for his part, is further surprised that the condemned man does not know that he has been condemned. He has had no opportunity to defend himself. He has been told neither the sentence, nor the punishment. That is how Kafka the practical joker plays in earnest. The traveller is like a bemused representative for the conventional point of view that has no room in the colonial bureaucracy.

The enactment of the Law is entirely in the hands of the officer. He is its eager tool. We can see how Kafka's tongue-in-cheek representation can stand in for the history of colonial officers posted overseas who were given powers inconceivable in their home countries. This young enforcer of the law upholds an astonishing principle: 'Guilt is always beyond question' (80). The traveller tries to get over his sense of discomfort at this with the conjecture that judicial processes in a colony might have to adopt militarist simplifications.

The previous commandant had created designs for how the Harrow would inscribe a sentence onto flesh. The soldier treats this like holy writ, with reverence. The beauty of the machine, its efficiency, the simplicity of the law he upholds and the literal process of its application are his primary focus. He attends to the machine with patience and care. The design takes time in killing the victim. The screaming is over within the first two hours, but the pain lasts for six hours and the entire job takes twelve hours to finish. The officer loves to watch the dawning recognition of what the sentence means in the eyes of the victim. He remembers the days when 'we all took in the look of transfiguration from the suffering face' (87). Kafka builds up the tension by withholding the horror most of us would experience under these circumstances. Colonialism, like the modern concept of law, has its roots in the ethos of the European Enlightenment. When abetted by the modernity of the machine, it could enact its purposes in a manner that called for Swiftian methods of indirectness in building up the horror.

It is only at this point that the reader is told that the traveller does not belong to the nation whose colony he visits. He is a witness, not an agent, and he is not sure if he can interfere. Kafka thus marginalises the scope for protest. Meanwhile the soldier confesses that he and his machine are isolated in the colony. The new commandant is 'soft', and advised by the women around him, while the machine is short of spare parts, and people no longer take much interest in the spectacle and performance. The focus shifts to accommodate some room for intervention. The traveller has been invited to visit the colony as 'a great Western expert' (89) and 'great scientist' (91), to make recommendations on the criminal justice procedure in the colony. The officer would like to enlist his support in blocking the new commandant's faction.

The traveller now declares his position unambiguously. He objects to the procedure and will indicate as much to the commandant, in private. Kafka thus sets up the narrative for the final surprise. The officer recognises that the traveller is adamant. He frees the condemned man, and then does something that is likely to catch most readers by surprise. He climbs up the machine to put a new injunction into the machine – 'Be just' – then strips and puts himself onto the Bed of the machine. We are told, without fuss or explanation, that 'in his place the traveller would not have acted differently himself' (95). As if this were not strange enough, the story arrives at an anti-climax: the machine malfunctions, a cog-wheel falls off and instead of working its normal, elaborate routine, the Harrow no longer writes, 'it only stabbed' (97). The officer is killed in a brutal manner quite contrary to the process intended by the old commandant. The supine officer does not get what he wanted: 'not a sign of the promised deliverance' that he had spoken of appears on his dead face. His self-sacrifice has been pointless. The traveller departs.

The ending seems to have left Kafka dissatisfied. The entry for 9 August 1917 in his diary is particularly interesting. In it Kafka records part of the narrative ending in draft form. As the traveller prepares to leave aboard a ship, he has a hallucinatory experience: the man carrying his baggage onto the ship is 'the condemned man'. He asks if the officer has perpetrated a conjuring trick. He is told by the officer: '"No . . . a mistake on your part; I was executed, as you commanded"' (Kafka 1972: 382). The fragment ends with this sentence: 'And all saw together how the officer passed his hand across his brow to disclose a pike crookedly protruding from his shattered forehead' (382). There is obviously more to the resonance of the narrative than an implied critique of colonial criminal justice, or of the hubris of colonial regimes. The strange logic with which the traveller confirms the officer's choice also haunts him with a sense of complicity. Through this emblematic colony, Kafka engages with the enigma of how suffering, even uncomprehending suffering, might be a form of distorted transfiguration, perhaps the only one allotted the modern condition.

Kafka and 'minor literature'

An entry dated 25 December 1910 in Kafka's diary is devoted to a discussion of the literary productions of minority cultures such as Jews in Warsaw and Prague. Kafka reflects, 'A small nation's memory is not smaller than the memory of a large one' (Kafka 1978: 149). He then proceeds to sketch an outline of the character of the literature of 'small peoples' (150). It is understandable if his sentiments should find echoes in the discourse of postcolonial studies.

The fictions by Kafka discussed above confirm the sense of a relation of correspondence and analogy between modernist and colonial (as well as postcolonial) predicaments. The idea of a literature of 'small peoples' was developed in the 1970s by Deleuze and Guattari into the idea of a 'minor literature'. They explain the term as follows: 'A minor literature doesn't come from a minor language; it is rather that which a minority constructs within a major language' (Deleuze and Guattari 1986: 16). Kafka writes in German without being German, as a Czech Jew, who uses Prague German as 'a deterritorialised language' (17). All such 'cramped' uses of language are necessarily political, 'because a whole other story is vibrating within it', and such uses take on 'a collective value' (17).

Deleuze and Guattari argue that in Kafka deterritorialisation, political immediacy and collective enunciation go together (18). With allowances for variations in history and circumstance, pretty much the same applies to postcolonial writing. What then can a discourse about the latter set of texts learn from this approach to Kafka? And what do we learn about Kafka from that connection? Deleuze and Guattari argue that writing which draws its revolutionary power by remaining 'minor' in relation to a 'major' tradition creates not only a line of escape (from dominance), but three kinds of freedom: of movement, statement and desire (65). They point to the fact that the German language in Czechoslovakia was intermixed with Czech and Yiddish, and thus became a flexible instrument in Kafka's hands, even though the German language as used in Prague had a limited vocabulary and an outmoded syntax, quite unlike the vernacular languages used by the region's rural communities, or Hebrew (23). They believe that the situation of the Habsburg Empire in Kafka's time provides opportunities for a new re-territorrialisation of language.

A contemporary Kafka expert, Stanley Corngold, objects to the notion of 'Prague German'. He argues that Kafka aspired in his published writings to a High German that had few marks of regional associations (Corngold 2004: 142–57). Corngold feels that Deleuze and Guattari politicised aspects of Kafka for purposes that do not fit Kafka's conception of his own work. Benjamin had described Kafka as having written 'fairy tales for dialecticians' (Benjamin 1999: 799). Corngold alludes to that reference to suggest that the alignment of Kafka with the idea of 'dialect' is not as convincing as Kafka's link with 'dialectic'. Regardless of the position we take on the debate, it remains viable to say that Kafka, in fictions such as that concerning China, mobilised a narrator whose sympathies are allied with the common folk of the South-east who feel themselves remote from the metropolitan centre of the empire. In that sense, issues of territory and resistance to marginalisation provide a bridge between the dominance of High German that Kafka worked with and against, and the dominance of colonial models that postcolonial writing works with and against.

Kafka's postcolonial interlocutors

In a 1921 essay on translation, Walter Benjamin argued for the necessity of literalness in 'The Task of the Translator' (1921) deploying an image that is as old as the Kabbalah tradition he drew upon. It is an image of recuperation concerning 'fragments of a vessel that are to be glued together [. . .] recognisable as fragments of a greater language' (Benjamin 1996: 260). This image from a Jewish contemporary of Kafka's finds an echo in the postcolonial writing of the Caribbean poet Derek Walcott (b. 1930). He used it tellingly in his Nobel Prize acceptance speech:

> Break a vase, and the love that reassembles the fragments is stronger than that love which took its symmetry for granted when it was whole [. . .] Antillean art is this restoration of our shattered histories, our shards of vocabulary, our archipelago becoming a synonym for pieces broken off from the original continent. (Walcott 1992: 8–9)

Walcott articulates a realisation of how postcolonial writers can turn the modernist sense of crisis into new opportunities applicable to their own situations in time and place. He reiterates the idea that the things of the world exist in nature more truly when their linguistic being is spoken. One of his poems treats the Caribbean as inconceivable because 'no one had yet written of this landscape / that it was possible' (Walcott 1986: 195). In the modernist-postcolonial epic poem, *Omeros*, he speaks of his boyhood as a time 'when I was a noun / gently exhaled from the palate of the sunrise' (Walcott 1990: 12). The poet is like an Adam whose task is 'giving things their names' (1986: 294), although the poet can also envisage a condition prior to the act of naming:

> My race began as the sea began,
> with no nouns [. . .] (1986: 305)

Thus, we see that from Hofmannsthal and the turn of the last century to Kafka and Benjamin to Derek Walcott in the 1960s and 1980s, the modernist-and-postcolonial preoccupation with the degeneracy and refurbishing of language remains a recurrent motif.[11]

In 'What is a Classic? A Lecture' (1993), the novelist J. M. Coetzee recounts that as a youth he was uninterested in music, until 1955, when he heard Bach, and found it a transfiguring experience. He recognised that Bach and his music grew from roots in a specific time and place, but the Bach he heard appealed at a level of humanity that transcended time and place. This made him realise that in his own writing he might handle the issue of rootedness in time and place in such a way as to reach across the specific and the contingent to the more general and universal dimension of the human condition.[12] His anecdote helps us appreciate the kind of distance his novels keep from Western realism. Coetzee notes the same tendency in the preference shown by the Egyptian novelist Naguib Mahfouz (1911–2006).

Coetzee's perception of Mahfouz's significance can be contrasted with the argument supported by many of the contributors to a special issue of *Modern Language Quarterly* (2012) on 'Peripheral Realisms', in which Joe Cleary, for example, laments that postcolonial writing of the post-modern and magical realism kind has been well-received by postcolonial critics, whereas many 'classics of anticolonial or postcolonial realism' (Cleary 2012: 265) have not been given their due. He cites Mahfouz as an example of such realism; however, that misrepresents the later work of the Egyptian novelist. More to the point, its desire to promote realism overstates the degree to which 'postcolonial studies has privileged modernist-associated terms such as hybridity, polyphony, pastiche, irony, and defamiliarisation rather than realist-associated conceptual categories such as historical transition, class consciousness and totality' (265). This argument underestimates the degree to which realism exercised over writers from the colonies a force that constituted a colonisation of literary forms and genres, and the degree to which the adaptation of modernist modes was in itself a kind of literary decolonisation.

The later work of Mahfouz adopts a symbolic and allegorical approach very different from the realism of his early novels. He began his long career with historical fiction; then wrote realist novels in a contemporary setting, of which his 'Cairo trilogy' of the 1950s is the most ambitious example. Then came the political revolution of 1952, and the disappointment that Abdul Nasser proved to be in his governance of Egypt. Mahfouz reconsidered his fictional repertoire, as if realism had served its purpose, and a new method had to be found to cope with changing circumstances and needs. With *Children of Gebelaawi* (*Awlad Haratina*, 1959), he showed a new approach to narrative technique: realism made way for a fluid movement between naturalistic detail and symbolic resonance. An ordinary alley in Cairo is observed in minute detail. The narrative unfolds the struggles of its inhabitants to restore their rights to a 'Trust Fund' set up by their ancestor Gebelaawi ('Old Man of the Jebel'). The alley is the world, and the events of the story are a moral drama with Cain and Abel, Muhammad and Jesus, and Adam and Eve as protagonists. The fable has a point to make: the urgent need for restoring God's legacy to the common people.[13]

The book shows how one can speak of God within a fictional context without overburdening the story. Such allegory accomplishes several goals not accessible to realism on its own. It can speak at once of two things (it can bring seemingly unrelated things together, revealing kinships where none might have been suspected). It can also conceal, and then reveal to appropriate reading practices, a deeper second sense underneath a surface layer that has its own appeal. In accomplishing such ends, we do not have to claim that he was indebted to Kafka. Each in his time and place discovers for himself a similar resource in allegory. This resource does not abandon the conventions of realism; instead, it uses closely observed circumstantial detail, but applied to an enlarged field of reference well beyond the scope of realism and its fidelity to the contingent and the quotidian.

Coetzee's novels of the 1980s show the success of applying realist means to allegorical ends. *Waiting for the Barbarians* (1980) grows its narrative from a kernel in C. P. Cavafy's well-known poem 'Waiting for the Barbarians' (1904). A feared invasion by barbarians rumoured to be at the borders of a sophisticated but decadent nation has failed to materialise. The poem concludes with a rhetorical question followed by a sardonic observation: 'Now what's going to happen to us without barbarians? / Those people were a kind of solution' (Cavafy 1975: 18). The novelist practises a similarly dead-pan irony in his fable of a border town and its commander.[14] The very title of *Life & Times of Michael K* (1983) makes an allusion to Kafka's 'K' from *The Trial* (1925) and *The Castle* (1926). Finally, consider *Foe* (1986). Here Coetzee deconstructs the fiction of survival created by Daniel Defoe's *Robinson Crusoe* (1719) by presenting us a 'Cruso' gone derelict and dejected. His apathy contrasts with the fervent desires of a female character, whose inclusion draws attention to the glaring absence of women from the Crusoe myth. She is obsessed with the desire to tell her story. Coetzee sets up the narrative at a level of generality that absorbs characters and events into a symbolic debate about gender, race and writing, which grows from a particular moment in the history of apartheid South Africa, but retains an application that is not bound to that time and place.

Mahfouz and Coetzee, each in his way, tackles a recurrent question: 'can a culture become modern without internalising the genealogy of modernity, that is, without living through the epistemological revolution, in all its implications, out of which Western scientific knowledge grew?' (Coetzee 1999: 226–7). The same question echoes in writing from Latin America and other parts of the formerly colonised world. The question keeps the conversation alive between postcolonial postmodernists and the Kafka whose life was confined to his corner of Europe, but whose imagination sought out the hidden corners of a larger world of modernity and crisis. As he put it in a letter to Felice Bauer, dated mid-May 1916 (Kafka 1978: 594): 'I imagine if I were a Chinese and were about to go home (indeed I am a Chinese and am going home), I would make sure of returning soon, and at any price.'

3. Modernism and Faith

> someone will forever be surprising
> A hunger in himself to be more serious,
> And gravitating with it to this ground,
> Which, he once heard, was proper to grow wise in,
> If only that so many dead lie round.

Philip Larkin

Of Manila and Mumbai

Whenever social modernity is treated as a secular phenomenon, the impact of modernisation on the role of religion in traditional modes of life is likely to be underestimated. Our final case study addresses the intersection of modernity and faith in postcolonial societies through a reading of two texts from Asia: Nick Joaquin's novel, *The Woman Who Had Two Navels* (1961) and Arun Kolatkar's sequence of poems, *Jejuri* (1976). We can treat them as representative of a common predicament, because there are many others like them who grapple with the question of how to retain faith, what to retain faith in, when that in which faith once reposed is dissolved by the forces of modernity. These forces redefine the terms on which faith and religion can relate. In the colonies and former colonies, the struggle acquires a particular tension because while the forces of modernity have become global in range, the religious impulse often remains indigenous or regional in its manifestations, and struggles to retain its identity under the onslaught of a homogenising modernity.

Joaquin's *The Woman Who Had Two Navels* began life as a short story undertaken in the aftermath of World War II.[15] By 1961 it had grown into a novel that narrates the struggle by a young Filipino woman, Connie Escobar, to escape the entrapments of her past. It is a struggle in which she discovers that the personal is inseparable from the familial, the communal and the national. For her, becoming modern entails a process of psychological self-transformation, and retaining faith becomes a matter of retrieving convictions. She must exorcise the past, and she must grapple with the impulse towards death. Her account is interwoven with the narrative of an old man, Dr Monson. He is a Filipino self-exile living in Hong Kong, away from the Manila where he had fought for Philippine independence (from the Americans) in his youth. He discovers too late that a fixation with the past has prevented him from coping with the present. In his case, becoming modern requires him to abandon an idealisation of nation and community nourished in the past. The shock of that realisation kills him, but not before he and Connie have met accidentally for a moment. In that brief encounter, a mysterious communion bridges the gap of more than a generation that separates their personal histories. The meeting brings each to the recognition that they had been seeking an absolution from their past as a way of preparing for the possibility of a redemptive future.

Arun Kolatkar's Commonwealth Poetry Prize winning poetic sequence *Jejuri* (1976) gives voice to a struggle between faith and modernity through the inability to believe in values and rituals from the past. A modern frame of mind finds communal religious practices untenable. Yet the past refuses complete erasure. An iconoclasm worn aggressively on his sleeve is continually nagged by the mythopoeic power of that which he would like to dismiss or mock. We suspect that the poet would like to recover the ability to have faith in something that might relieve him of the need to mock. If Joaquin's protagonist struggles with despair in her search for a ground on which faith might stand, Kolatkar's protagonist hovers over his own desire to shed his edgy insouciance.

The Philippine context

The Philippines as a nation is distinguished in the history of colonisation for its two-layered experience of colonialism. Ferdinand Magellan, a Portugal-born navigator sailing under the Spanish flag, landed on one of the Philippine islands in 1521. Thereafter, a Spanish colony was established on the island of Cebu by Miguel López de Legazpi shortly after his arrival in the archipelago in 1565. Three hundred years of Spanish rule followed, lasting until the end of the nineteenth century.

The long period of Spanish rule ensured the assimilation of Roman Catholicism by the Philippines. Indigenous belief systems either made way for or combined with the doctrines and dogmas of Christianity in most parts of the archipelago. In the southern region of Mindanao, however, the influence of Islam has remained dominant from the fourteenth century to this day. Spanish colonialism also introduced the Philippines to European technologies (including printing), the Spanish language and the cultural values and practices of the Hispanic world in their colonial guise. In the 1890s, the Filipinos challenged Spanish rule. The ensuing conflict was brought to an abrupt halt by US naval and military invention in 1898.

Claiming that the Philippines lacked the modernity of systems that could ensure stable self-rule, the Americans stepped into the gap that they had created, and stayed there for almost half a century. The Philippines thus underwent a double-colonisation with the transfer of colonial power from the Spanish to the Americans.[16] The Philippines underwent various kinds of modernisation under both the Spanish and the Americans: slowly, in the first instance; rapidly, in the second case. American colonialism lasted until 1946, interrupted only by the short and savage occupation of the Philippines by Japan during World War II. The Americans insisted on seeing themselves as benevolent. President McKinley declared in a 1903 interview that once the Spanish had been ejected, 'there was nothing left for us to do but to take them all, and to educate the Filipinos, and uplift and civilise and Christianise them' (Tucker 2009: 92).

Joaquin's novel embeds its drama of personal crises amidst the aftermath of the most decisive phase of Filipino history. This phase started with the revolution of 1896. It led to a declaration of independence in 1898, and that would have been a kind of culmination for the struggle to decolonise, had it not been for the subsequent annexation of the Philippines. The resistance offered by the newly declared republic to the Americans died down gradually by 1913.

The novel has a range of historical references that extends across the entire period from the late nineteenth century to the end of World War II. The early part of this history provides the backdrop for the growing up into adulthood of the protagonist's mother, Concha Vidal. The decline of Spanish influence during this period was accompanied by the growth of nationalist optimism. The critic Epifanio San Juan, Jr, in an essay of 1967, describes the ethos as 'the disintegrating world of the Filipino petty bourgeoisie' (San Juan, Jr 1984: 146). The present tense of the novel evokes the raw newness of life after the ejection of the Japanese from the Philippines at the end of World War II. That constitutes the context for the growth of Connie into adulthood.

Manila and Hong Kong

Joaquin's novel is urban in setting, haunted by the city of Manila. It is like a microcosm for the transition of the Philippines from the colonial to the postcolonial era. One of the characters, the Hong Kong based musician Paco Texeira, compares the city to a woman who can suggest 'that combination of primitive mysticism and slick modernity which he felt to be the special temper of the city and its people' (Joaquin 1972: 27). Manila is like a ghostly presence throughout the novel, but the main plot is set in Hong Kong. Throughout its history, this port city has served as a haven for exiles, refugees and migrants of all the regions from the Philippines to China. In the novel, it provides a geographical symbol for the merging of the colonial and the modern in Southeast Asia. Its liminal space, globally well connected yet regionally distinctive, provides the distance from, and proximity to, the home that Connie and her mother need to conclude their struggle for the right to love and be loved.

It was in Hong Kong that the subsequently mythologised Filipino patriot and hero José Rizal (1861–96) worked for several years after leaving Europe in 1891, before returning to the Philippines for what became a swift and tragic martyrdom. He believed that though the Philippines deserved independence, the time was not right for it in the 1890s. Nevertheless, the Spanish executed him in 1896 on the charge of having fomented rebellion. Joaquin remarks of his fate, in an essay on the 'Anatomy of the Anti-Hero', that Rizal's 'condemnation of the Revolution as "absurd" has an uncanny echo in the "theatre of the absurd"' which we discover in modern existentialists from Kierkegaard to Kafka to Sartre. Rizal's fate makes him apt for the community of 'modern man aghast at the world he has made' (Joaquin 1977: 66).[17]

We have noted that the novel works out an intersection between two plots: one concerns Connie; the other features Dr Monson, the defeated revolutionary who chose self-exile in Hong Kong, and waited interminably for a resumption of the idealised first republic that the Americans had thwarted. It is to this Hong Kong that the other Filipino hero of history, Emilio Aguinaldo (1869–1964), retired in 1897, to wait for the resumption of the republic. It is to this Kong Kong that Connie is brought by a plot that weaves moral dilemmas into a meditation on the history of individuals and nations struggling to arrive at a conjunction between modernity and freedom. Joaquin succeeds in combining realist detail in his evocation of time and place with a metaphorical-allegorical handling of psychological and existential dilemmas. The same ability to combine the cumulative effects of metonymic detail with the transforming force of allegory also distinguishes his drama *A Portrait of the Artist as Filipino* (1966).

As a young man, Joaquin had studied for the priesthood in Hong Kong (1947–50). The monastery of St Andrews, atop Holy Cross Hill in Hong Kong, provides the setting for the intense debates carried on by Connie within her head, which the author shares with his readers through the stream-of-consciousness technique. Connie has come to Hong Kong to pursue an association with the musician Paco. Her mother introduced them to one another in Manila. In that brief period, they both fought and made violent love. Connie's worried husband follows her to Hong Kong, where her mother has already come on vacation. The novel begins with Connie seeking a professional remedy from one of Dr Monson's sons, Pepe, a veterinarian, for an unusual problem: she claims that she has two navels. He refers her to his brother Tony instead (who happens to be a priest) because he thinks that the solution to her problem is not surgery but spiritual counselling. Through the device of a double-plot Joaquin is able to use the Monson family as a vital link between the dilemma confronting Dr Monson and the conflicts besetting young Connie, who thinks of the navels as stigmata or emblems of the suffering for which she thinks she has a calling.

Connie's closeness to her mother Concha Vidal was destroyed when she discovered letters exchanged prior to her marriage between her mother and her husband, Macho Escobar. Macho is the hedonistically self-indulgent son of a formerly wealthy Southern plantation owner. When Connie was still a small girl, he had been her mother's lover (under the knowing but indifferent eyes of Concha's second husband, Manolo Vidal, former abortionist and current politician, who was always more interested in his political career than in his wife's infidelities or his daughter's neuroses). Guilt eventually made Concha Vidal give up her lover, and anxiety made her persuade him to marry Connie. As the plot thickens, Connie's claim of having two navels is treated with deliberate ambiguity by Joaquin: a surreal claim is treated as if it were a mundane phenomenon. The narrative technique moves constantly between reporting actions or speech and dramatising inner thoughts, which are presented to readers as internal brooding by Connie, or as vivid scraps of montage from the narrator.

Modernist allegory

The novel develops an allegory in which Connie's claim to possess two navels embodies a range of possible symbolic meanings, including her complex relation to her parents: a mixture of love and loathing, need and bondage. The two navels also point to a specific association. As a child, Connie had become very fond of a 'billikin' figure of the kind popular among children during the 1920s and 1930s in Manila. In Hong Kong, Connie keeps visiting a dilapidated shelter where this

'Biliken [sic]' is housed. This carnival statue was once housed in her family garden in Manila. After the war it was moved to Hong Kong. Seated, smiling, pot-bellied, long-eared and droll, it provides her with silent companionship and solace. The attachment began during her lonely childhood in Manila.[18] In the war, the statue was grazed by stray bullets and sustained damage around its belly. The scars make it appear as if it has two navels. The allegory of the two navels thus alludes to her dependency on a surrogate figure, a substitute for the absence of the companionship a father, sibling, or friend might have provided. The figure also serves as a kind of umbilical connection to the past, a time before the process of growing up had brought all its miseries upon her.

As the novel progresses, the two navels recede in significance. Some interpreters even insist that eventually Connie comes to accept her own claim as a fiction.[19] Regardless of how we read the symbolism, the story reaches a climax when Connie drives up to the monastery at night, in thick fog, either to consult the priest, or to commit suicide by driving off the cliff. While racing feverishly uphill, she goes over all the conflicts besetting her. During this internal drama of voices, she engages in what appears to be animated conversation with the three people she has loved most who have all hurt her in different ways: father, mother and husband. What happens in her internal colloquy is the heart of the novel. In her essay on the novel, Thelma Kintanar points out, 'Connie makes peace with her personal past by dying in each of her dream encounters with the people and events of her past life. The manner of each death is clearly symbolic: death by land, by water, by air' (Kintanar 1992: 135). There is also death by fire, which she averts when she falls out of the car as it goes over the cliff. Thus, Christian symbolism is woven into this modern fable. For Connie, coming to Hong Kong turns out to have been her bid for a new life, a risky undertaking that is not without cost.[20]

Her choice leads to a mixed outcome: she lives, and finds freedom from her three bonds, but her freedom has a cost. Others have to suffer; her husband chooses death. If she finds release from bondage in averting death, Dr Monson finds his release in death. It frees him from the phantasmal imprisonment produced by his half-century- old dream of revolution.[21] In contrast, Connie's decision becomes a token of the author's hope for the future; not for his protagonist alone, but for her generation and for the Philippines (a people awaiting the realisation of their true nationhood). That is how the story becomes an allegory of the nation. The past can both haunt and enrich. The future is secured as a viable option only when the strands that entangle people in the past can be disentangled. In her freedom Joaquin projects his fears and hopes for a modern Philippines moving forward towards a sustainable modernity.

Modernity and allegories of nation

We encountered the idea of a national allegory in the first section of Chapter 2. We return to Fredric Jameson's hypothesis that postcolonial writers seem drawn to allegorising nation in their narratives. San Juan, Jr, for instance, reads the novel as a 'national allegory of the Filipino condition' (San Juan, Jr 1988: 145). We can see how Connie's turn to the future and Dr Monson's acceptance of death both form part of this design. If her fate represents hope, his represents the idealism that lost its way along the twisted paths of history in the first decade of the twentieth century, when the last vestiges of resistance to the American occupation were snuffed out.

The Filipino historian O. D. Corpuz concludes his account of *The Roots of the Filipino Nation* (2006) on a note of melancholic irony: 'The fading away of nationalism as the guiding spirit and paramount value in Filipino politics might be said to have begun with the founding of the Nacionalista Party of 1907' (Corpuz 2006: 670). The story of the decline of nationalism, from 1906 to 1941, is little more than 'a story of the continuing erosion of the ideals of the nationalist Revolution and the First Republic' (657). No wonder then that Dr Monson is pushed into his grave by the shock of his belated realisation. Joaquin treats it as an honourable release from a faded illusion that had kept him in thrall far too long. As the spirit of nationalism died, the Philippines embarked upon its modernity willy-nilly, through the second colonialism of a modernisation devoid of the ideals of the past. The ironies of this inadvertent modernity become the underlying preoccupation of Joaquin's novel. The inception of a new world of possibility needs the clearing away of the old world.

The contemporary Filipino writer and critic Jaime an Lim notes that 'The convergence of humanitarian sentiment and aggressive temper which characterised American policy toward the Philippines was, in the final analysis, not much different from that of Spain's, although one called its gift the True Faith and the other called it Progress and Modernisation' (an Lim 1993: 49). What did American-styled modernity entail in a context at once colonial and postcolonial? The answer: the division of Church from State; an increasing role for Filipinos in local government; mass education in English; the building of roads and bridges; the expansion of transportation facilities; rationalised and nationalised banking and finance; and agriculture revitalised. All the processes associated with developing nations everywhere in the post-colonial world. Joaquin's reaction to this modernity was an explicit attempt to keep some sense of a vital connection between the past and the present alive for the kind of future in which Philippine society would regain or acquire the coherence and integration that many felt had slipped from its grasp when Americans took over where the Spanish had left off. In 1977, for example, Joaquin wrote of his own role in all this:

> I think it was this reaction, this obscure yearning or nostalgia for what we had set aside in favour of Hollywood and Manhattan, that was bound to break out sooner or later. I just happened to be around when it was bound to happen [. . .] you and I were wanting to express what had to be expressed – if Filipino culture is to achieve a reintegration. If we are to rediscover our grandfather [. . .] (Joaquin 1977: 16)

In an essay titled 'Sa Loob ng Maynila' ('Inside Manila'), Joaquin expressed similar sentiments about a Philippine nation-community torn asunder by the kind of modernity enforced by the Americans. In all his writing, nostalgia for the Spanish era co-exists with ambivalence about the transformations wrought in the Philippines under American patronage. Joaquin's father had served as a colonel in the revolution: an old-world gentleman rather like Dr Monson. Connie recognises in Dr Monson 'the hero they had all betrayed' (Joaquin 1972: 204). Such heroes had cherished a dream. The nation has not succeeded in realising this dream. That is why the present and the future owe an apology to that past, even though apologies do not suffice for what amounts to a continued deferral. This deferral feels like a betrayal of aspirations and sacrifices by preceding generations. That is the moral burden of the novel on behalf of the Philippine people.

The Indian context: modernity and caste

From Manila to Mumbai, the cultural contrast is considerable, yet the underlying factors reveal many similarities. Arun Kolatkar (1932–2004) was a bilingual poet who wrote in English and Marathi, and also worked as a graphic artist. He was one among several writers from mid-twentieth-century India to succeed in adapting a modernist outlook to his times and circumstances. Born in Kolhapur (in the state of Maharashtra) into a middle-class Hindu family, he studied art in Mumbai and worked most of his professional life in advertising. Intensely private in nature and bohemian by temperament, he shunned publicity, read eclectically, published sporadically and developed the attitude of a *flâneur* browsing the street-life of Mumbai. For many years he frequented its humble cafés, and from such vantage points wrote poems that provide a sardonic collection of marginalia on the cultural transformations undergone by his corner of contemporary Asia, refracted through a temperament impatient of cant, indifferent to bourgeois attitudes and sceptical of much that passes for tradition in India. His work can be said to imply a search for values in a world where the conventions and orthodoxies of the past no longer appeal or apply. It is also of particular significance for the theory and practice of self-translation, given that it was his regular habit to write a poem in one language, and then recreate it, concurrently, or many years later, in his other language. Kolatkar practised this form of bilingual creativity without any apparent sense of cultural duality or schizophrenia.

His writing is notable for its affinity to the vernacular tradition of *Bhakti* (devotional) poetry in Marathi, from which he often translated. In tone, his poems can appear casual and almost inconsequential. His laid-back manner belies a seriousness of intent that can be scathing in satire, unsparing in its honesty and consistent in its sympathy for the underdog. His style keeps close to the rhythms and vocabulary of contemporary speech. The language is often spiced by locutions typical of contemporary Mumbai. The humour – and there is plenty – is of the laconic kind, clear-eyed and dry. The writing is sharp in its distaste for all forms of social totalisation, including the kinds perpetrated in India by caste prejudice and Brahminism. Kolatkar's style accommodates a wide variety of international influences, including American popular genres (from beat to jazz to blues). His work also shows a special attraction to what the novelist and critic Amit Chaudhuri describes as the 'proximity of the disreputable, the culpable, and the religious' (Kolatkar 2005: xiii).[22]

Early work in Marathi was collected in *Arun Kolatkarchya Kavita* (*Arun Kolatkar's Poems*, 1977). The same year he won the Commonwealth Poetry Prize for a volume in English, *Jejuri* (1976). Its loose sequence constitutes a kind of pilgrim's progress for agnostics. A visit to a temple mixes the evocation of myth and scepticism in noting the dereliction of religion amidst a social ethos in which such needs were once fulfilled for many by traditional religion. Decades of apparent silence were followed in 2003–4 by a spate of books in both languages: four in Marathi and one in English. These appeared just as the poet succumbed to stomach cancer. They add to the historical scope and range covered by his work, especially in Marathi, which engages more intensively than the work in English with the critical residue of his cultural inheritance. Kolatkar had worked for many years on the Marathi versions of the *Jejuri* poems, which he probably wrote first in English. The Marathi collection was published posthumously, in 2011.

Long admired by a small circle of friends and writers, his books had circulated during his lifetime from Mumbai and Pune. Posthumously, his reputation has become international. The belatedness of this recognition is ironic, given the tension in his career between reticence and the impulse to create, between the urgency to share a unique perspective on experience, and his acute wariness about the likelihood of complicity with the culture industry.

The caste system that Kolatkar looked upon with distaste has been a part of the interface that has linked religion to social organisation for several thousand years in India. It has ensured that worship split into two antithetical traditions: a mainstream tradition accessible throughout the country to people of Brahmin caste, and a set of regional alternatives, created by the 'lower' castes, who did not have access to Brahmin temples and rituals. The latter drew sustenance from the work of dissident poet-saints from the Indian vernacular languages. Over a period extending from the twelfth to the eighteenth century, these poets created a large corpus of oral and written poetry devoted to the gods of the 'lower' castes. Often these gods were regional variants of the Hindu gods worshipped by Brahmins, but with local names and modes of worship unique to each region and its language. Kolatkar sympathised with that tradition, and admired and translated into English from the non-Brahmin Marathi poetic tradition.[23]

It may have suited an Anglo-American modernist like T. S. Eliot to invoke the Hindu *Upanishads* as an alternative source of mythopoeic and spiritual sustenance, but for Kolatkar, born into the Brahmin caste, and aware of the inequities and atrocities of the caste system, it was impossible to endorse a Brahmin lineage. Kolatkar's work is based on an intellectual and emotional antipathy to orthodox Hindu worship and the traditional dominance of Brahmins in most walks of life. This orientation was reinforced by his openness to Western influences. He was a keen reader of modernist writing in English, and translations into English from Europe and Latin America. His eclecticism went hand in hand with a conviction that 'Some of the finest poetry in India, or indeed the world, has come from a sense of alienation' (Kolatkar 2009: 223).[24]

A poetics of translation

Kolatkar's sympathies for the vernacular tradition of devotional poetry in Marathi temper his Westernised rational scepticism. The combination enables him to engage with what the dereliction of faith has meant to an anti-intellectual intellectual like himself and others like him, especially from the metropolitan centres that are the most susceptible to Westernisation. We can discover a dual logic in his visit to the pilgrimage centre of Jejuri. On the one hand, he seems eager to elaborate on his rejection of traditional and popular modes of worship. On the other hand, he is not without awareness of something significant that vanishes in consequence, for which scepticism is not the antidote.

Jejuri is a Hindu shrine two hundred kilometres south-east of Mumbai and forty kilometres south-east of Pune. It has long been a destination for pilgrims throughout the state of Maharashtra. Their object of worship is the regional deity Khandoba. Worshipped by shepherds and other rural people, from the tenth century AD onwards, he became the most popular local deity of the region, along with the less fierce deity known as Vithoba or Vitthal. These two deities continue to be the objects of popular worship by millions of people from the Marathi and Kannada speaking parts of India. Over the years, Khandoba acquired a rich mythology, demanding rituals and a host of narratives concerning his several wives. He is celebrated as the destroyer of the demon Malla, and is often described as accompanied on his frequent hunts by one of his wives. His shrines (and there are many) require strict worship and ritual offerings. Worshippers believe that he is both munificent to and fierce with his devotees.

Kolatkar visited the set of temples and the hillside village where they are situated, with a friend, in the 1960s. The visit led to poems in both English and Marathi. The English collection was published first in a periodical in 1974, and then in book form in 1976. It was his first book-length publication in either language. The English and Marathi versions of the sequence are generally comparable in intent and execution within the context of their respective linguistic cultures. They also offer much of interest to those interested in the theory and practice of translation, as well as those appreciative of bilingual creativity of the utmost originality. Here we focus on the English poems.

The sequence comprises thirty-one relatively short poems, the last in six semi-autonomous sections. They follow a loose narrative line, from arrival at the shrine by bus from Mumbai, to departure by train. In between, we encounter a number of people both unique and typical, such as the local priest and an old beggar woman. We also get accounts of what the poetic persona saw and thought as he moved from individual temple to adjacent temple or from temple compound to a contemplation of the surrounding hilly landscape, and the routine life of the village in which the temples are situated. Throughout the sequence, we have a sense of someone at once uncomfortable about the fact that he is making the trip at all, and yet drawn despite himself to reflections on what the place once meant to the tradition of worship he finds himself unable to believe in.

The visit to the temple

It takes a long bus trip to get to the temple site: an uncomfortable journey in a blue-painted state transport vehicle, dusty and crowded, which has passengers facing each other for the duration of the trip in two or three seat rows.

> Your own divided face in a pair of glasses
> on an old man's nose
> is all the countryside you get to see.

> You seem to move continually forward
> towards a destination
> just beyond the caste mark between his eyebrows.
>
> (Kolatkar 1976: 9)

The poet sketches a sardonic and surreal image of his face reflected in each of the two sides of the glasses worn by the old man facing him, a token for a divided self (Raykar 1995: 7). The visual geometry is telling: the poet does not face the destination; he only sees it as reflected in a devotee's glasses. The allusion to the 'caste mark' is misleading, since what the mark denotes is devotion, not caste. Whether the error is inadvertent or deliberate, the informed reader can infer that the speaker does not actually know what the mark signifies. Since most Marathi-speaking persons would know what the mark signified, the speaker's ignorance identifies him as city-bred and Westernised.

Next, we meet the priest, who waits for the pilgrims as a cat for its prey. For him religion is a livelihood, and he, more than the gods whose rituals he officiates, needs pilgrims, for he is a professional parasite. The speaking voice of the poem wears its antipathies openly on its sleeve. The co-presence of a mongrel dog and her puppies amidst the lesser and greater gods in the temple complex introduces a recurrent feature of the sequence: Kolatkar's way of juxtaposing visual notation of neglect and disrepair with recognition that animals need only food and shelter, not gods and religion. The spirit that once animated religious belief seems to have fled from this temple. Most Hindu shrines in Maharashtra (and elsewhere in India) use stone for their temple statuary (occasionally, the more recent ones use metal). Such statues are often daubed red or turmeric yellow (as shown in the image used for the cover of this book, which is a photograph of one of the shrines at Jejuri).

The poet wonders why a stone need be a god at all. It is worth noting here that the American modernist William Carlos Williams declared his motto in 'A Sort of a Song' (1940) through the emblematic use of a flower: 'Saxifrage is my flower that splits / the rocks' (Williams 1991: 55). Kolatkar provides a postmodern echo of this declaration in his image of orange *jhendu* flowers, which he is willing to scatter on the rock without needing it to be a god of any kind: not ideas about the thing but the thing itself, as another American poet, Wallace Stevens, said in the last of his *Collected Poems*. He too had meditated in 'The Rock' (1950) about the need for a final 'cure of the ground / or a cure of ourselves, that is equal to a cure / Of the ground' (Stevens 1997: 324–5).

Of stones, gods, beggars and butterflies

The promenade continues. The poet finds it difficult to work out if a goddess in her dark shrine has eight or eighteen arms. The patterns on divine tortoises seem to have faded in time, making room for more mundane routines. Some shelters turn out to be cowsheds that looked like temples. And then, there are the beggars: more ubiquitous in Indian temples than the divinities they house. The poet may experience difficulty accepting the metaphysical, but he has an eye for the physical. In a series of stanzas that evoke vivid cinematic memories of Sergei Eisenstein's silent explosions from the film *Battleship Potemkin* (1925) and Francis Bacon's post-1935 variations on the image of the screaming nurse from that film, Kolatkar captures the sense of horror with which a genteel bourgeois sensibility reacts to the 'An Old Woman':

> An old woman grabs
> hold of your sleeve
> and tags along.
>
> [. . .]
>
> And as you look on
> the cracks that begin around her eyes
> spread beyond her skin.

And the hills crack.
And the temples crack.
And the sky falls

(Kolatkar 1976: 22)

After this explosive moment, the sequence changes tack for a while. The speaking voice engages more willingly with some of the traditional myths that endow the stark landscape with mythopoeic resonances. The anthropomorphism and personifying power of the imaginative faculty are accommodated by a playing with the notion that the hills surrounding the temple are like the demons that Khandoba is said to have subjugated. The poet has allowed his fancy to roam freely for a while and now pulls it short by asking the priest's son if he believes the stories. The answer in the poem is not very different from the one that Amit Chaudhuri reports Kolatkar having given when asked if he believed in a god: 'I leave the question alone' (Kolatkar 2005: xvii).

At the centre of the sequence, we encounter 'The Butterfly': 'just a pinch of yellow'. We scarcely notice it, and it is gone. Yet it is intensely alive in all its fragility and its vivid yellow: the poet is reminded of the yellow of turmeric powder. Turmeric has medicinal properties, and it is used routinely in worship, so that a stone deity ends up being covered in yellow. The two yellows are utterly unlike one another: one is stone, even if treated as sacred; the other celebrates a living creature in its vivid and momentary aliveness. The poet uses natural yellow to displace the yellow of ritual. His celebration of the tactile, phenomenal and fugitive aspect of the concretely particular renders the yellow into an emblem of evanescent reality.

Just a pinch of yellow
it opens before it closes
and closes before it o

where is it

(Kolatkar 1976: 27)

The imagery and its logic coincides with the ideas about concrete imagery promoted by the Imagist movement gathered in London before World War I, and the American modernists Williams and Stevens, who professed a similar doctrine in their early poems: no ideas but in things. Kolatkar's poem enjoins us, by implication, to merge all ideas into the phenomenal. The butterfly takes 'these wretched hills' under its wings: this is both a simple visual illusion of perspective and a symbol, like the holy dove brooding over an abyss. The mundane is sacred in itself, and needs to be sequestered from the sacralising tendency of religion. The butterfly is the priest of the natural and the real. It is fragile, but alive. In contrast, and robbed of their mythology, the hills are merely 'wretched'. It is myths that reduced them to wretchedness, and it is the sheer facticity of the butterfly, in all its mutability, that seems more real than those myths.

The sequence again changes direction. It plunges with zest into another set of myths with which Jejuri and Khandoba are invested: shepherds who must appease tigers in order to keep the peace; the songs we might sing for the male and female servants attached to Khandoba as Vaghyas and Murlis, whose turmeric and oil-lit lamps keep the worshipped god in place. A stroll past one of the minor temples, dedicated to the 'Yashwant Rao', provides occasion to enumerate the practices religion requires of its devotees as proof of their faith in this or that deity: a litany of sarcastic complaints. The poet shifts from one spot to another within the temple complex, mixing willingness to reanimate the myths of the old religion with his recurrent scepticism. Finally, making his way from the temple and through the adjacent village, the poet arrives at the railway station, where he encounters a familiar air of dereliction. This is modern India: unorganised, messy, unkempt. The clock dials have given up on telling the time. The station dog does not like to be patted or blessed. You may or may not get tea at the tea stall. The train may or may not arrive on time. The poet falls back on wryness in dealing with a situation that would otherwise frustrate or infuriate. The sequence ends on the hope that the train will arrive, but mindful that it is impossible to say when.

Standing back, looking forward

Standing back from the sequence, we note that it never sheds its air of reporting on a tourist trip from metropolis to village shrine, from urban rationalism to rural traditions of faith and worship, from a willing assimilation of Western-sceptical-rationalist assumptions and values to revisiting the origins where folk tales and myths turn to rituals of worship. The Marathi novelist Bhalchandra Nemade described this element in 1985 as a limitation to the significance of Kolatkar's achievement in English (Kolatkar 2005: xvii). On the other hand, Amit Chaudhuri argues with plausibility that Kolatkar's kind of ironic *flânerie* has greater enabling power (which other writers can learn from) than Rushdie's monumentalising forays into India history and society. There are affinities between Dalit writing and Kolatkar's work in Marathi and English, but they differ in two respects: Dalit literature is militant, whereas Kolatkar explores the spectrum of irony rather than indignation; and the Dalits write about the harm done to India by caste from outside Brahminism, he from within.

Another way of reflecting on Kolatkar's and Joaquin's significance in the context of Mumbai and Manila respectively is to recognise the manner in which, and the degree to which, each author has a divided attitude to his society's history and investment in religious belief. In a curious sense, they are both grateful for having been intellectually colonised, one by a broadly Anglo-American (and European) modernity, the other by the more specific influence of Hispanic culture and religion. Both welcome what constitutes for their time and place a specific kind of modernity; both apply modernist techniques in belated fashion to their predicaments, adapting them to local contexts with skill and energy. Each illustrates the asynchronous nature of postcolonial modernity, its capacity to show how derivativeness and innovativeness work together to produce literary artefacts that are hybrid in terms of technique. Each also shows how the desire to become modern leads to outcomes in the former colonies, which leaves authors ambiguous about what they accomplish, just as it leaves them ambivalent about what has had to be moulted off in the undertaking.

Kolatkar and Joaquin, in their different ways, exemplify what Homi Bhabha describes as the power of 'postcolonial translation'.[25] They also exemplify the condition of being translated selves, such that the will to decolonise works dialectically with and against the will to modernise. Joaquin's text belongs to the period of the 1940s-60s, Kolatkar's to the late 1960s. In the half-century since then, the significance of their work has grown. The sense in which it applies to more than their respective times and places has also grown. Work such as theirs confirms the sense in which 'modern' and 'colonial', 'postmodern' and 'postcolonial' are complexly interrelated, then and now.

Notes

1. For histories of the Suffragette Movement in England, see Diane Atkinson (1992) and Melanie Phillips (2004).
2. Cf. Quentin Bell (1972, 1990), Hermione Lee (1997), Katherine Dalsimer (2002) and Julia Briggs (2005).
3. Rhys first met Ford in Paris in 1924. He may have had a hand in helping shape her early work. They had an affair at about this time, but it ended badly (Athill 1984: 10). It provides some of the plot material for her novel *Postures* (1928, titled *Quartet*, 1929). Virginia Woolf's awareness of impressionism and post-impressionism came from a different source: Roger Fry (1866–1934), who joined the Bloomsbury circle that Virginia and Vanessa were associated with

in 1910. Conversations with Fry and Clive Bell brought the achievement of the Post-Impressionists to Virginia's attention during the period of composition of *The Voyage Out*, along with issues 'of colour, form, and "texture"' (Lee 1997: 286). These were frequent topics of discussion between the two sisters and their circle of friends. Lee notes that Fry's critique of photographic realism, as in the art of Sargent and Alma Tadema, had natural affinities with her attack on Edwardian materialism.

4. Rhys was to recollect, late in life: 'Our cook at Bona Vista was an obeah woman called Ann Tewitt. Obeah is a milder form of voodoo, and even in my time nobody was supposed to take it very seriously. Yet I was told about her in a respectful, almost awed tone' (Rhys 1979: 22). She also adds that her fictional depiction of the house and estate where her protagonist grew up, Coulibri, was derived from her memory of her mother's family home in Dominica, Geneva estate (33).

5. Cf. Keith A. Russell II: 'the establishment of Christophine's languages under-scores her ability to seamlessly flow between different cultural and lingual groups. She alters her speech to have the most impact in a given situation: English to quarrel with Antoinette's husband or berate the servant, Amelie; French-flavoured songs to soothe Antoinette; and, Creole to blend with the locals' (Russell II 2007: 93–4).

6. The incident offers the most naked example of interpellation (the projection of an identity upon someone by associating that person with the name you impose on that person, without the victim having any reciprocal power to name you):
   '"Bertha," I said.
   "Bertha is not my name. You are trying to make me into someone else, calling me by another name. I know that's obeah too."' (147).

7. Kathy Phillips notes how *The Voyage Out* provides 'links between the institu-tion of marriage and capitalism, colonies, and militarism', and musters detailed evidence from the novel for the claim that 'the Empire and its underlying values [. . .] set the stamp on all the individuals in the novel and their relations as couples' (Phillips 1994: 52, 71).

8. At the very outset of *Religious Experience and the Modernist Novel* (2010), Pericles Lewis emphasises that 'Woolf described the work of the modernists (specifically Joyce's *Ulysses*) as a return of the "spiritual" in response to the "materialism" of their Edwardian predecessors, and the modern novel is strik-ingly engaged with the spiritual aspects of life' (5).

9. Maurice Blanchot explains the importance attached by Kafka to creating a sem-blance of coherence in his narratives: 'Those who inhabit reality have no need for all those details which, as we know, do not correspond in any way to what is really seen. But those who dwell in the unrestricted depth of beyond, in the distress of measurelessness, those are indeed condemned to excessive restraint and to a faultless, unbroken, unencumbered coherence. And condemned is pre-cisely what they are' (Blanchot 1982: 141).

10. F. T. Marinetti, 'A Futurist Manifesto' (1909).

11. For a fuller development of the theme in Walcott see Patke (2006: 164–71).

12. Coetzee writes: 'is there some non-vacuous sense in which I can say that the spirit of Bach was speaking to me across the ages, across the seas, putting before me certain ideals; or was what was really going on at that moment that I was symbolically electing High European culture, and command of the codes of that culture, as a route that would take me out of my class position in white South African society and ultimately out of what I must have felt, in terms however obscure or mystified, as an historical dead end' (Coetzee 1999: 11).

13. Here, for example, is how the Trust Fund is spoken of in one exchange:

– What Trust is this?

Hamdan tried to prevent Digger from speaking, but the words poured out as if he were drunk.

The great Trust! Don't get angry your Honour! The great Trust that belongs to everybody in our Alley from the highest to the lowest, that includes every holding in the desert round about: Gebelaawi's Trust, your Honour! (1997: 109)

14. For example, from Chapter 5: 'Nearly three months since it departed, and still there is no news of the expeditionary force. Instead, terrible rumours everywhere: that the force has been lured into the desert and wiped out; but unknown to us it has been recalled to defend the homeland, leaving the frontier towns for the barbarians to pick like fruit whenever they choose to' (Coetzee 1980: 130).

15. Reprinted in Joaquin's *Tropical Gothic* (2003: 183–242).

16. Before 1898, the only interruption to Spanish rule was a short period of British control over Manila during 1762–4 (Zaide 1957: 12–16).

17. Jaime an Lim remarks, in *Literature and Politics* (1993) that Rizal's two novels in Spanish, *Noli Me Tangere* (1887) and *El Filibusterismo* (1891), 'helped fuel the Philippine revolution of 1896 which implicated him as its political leader and instigator. He was not, but the popular identification of Rizal with the reform and the revolutionary movements was so strong that he might just as well have been its spiritual and true leader. On December 30, 1896, after a mock military trial, Rizal was executed for rebellion and subversive association' (1993: 6–7). Benedict Anderson's 2005 overview of Rizal would seem to confirm the general perception of his exemplary status in all anti-colonial movements, but his more recent book (2009) draws attention to the ambiguities of Rizal's position on race, nation and modernity, and also cautions against reading his novels as straightforward 'ethico-political treatises' (Anderson 2009: 1).

18. San Juan, Jr interprets 'Biliken' as 'the presiding carnival deity representing the folk affirmation of the communal body (Bakhtin) and negation of the deceitful order of patriarchal law' (San Juan, Jr 1988: 145).

19. Sylvia Mendez Ventura writes: 'After a series of confrontations, he [Father Tony] manages to make Connie accept the fact that she has only one navel' (Ventura 1993: 74).

20. San Juan, Jr interprets the characterisation of Macho as one who accepted marriage with Connie 'not as a substitute but as fetish', thus becoming a classic example of someone 'pursuing the phantasmal object which originally linked the child to the mother's body' (San Juan, Jr 1988: 146).

21. In his formalist essay of 1967, San Juan, Jr indicts Joaquin on several grounds, among them the alleged failure 'to tell us anything actually happening in the Philippines before and after the war – the renewed insurgency of the masses, the awakening of nationalism resisted by neo-colonial collaborators of American imperialism, the fascism of the landlords and comprador-bureaucrats. Joaquin sacrifices the rich texture of historical experience for the specious labyrinthine doubts and ennui of his exiles' (San Juan, Jr 1984: 149). He may well be entitled to his view that Joaquin focuses on the petty bourgeoisie rather than the masses, but the moral crises represented by Joaquin are confirmed as the issues most relevant for the nation by the history of almost continuous political misrule in the Philippines since the book was published.

22. The poet Arvind Krishna Mehrotra, at whose suggestion Kolatkar embarked on *Jejuri* in late 1973, reports in his introduction to *the boatride* (2009) on a conversation with Kolatkar shortly before his death: 'He spoke about American popular music and its influence on him. He said that gangster films, cartoon strips, and blues had shaped his sense of the English language and he felt closer

to the American idiom, particularly Black American speech, than to British English. He mentioned Bessie Smith, Big Bill Broonzy, and Muddy Waters – "Their names are like poems"' (Kolatkar 2009: 26).

23. See Zelliot (1976: 154–7) on the vernacular poet-saints of the Marathi-speaking state of Maharashtra within the larger tradition of the *Bhakti* movement in India.

24. For example, the *Encyclopaedia of Dalits in India* notes that 'Brahmans occupying less than four per cent of the total population of Maharashtra had obtained an important position with economic, political as well as socio-cultural prerogatives under Peshwa rule [during the eighteenth century] and also under British rule since the early nineteenth century' (Paswan and Jaideva 2003: 99). See L. and S. Rudolph (1984) on the relation of modernisation to the politics of caste and identity in India.

25. 'The power of the postcolonial translation of modernity rests in its performative, deformative structure that does not simply revalue the contents of a cultural tradition, or transpose values "cross-culturally"' (Bhabha 1994: 346).

Bibliography

Achebe, Chinua (1988), *Hopes and Impediments: Selected Essays*, New York: Doubleday.

Adhikari, Mohamed (2008), '"Of Blood and Streams of Money": New Perspectives on the Annihilation of the Herero and Nama Peoples of Namibia, 1904–1908', *Kronos: Journal of Cape History* 34: 303–20.

Adorno, Theodor, Ernst Bloch, Georg Lukács and Bertolt Brecht (1977), *Aesthetics and Politics*, trans. Ronald Taylor, London and New York: Verso.

Adorno, Theodor W. [1967] (1981), 'Notes on Kafka', in *Prisms*, trans. Sam Weber, Cambridge, MA: MIT Press, pp. 245–71.

Ahmad, Aijaz (1987), 'Jameson's Rhetoric of Otherness and the "National Allegory"', *Social Text* 17 (Autumn): 3–25.

—(1992), *In Theory: Classes, Nations, Literatures*, London: Verso; Bombay: Oxford University Press.

al-Halool, Musa (2008), 'The Nature of the Uncanny in *Season of Migration to the North*', *Arab Studies Quarterly* (Winter), <http://findarticles.com/p/articles/mi_m2501/is_1_30/ai_n27964254/?tag=content;col1> (accessed 23 December 2011).

Allison, Jonathan (ed.) (1996), *Yeats's Political Identities: Selected Essays*, Ann Arbor: The University of Michigan Press.

Alvarez, A. (ed.) (1962), *The New Poetry*, Harmondsworth: Penguin.

Anderson, Benedict R. O'Gorman (2005), *Under Three Flags: Anarchism and the Anti-Colonial Imagination*, London and New York: Verso.

—(2009), *Why Counting Counts: A Study of Forms and Consciousness and Problems of Language in 'Noli Me Tangere' and 'El Filibusterismo'*, Manila: Ateneo de Manila University Press.

Anderson, Perry (1984), 'Modernity and Revolution', *New Left Review* 1.144 (March–April): 96–113.

Angier, Carole (1991), *Jean Rhys: Life and Work*, New York: Little, Brown.

an Lim, Jaime (1993), *Literature and Politics: The Colonial Experience in Nine Philippine Novels*, Quezon City: New Day Publishers.

Appiah, Kwame Anthony (1992), *In My Father's House: Africa in the Philosophy of Culture*, New York and Oxford: Oxford University Press.

Artaud, Antonin (1989), *Artaud on Theatre*, ed. Claude Schumacher, London: Methuen.

Ashcroft, Bill, Gareth Griffiths and Helen Tiffin (1998), *Key Concepts in Post-Colonial Studies*, London and New York: Routledge.

Athill, Diana (1984), *Jean Rhys: The Early Novels*, London: André Deutsch.

Atkinson, Diane (1992), *Suffragettes in the Purple, White and Green: London 1906–1914*, London: Museum of London.

Ballantyne, Tony (2002), *Orientalism and Race: Aryanism in the British Empire*, Basingstoke and New York: Palgrave.

Baudelaire, Charles (1995), *The Painter of Modern Life and Other Essays*, trans. and ed. Jonathan Mayne, London: Phaidon Press.

Bell, Quentin (1972), *Virginia Woolf: A Biography*, Orlando: Harcourt, Brace and Co.

—[1970] (1990), *Virginia Woolf: A Biography*, London: Hogarth Press.

Benjamin, Walter (1973), *Charles Baudelaire: A Lyric Poet in the Era of High Capitalism*, trans. Harry Zohn, London and New York: Verso.

—(1977), *The Origins of German Tragic Drama*, trans. John Osborne, with an introduction by George Steiner, London: Verso.

—(1996), *Walter Benjamin: Selected Writings, Volume 1, 1913–1926*, ed. Marcus Bullock and Michael W. Jennings, Cambridge, MA and London: The Belknap Press of Harvard University Press.

—(1999), *Walter Benjamin: Selected Writings, Volume 2, 1927–1934*, ed. Michael W. Jennings, Howard Eiland and Gary Smith, trans. Rodney Livingstone, Cambridge, MA: The Belknap Press of Harvard University Press.

Bennett, Tony, Lawrence Grossberg and Meaghan Morris (eds) (2005), *New Keywords: A Revised Vocabulary of Culture and Society*, Malden, MA: Blackwell.

Berger, Klaus [1980] (1992), *Japonisme in Western Painting from Whistler to Matisse*, trans. David Britt, Cambridge: Cambridge University Press.

Berman, Marshall (1984), 'The Signs in the Street – A Response to Perry Anderson', *New Left Review* 1.144 (March–April): 114–23.

Bhabha, Homi (1986), 'Foreword: Remembering Fanon', in Frantz Fanon, *Black Skin, White Masks*, London: Pluto Press, pp. vii-xxv.

—(1994), *The Location of Culture*, London and New York: Routledge.

Blanchot, Maurice [1955] (1982), 'Kafka or the Demands of Literature', in Gabriel Josipovici (ed.), *The Sirens' Song: Selected Essays by Maurice Blanchot*, Brighton: The Harvester Press, pp. 121–43.

Bongie, Chris (1991), *Exotic Memories: Literature, Colonialism, and the Fin de Siècle*, Stanford: Stanford University Press.

Brantlinger, Patrick (1985), 'Victorians and Africans: The Genealogy of the Myth of the Dark Continent', *Critical Inquiry* 12.1 (Autumn): 166–203.

—(2009), *Victorian Literature and Postcolonial Studies*, Edinburgh: Edinburgh University Press.

Briggs, Julia (2005), *Virginia Woolf: An Inner Life*, Orlando: Harcourt, Brace.

Bührer, Tanja (2008), 'Berlin Conference', in Prem Poddar, Rajeev S. Patke and Lars Jensen (eds), *A Historical Companion to Postcolonial Literatures: Continental Europe and its Empires*, Edinburgh: Edinburgh University Press, pp. 210–11.

Bush, Andrew (1996), 'Lyric Poetry of the Eighteenth and Nineteenth Centuries', in Roberto González Echevarría and Enrique Pupo-Walker (eds), *The Cambridge History of Latin American Literature*, vol. 1, Cambridge: Cambridge University Press, pp. 375–400.

Cain, P. J. and A. G. Hopkins [1993] (2002), *British Imperialism 1688–2000*, 2nd edn, Harlow: Pearson Education Ltd.

Cascardi, Anthony J. (1992), *The Subject of Modernity*, Cambridge: Cambridge University Press.

Casillo, Robert (1988), *The Genealogy of Demons: Anti-Semitism, Fascism, and the Myths of Ezra Pound*, Evanston, IL: Northwestern University Press.

Cavafy, C. P. (1975), *Collected Poems*, ed. George Savidis, trans. Edmund Keeley and Philip Sherrard, Princeton: Princeton University Press.

Césaire, Aimé [1955] (1972), *Discourse on Colonialism*, trans Joan Pinkham, New York and London: Monthly Review Press.

Chamberlin, J. Edward (1993), *Poetry and West Indies*, Champaign: University of Illinois Press.

Chaudhuri, Amit (2005), 'On strangeness in Indian writing', *The Hindu* (Sunday, 2 October), <http://www.hindu.com/lr/2005/10/02/stories/2005100200130300.htm> (accessed 2 April 2012).

Cheyfitz, Eric [1991] (1997), *The Poetics of Imperialism: Translation and Colonisation from The Tempest to Tarzan*, Philadelphia: University of Pennsylvania Press.

Childs, Peter (2000), *Modernism: New Critical Idiom Series*, London and New York: Routledge.

Clark, T. J. (1985), *The Painting of Modern Life: Paris in the Art of Manet and his Followers*, New York: Knopf; London: Thames and Hudson.

—(1999), *Farewell to an Idea: Episodes from a History of Modernism*, New Haven, CT and London: Yale University Press.

Cleary, Joe (2012), 'Foreword', *Modern Language Quarterly* 73.3 (September): 255–68.

Coetzee, J. M. (1980), *Waiting for the Barbarians*, Harmondsworth: Penguin.

—(1999), *Stranger Shores: Essays 1986–1990*, London: Secker and Warburg.

Confucius (1951), *The Great Digest & Unwobbling Pivot*, trans. and commentary by Ezra Pound, London: Peter Owen.

Conrad, Joseph [1898] (1920), *Tales of Unrest*, New York: Doubleday.

—[1899] (1999), *Heart of Darkness*, London and New York: Penguin.

—[1990] (2002), *Heart of Darkness and Other Tales*, ed. Cedric Watts, New York: Oxford University Press.

—(2008), *A Personal Record*, ed. Zdzisław Najder and J. H. Stape, Cambridge: Cambridge University Press.

Corngold, Stanley (2004), *Lambent Traces: Franz Kafka*, Princeton and Oxford: Princeton University Press.

Corpuz, O. D. (2006), *The Roots of the Filipino Nation, Vol. 2*, Quezon City: The University of the Philippines Press.

Cullingford, Elizabeth (1981), *Yeats, Ireland and Fascism*, London: Macmillan.

Dalsimer, Katherine (2002), *Virginia Woolf: Becoming a Writer*, New Haven, CT: Yale University Press.

Dasenbrock, Reed Way (2001), 'Why the Post in Post-colonial is not the Post in Post-modern: Homer. Dante. Pound. Walcott', in Michael Coyle (ed.), *Ezra Pound and African American Modernism*, Orono, ME: The National Poetry Foundation, pp. 111–22.

Davie, Donald (1973), *Thomas Hardy and British Poetry*, London: Routledge.

Deleuze, Gilles and Félix Guattari [1975] (1986) *Kafka: Toward a Minor Literature*, trans. D. Polan, Minneapolis: University of Minnesota Press.

DeSalvo, Louise A. (1980), *Virginia Woolf's First Voyage: A Novel in the Making*, New York: Rowman and Littlefield; London and Basingstoke: Macmillan.

de Gruchy, John Walter (2003), *Orienting Arthur Waley: Japonism, Orientalism, and the Creation of Japanese Literature in English*, Honolulu: University of Hawai'i Press.

de Man, Paul (1970), 'Literary History and Literary Modernity', *Daedalus* 99.2 (Spring): 384–404.

Eagleton, Terry (1996), 'Introduction', in Terry Eagleton and Drew Milne (eds), *Marxist Literary Theory: A Reader*, Oxford and Cambridge, MA: Blackwell, pp. 1–15.

Eliot, T. S. (1933), *After Strange Gods: A Primer of Modern Heresy*, New York: Harcourt, Brace.

—(1962), *George Herbert*, London: Longmans, Green.

—[1928] (1987), 'Introduction', in *Selected Poems of Ezra Pound*, New York: New Directions.

—(1988), *The Letters of T. S. Eliot, Volume 1: 1898–1922*, ed. Valerie Eliot, London: Faber.

—(1996), *Inventions of the March Hare: Poems 1909–1917*, ed. Christopher Ricks, London: Faber.

Enright, D. J. (1960), *Robert Graves and the Decline of Modernism*, Singapore: University of Malaya.

Esty, Jed (2004), *A Shrinking Island: Modernism and National Culture in England*, Princeton: Princeton University Press.

—(2007), 'Virginia Woolf's Colony and the Adolescence of Modernist

Fiction', in Richard Begam and Michael Valdez Moses (eds), *Modernism and Colonialism: British and Irish Literature, 1899–1939*, Durham, NC and London: Duke University Press, pp. 70–90.

—and Colleen Lye (2012), 'Peripheral Realisms Now', *Modern Language Quarterly* 73.3 (September): 269–88.

Everdell, William R. (1997), *The First Moderns: Profiles in the Origins of Twentieth-century Thought*, Chicago and London: The University of Chicago Press.

Fanon, Frantz [1961] (1963) *The Wretched of the Earth*, trans. C. Farrington, New York: Grove Press.

—[1952] (1967), *Black Skin, White Masks*, trans. C. L. Markmann, New York: Grove Press.

—[1961] (2005), *The Wretched of the Earth*, trans. Richard Philcox, New York: Grove Press.

Fenollosa, Ernest and Ezra Pound (2008), *The Chinese Written Character as a Medium for Poetry: A Critical Edition*, ed. Haun Saussy, Jonathan Stalling and Lucas Klein, New York: Fordham University Press.

Forster, E. M. [1927] (1956), *Aspects of the Novel*, Orlando: Mariner Books.

Foucault, Michel (1984), 'What is Enlightenment?', in P. Rabinow (ed.), *The Foucault Reader*, New York: Pantheon Books, pp. 32–50.

—[1978] (1996), 'What is Critique?', in James Schmidt (ed.), *What Is Enlightenment? Eighteenth-century Answers and Twentieth-century Questions*, Berkeley and Los Angeles: University of California Press, pp. 382–98.

Frost, Robert (1995), *Collected Poems, Prose, and Plays*, ed. Richard Poirier and Mark Richardson, New York: Library of America.

Fuentes, Carlos (1988), *Myself with Others; Selected Essays*, New York: Farrar Straus and Giroux.

Gallagher, John and Ronald Robinson (1953), 'The Imperialism of Free Trade', *The Economic History Review*, second series 6.1: 1–15.

Gaonkar, Dilip Parameshwar (ed.) (2001), *Alternative Modernities*, Durham, NC and London: Duke University Press.

Geertz, Clifford (1995), *After the Fact: Two Countries, Four Decades, One Anthropologist*, Cambridge, MA: Harvard University Press.

Gilroy, Paul (2005), *Postcolonial Melancholia*, New York: Columbia University Press.

Goebel, Rolf J. (1997), *Constructing China: Kafka's Orientalist Discourse*, Columbia, SC: Camden House.

—(2002), 'Kafka and Postcolonial Critique: "Der Verschollene", "In der Strafkolonie", "Beim Bau der chinesischen Mauer"', in James Rolleston (ed.), *A Companion to the Works of Franz Kafka*, Rochester, NY: Camden House, pp. 187–212.

Goldberg, David Theo (2002), *The Racial State*, Malden, MA: Blackwell.

—(2009), *The Threat of Race: Reflections on Racial Neoliberalism*, Malden, MA: Wiley-Blackwell.

Goonetilleke, D. C. R. A. (2007), *Joseph Conrad's 'Heart of Darkness': A Routledge Study Guide*, New York: Routledge.

Graves, Robert (1962), *Oxford Addresses on Poetry*, London: Cassell.

Griffith, John W. (1995), *Joseph Conrad and the Anthropological Dilemma: 'Bewildered Traveller'*, Oxford: Clarendon Press.

Guha, Ranajit (ed.) (1997), *A Subaltern Studies Reader, 1986–1995*, Minneapolis and London: University of Minnesota Press.

Hall, Timothy and Timothy Bewes (eds) (2011), *Georg Lukács: The Fundamental Dissonance of Existence. Aesthetics, Politics, Literature*, London and New York: Continuum Books.

Hardt, Michael and Antonio Negri (2000), *Empire*, Cambridge, MA and London: Harvard University Press.

Harris, Wilson (1981), 'The Frontier on which *Heart of Darkness* Stands', *Research in African Literatures* 12.1 (Spring): 86–93.

Hassan, Waïl S. (2003), *Tayeb Salih: Ideology and the Craft of Fiction*, New York: Syracuse University Press.

Haule, James M. (1996), 'Virginia Woolf's Revisions of *The Voyage Out*: Some New Evidence', *Twentieth Century Literature* 42.3 (Autumn): 309–21.

Hayot, Eric (2003), *Chinese Dreams: Pound, Brecht, Tel quel*, Ann Arbor: University of Michigan Press.

Hegel, G. W. F. [1830] (1971), *Hegel's Philosophy of Mind: Part Three of the Encyclopaedia of the Philosophical Sciences*, trans. William Wallace, Oxford: Clarendon Press.

—[1837] (2001), *The Philosophy of History*, trans. J. Sibree, Kitchener: Batoche Books.

Hill, Geoffrey (2008), *Collected Critical Writings*, ed. Kenneth Haynes, Oxford: Oxford University Press.

Hobsbawn, Eric (1989), *The Age of Empire, 1875–1914*, New York: Vintage Books.

Hobson, J. A. (1902), *Imperialism: A Study*, London: George Allen and Unwin.

Hofmannsthal, Hugo von [1902] (2005), *The Lord Chandos Letter and Other Writings*, trans. Joel Rotenberg, intro. John Banville, New York: New York Review of Books.

Howe, Stephen (2002), *Empire: A Very Short Introduction*, Oxford: Oxford University Press.

Huggan, Graham (2001), *The Postcolonial Exotic: Marketing the Margins*, London and New York: Routledge.

Jakobson, Roman (1956), 'Two Aspects of Language and Two Types of Aphasic Disturbances', in Roman Jakobson and Morris Halle, *Fundamentals of Language*, The Hague and Paris: Mouton, pp. 55–82.

Jameson, Fredric (1986), 'Third-World Literature in the Era of Multinational Capitalism', *Social Text* 15 (Autumn): 65–88.

—(1987), 'A Brief Response', *Social Text* 17 (Autumn): 26–7.

—(1990), 'Modernism and Imperialism', in Terry Eagleton, Fredric Jameson and Edward W. Said, *Nationalism, Colonialism, and Literature*, Minneapolis: University of Minnesota Press, pp. 43–66.

—(2002), *A Singular Modernity: Essay on the Ontology of the Present*, London and New York: Verso.

—(2012), 'Afterword', *Modern Language Quarterly* 73.3 (September): 475–85.

Joaquin, Nick [1961] (1972), *The Woman Who Had Two Navels*, Manila: Solidaridad Publishing House.

—(1977), *A Question of Heroes*, Metro Manila: National Book Store, Inc.

—[1972] (2003), *Tropical Gothic*, Manila: Anvil.

Joyce, James [1914] (2000), *A Portrait of the Artist as a Young Man*, ed. Jeri Johnson, Oxford and New York: Oxford University Press.

Kafka, Franz [1948–9] (1972), *The Diaries of Franz Kafka 1910–1923*, ed. Max Brod, Harmondsworth: Penguin.

—(1977), *Franz Kafka: Letters to Friends, Family, and Editors*, trans. Richard and Clara Winston, New York: Schoken Books.

—(1978), *Franz Kafka: Letters to Felice*, trans. Erich Heller and Jürgen Born, with *Kafka's Other Trial*, by Elias Canetti, trans. Christopher Middleton, Harmondsworth: Penguin [abridged version of *Letters to Felice*, first published New York: Schocken Books, 1973].

—(1983), *The Penguin Complete Short Stories of Franz Kafka*, ed. Nahum N. Glatzer, London: Allen Lane.

—(2009a), *Franz Kafka: The Metamorphosis and Other Stories*, trans. Joyce Crick, notes by Ritchie Robertson, Oxford and New York: Oxford University Press.

—(2009b), *Franz Kafka: The Office Writings*, ed. Stanley Corngold, Jack Greenberg and Benno Wagner, trans. Eric Patton with Ruth Hein, Princeton: Princeton University Press.

Kant, Immanuel [1784] (1996), 'An Answer to the Question: What is Enlightenment?', in James Schmidt (ed.), *What is Enlightenment? Eighteenth-century Answers and Twentieth-century Questions*, Berkeley, Los Angeles and London: University of California Press, pp. 58–64.

Kaul, Suvir (2009), *Eighteenth Century British Literature and Postcolonial Studies*, Edinburgh: Edinburgh University Press.

Kelley, Theresa M. (1997), *Reinventing Allegory (Cambridge Studies in Romanticism)*, Cambridge: Cambridge University Press.

Kennedy, George A. (1964), 'Fenollosa, Pound and the Chinese Character', in Tien-ti Lee (ed.), *George A. Kennedy: Selected Works*, New Haven, CT: Far Eastern Publications, pp. 443–62.

Kermode, Frank (1990), *Modern Essays*, Glasgow: Fontana Press.

Kiberd, Declan [1995] (1996), *Inventing Ireland: Literature of the Modern Nation*, New York: Vintage.

—(1997), 'From Nationalism to Liberation', in Susan Shaw Sailer (ed.), *Representing Ireland: Gender, Class, Nationality*, Gainesville: University Press of Florida, pp. 17–28.

Kintanar, Thelma B. (1992), 'From Formalism to Feminism: Rereading Nick Joaquin's *The Woman Who Had Two Navels'*, in *Women Reading: Feminist Perspectives on Philippine Literary Texts*, Quezon City: The University of the Philippines Press and the University Center for Women's Studies, pp. 131–45.

Kipling, Rudyard (1982), *The Portable Rudyard Kipling*, ed. Irving Howe, New York: Penguin Books.

Kolatkar, Arun (1976), *Jejuri*, Bombay: Clearing House.

—(2004) 'No easy answers: Gowri Ramnarayan interviews the "inaccessible" bilingual poet, Arun Kolatkar', *The Hindu* (Sunday, 5 Sept.), <www.hindu.com/lr/2004/09/05/stories/2004090500110100.htm (accessed 2 April 2012).

—(2005), *Jejuri*, introduction by Amit Chadhuri, New York: New York Review of Books.

—(2009), *the boatride and other poems*, ed. Arvind Krishna Mehrotra, Mumbai: Pras Prakashan.

Koselleck, Reinhart [1979] (2004), *Futures Past: On the Semantics of Historical Time*, trans. Keith Tribe, New York: Columbia University Press.

Kramnick, Isaac (ed.) (1995), *The Portable Enlightenment Reader*, New York: Penguin.

Kwame, Anthony Appiah (1991), 'Is the "Post" in "Postcolonial" the "Post" in "Postmodern?"', *Critical Inquiry* 17 (Winter): 336–57.

—(1992), *In My Father's House: Africa in the Philosophy of Culture*, New York and Oxford: Oxford University Press

Larsen, Neil (2001), *Determinations: Essays on Theory, Narrative and Nation in the Americas*, London and New York: Verso.

Lawrence, D. H. (1932), *The Letters of D. H. Lawrence*, ed. Aldous Huxley, New York: Viking Press.

—(1959), *Sex, Literature and Censorship*, ed. Harry T. Moore, New York: Viking Press.

—[1927] (1960), *Mornings in Mexico, Etruscan Places*, Harmondsworth: Penguin Books.

—(1961), *Phoenix: The Posthumous Papers of D. H. Lawrence*, ed. Edward D. McDonald, London: Heinemann.

—[1923] (1966), *Studies in Classic American Literature*, New York: Viking Press.

—(1968), *Phoenix II: Uncollected, Unpublished and Other Prose Works by D. H. Lawrence*, ed. Warren Roberts and Harry T. Moore, London: Heinemann.

—(1970), *The Quest for Rananim; D. H. Lawrence's Letters to S. S. Koteliansky, 1914–1930*, ed. George J. Zytaruk, Montreal: McGill-Queen's University Press.

—[1923] (2002), *Kangaroo*, ed. Bruce Steele, The Cambridge Edition of the Works of D. H. Lawrence, Cambridge: Cambridge University Press.

Lazarus, Neil (2011), *The Postcolonial Unconscious*, Cambridge: Cambridge University Press.

Lee, Hermione [1997] (1999), *Virginia Woolf*, New York: Knopf.

Lenin, V. I. [1917] (1969), *Imperialism: The Highest State of Capitalism*, New York: International Publishing Company, Inc.

Levenson, Michael (2005), 'Modernism: Overview', in Maryanne Cline Horowitz et al. (eds), *Gale New Dictionary of the History of Ideas*, vol. 4, Detroit: Thomson Gale, pp. 1465i–1469i.

Lewis, Pericles (2010), *Religious Experience and the Modernist Novel*, Cambridge: Cambridge University Press.

—(2011), 'Modernism and Religion', in Michael Levenson (ed.), *The Cambridge Companion to Modernism*, 2nd edn, Cambridge: Cambridge University Press, pp. 178–96.

Light, Alison (2007), *Mrs Woolf and the Servants: An Intimate History of Domestic Life in Bloomsbury*, London: Fig Tree.

Lionnet, Francoise (2008), '"The Indies:" Baudelaire's Colonial World', *PMLA* 123. 3 (May): 723–36.

Lloyd, David (1993), 'The Poetics of Politics: Yeats and the Founding of the State', in *Anomalous States: Irish Writing and the Post-Colonial Moment*, Dublin: Lilliput, pp. 59–87.

Longenbach, James (1988), *Stone Cottage: Pound, Yeats, and Modernism*, New York and Oxford: Oxford University Press.

Longley, Edna (1994), *The Living Stream: Literature and Revisionism in Ireland*, Newcastle upon Tyne: Bloodaxe Books.

Lukács, György [1958] (1963), *The Meaning of Contemporary Realism*, trans. John and Necke Mander, London: Merlin Press.

—[1922] (1983), *Reviews and Articles from 'Die rote Fahne'*, trans. Peter Palmer, London: Merlin Press.

Macey, David (2000), *Frantz Fanon: A Biography*, New York: Picador.

MacIver, R. M. [1926] (2003), 'Formation and Dissolution,' in Chris Jenks (ed.), *Critical Concepts in Sociology*, vol. 1, London and New York: Routledge, pp. 90–100.

MacPhee, Graham (2011), *Postwar British Literature and Postcolonial Studies*, Edinburgh: Edinburgh University Press.

Mahfouz, Naguib (1997), *Children of Gebelaawai*, revised translation of augmented edition (translation first published 1981, original Arabic first published in 1959, *Awlad Haratina*), Pueblo, CO: Passeggiata Press.

Marinetti, F. T. (1909) 'A Futurist Manifesto', <http://cscs.umich.edu/~crshalizi/T4PM/futurist-manifesto.html> (accessed 12 February 2012).

McIntire, Gabrielle (2008), *Modernism, Memory, and Desire: T. S. Eliot and Virginia Woolf*, Cambridge: Cambridge University Press.

Mignolo, Walter (2008), 'Preamble: The Historical Foundation of Modernity/ Coloniality and the Emergence of Decolonial Thinking', in Sara Castro-Klaren (ed.), *A Companion to Latin American Literature and Culture*, Malden, MA; and Oxford: Blackwell, pp. 12–32.

Miller, J. Hillis (1996), 'Reading and Periodization: Wallace Stevens' "The Idea of Order at Key West"', in Lawrence Besserman (ed.), *The Challenge of Periodization: Old Paradigms and New Perspectives*, New York: Routledge, pp. 197–216.

Ming Xie (1999), 'Pound as Translator', in Ira B. Nadel (ed.), *The Cambridge Companion to Ezra Pound*, Cambridge: Cambridge University Press, pp. 204–23.

Mitter, Partha (2007), *The Triumph of Modernism: India's Artists and the Avant-garde, 1922–1947*, London: Reaktion Books.

Moody, A. David (2007), *Ezra Pound, Poet, Vol. I: The Young Genius, 1885–1920*, Oxford: Oxford University Press.

Murti, Kamakshi P. (2001), *India: The Seductive and Seduced 'Other' of German Orientalism*, Westport, CT: Greenwood Press.

Naipaul, V. S. (1967), *The Mimic Men*, Harmondsworth: Penguin.

Nandy, Ashis (2004), *Bonfire of Creeds: The Essential Ashis Nandy*, New Delhi: Oxford University Press.

O'Brien, Conor Cruise [1965] (1988), 'Passion and Cunning: An Essay on the Politics of W. B. Yeats', in *Passion and Cunning and Other Essays*, New York: Simon and Schuster, pp. 8–61.

Ortega y Gasset, José [1925] (1948), *The Dehumanization of Art and Notes on the Novel*, trans. Helene Weyl, London: Oxford University Press.

Orwell [1943] (1968), 'W. B. Yeats', in Sonia Orwell and Ian Angus (eds), *The Collected Essays, Journalism and Letters of George Orwell, Vol. 2: My Country Right or Left, 1940–1943*, New York: Harcourt, Brace and World, pp. 271–6.

Osborne, Peter (1992), 'Modernity is a Qualitative, Not a Chronological Category: Notes on the Dialectic of Differential Historical Time', in Francis Barker, Peter Hulme and Margaret Iversen (eds), *Postmodernism and the Re-reading of Modernity*, Manchester: Manchester University Press, pp. 23–45.

—(2000), 'Modernism as Translation', in *Philosophy in Cultural Theory*, London and New York: Routledge, pp. 53–62.

Paswan, Sanjay and Paramanshi Jaideva (eds) (2003), *Encyclopaedia of Dalits in India, Volume 13*, Delhi: Kalpaz Publishers.

Patke, Rajeev S. (2006), *Postcolonial Poetry in English*, Oxford and New York: Oxford University Press.

Phillips, Kathy J. (1994), *Virginia Woolf against Empire*, Knoxville: The University of Tennessee Press.

Phillips, Melanie (2004), *The Ascent of Woman: A History of the Suffragette Movement*, London: Abacus.

Pound, Ezra (1931), *How to Read*, London: Desmond Harmsworth.

—(1948), *Ezra Pound: Selected Poems*, ed. T. S. Eliot, London: Faber.

—[1934] (1951), *ABC of Reading*, London: Faber.

—(1971), *Selected Letters of Ezra Pound*, ed. D. D. Paige, New York: New Directions.

—(1972), *The Cantos*, New York: New Directions.

—(1973), *Selected Prose, 1909–1965*, ed. William Cookson, London: Faber.

—(1991), *Ezra Pound's Poems and Prose Contributions to Periodicals in Ten Volumes*, ed. Lea Baechler, A. Walton Litz and James Longenbach, vol. 1, New York and London: Garland Publishing.

—(2003), *Ezra Pound: Poems and Translations*, sel. Richard Sieburth, New York: Library of America.

Pratt, Mary Louise [1992] (2008), *Imperial Eyes: Travel Writing and Transculturation*, London and New York: Routledge.

Press, John (1969), *A Map of Modern English Verse*, Oxford: Oxford University Press.

Rao, Raja [1938] (1970), *Kanthapura*, New Delhi: Orient Paperbacks.

Raykar, Shubhangi (ed.) (1995), *'Jejuri': A Commentary and Critical Perspectives*, Pune: Prachet Publications.

Retamar, Roberto Fernández (1995), 'These Are the Times We Have to Live in: An Interview with Roberto Fernández Retamar', interview by Goffredo Diana and John Beverley, *Critical Inquiry* 21.2 (Winter): 411–33.

Rhys, Jean (1979), *Smile Please: An Unfinished Autobiography*, London: Andre Deutsche.

—[1966] (1982), *Wide Sargasso Sea*, New York and London: Norton.

—(1984), *The Letters of Jean Rhys*, ed. Francis Wyndham and Diana Melly, New York: Viking.

Ricks, Christopher (1988), *T. S. Eliot and Prejudice*, London and Boston: Faber.

Rudolph, Lloyd I. and Susanne Hoeber Rudolph [1967] (1984), 'The Politics of Caste', in *The Modernity of Tradition: Political Development in India*, London and Chicago: The University of Chicago Press, pp. 64–87.

Rushdie, Salman [1981] (1991), *Midnight's Children*, New York: Penguin.

Russell II, Keith A. (2007), '"Now every word she said was echoed, echoed loudly in my head": Christophine's Language and Refractive Space in Jean Rhys's *Wide Sargasso Sea*', *Journal of Narrative Theory* 37.1 (Winter): 87–103.

Said, Edward (1975), *Beginnings: Intention and Method*, New York: Basic Books.

—[1978] (1979), *Orientalism*, New York: Vintage.

—(1990), 'Yeats and Decolonisation,' in Terry Eagleton, Fredric Jameson and Edward Said, *Nationalism, Colonialism, and Literature*, Minneapolis: University of Minnesota Press, pp. 69–98.

—(1993), *Culture and Imperialism*, New York: Knopf.

—and Tariq Ali (2005), *Conversations with Edward Said*, New York: Seagull Books.

Salih, Tayeb [1966] (2003), 'Introduction' in *Season of Migration to the North*, trans. Denys Johnson-Davies, London: Penguin, pp. v–x.

—[1966] (2009), *Season of Migration to the North*, trans. Denys Johnson-Davies, intro. Laila Lalami, New York: New York Review of Books.

San Juan, Jr, Epifanio (1984), *Toward a People's Perspective: Essays in the Dialectics of Praxis and Contradiction in Philippine Writing*, Quezon City: The University of the Philippines Press.

—(1988), *Subversions of Desire: Prolegomena to Nick Joaquin*, Honolulu: University of Hawaii Press.

Sinfield, Alan (1989) *Literature, Politics, and Culture in Postwar Britain*, Berkeley and Los Angeles: University of California Press.

Stamy, Cynthia (1999), *Marianne Moore and China: Orientalism and a Writing of America*, Oxford and New York: Oxford University Press.

Stevens, Wallace (1997), *Collected Poetry and Prose*, ed. Frank Kermode and Joan Richardson, New York: The Library of America.

Storey, Mark (ed.) (1988), *Poetry and Ireland since 1800: A Source Book*, London and New York: Routledge.

Tagore, Rabindranath (2001), *The Oxford Tagore Translations: Selected Writings on Literature and Language*, gen. ed. Sukanta Chaudhuri, New Delhi: Oxford University Press.

Tapscott, Stephen (ed.) (1996), *Twentieth-century Latin American poetry: A Bilingual Anthology*, Austin: University of Texas Press.

Taylor, Charles (1995), 'Two Theories of Modernity,' *The Hastings Center Report* 25: 24–33.

Todorov, Tzvetan [2008] (2010), *The Fear of Barbarians: Beyond the Clash of Civilisations*, trans. Andrew Brown, Chicago: The University of Chicago Press.

Torgovnick, Marianna (1990), *Gone Primitive: Savage Intellects, Modern Lives*, Chicago and London: The University of Chicago Press.

Trilling, Lionel [1961] (1965), 'On the Teaching of Modern Literature', in *Beyond Culture: Essays on Literature and Learning*, New York: The Viking Press, pp. 3–30.

Tucker, Spencer (ed.) (2009), *The Encyclopedia of the Spanish-American and Philippine-American Wars: A Political, Social, and Military History, Vol. 1*, Denver and London: ABC-CLIO.

Velez, Mike (2010), 'On Borderline between Shores: Space and Place in *Season of Migration to the North*', *College Literature* 37.1 (Winter): 190–203.

Ventura, Sylvia Mendez (1993), 'Nick Joaquin's Batwoman: Revaluating "The

Legend of Doña Jeronima"', *Journal of English Studies* 1.2 (December): 74–87.

Walcott, Derek (1986), *Collected Poems 1948-1984*, New York: The Noonday Press/Farrar, Straus and Giroux.

—(1990), *Omeros*, London and Boston: Faber and Faber.

—(1992), *The Antilles: Fragments of Epic Memory*, New York: Farrar, Strauss and Giroux.

Weber, Max [1917] (1958a), "Science as a Vocation,' in H. H. Gerth and C. Wright Mills, ed. and trans., *From Max Weber: Essays in Sociology*, New York: Oxford University Press, pp. 129–56.

—[1930] (1958b), *The Protestant Ethic and the Spirit of Capitalism* [1920–1], first trans. Talcott Parsons, New York: Scribner's.

—(1968), *Economy and Society*, ed. Guenther Roth and Claus Wittich, Berkeley and Los Angeles: University of California Press.

Weber, Samuel (1991), 'Genealogy of Modernity: History, Myth and Allegory in Benjamin's *Origin of the German Mourning Play*', *MLN* 106.3 (April): 465–500.

Wilhelm, J. J. (1990), *Ezra Pound in London and Paris (1908–1925)*, University Park and London: The Pennsylvania State University Press.

Williams, Raymond (1989), *The Politics of Modernism: Against the New Conformists*, London and New York: Verso.

Williams, William Carlos (1991), *The Collected Poems, Vol. 2: 1939–1962*, ed. Christopher MacGowan, New York: New Directions.

Woolf, Virginia (1975), *The Letters of Virginia Woolf, Volume I: 1888–1912 (Virginia Stephen)*, ed. Nigel Nicolson, New York and London: Harcourt Brace Jovanovich.

—[1915] (2001), *The Voyage Out*, ed. Lorna Sage, Oxford: Oxford University Press.

Yeats, W. B. (1961), *Essays and Introductions*, London: Macmillan.

—(1997), *The Collected Works of W. B. Yeats, Vol. 1: The Poems*, ed. Richard J. Finneran, 2nd edn, New York: Scribner.

—(2008), *The Collected Works of W. B. Yeats Volume XIII: 'A Vision:' The Original 1925 Version*, ed. Catherine E. Paul and Margaret Mills Harper, New York: Scribner.

Yoon Sun Lee (2011), 'Temporalized Invariance: Lukács and the Work of Form', in Timothy Hall and Timothy Bewes (eds), *George Lukács: The Fundamental Dissonance of Existence*, London and New York: Continuum Books, pp. 17–35.

—(2012), 'Type, Totality, and the Realism of Asian American Literature', *Modern Language Quarterly* 73.3 (Sept.): 415–32.

Zaide, Gregorio F. (1957), *Philippine Political and Cultural History, Volume 2*, Manila: Philippine Education Co.

Zelliot, Eleanor (1976), 'The Medieval Bhakti Movement in History: An Essay on the Literature in English', in Bardwell L. Smith (ed.),

Hinduism: New Essays in the History of Religions, Leiden: E. J. Brill, pp. 143–66.

Zhaoming Qian (1995), *Orientalism and Modernism: The Legacy of China in Pound and Williams*, Durham, NC and London: Duke University Press.

—(2003), *The Modernist Response to Chinese Art: Pound, Moore, Stevens*, Charlottesville and London: University of Virginia Press.

Zhuwarara, Rino (1994), '*Heart of Darkness* Revisited: The African Response', *Kunapipi* 16.3: 21–37.

Ziogas, Ioannis (n.d.), 'Ovid in Rushdie, Rushdie in Ovid: A Nexus of Artistic Webs', *Arion*, Boston University, College of Arts and Science, < http://www.bu.edu/arion/ovid-in-rushdie-rushdie-in-ovid-a-nexus-of-artistic-webs/> (accessed 28 September 2012).

Further Reading

Bartolovich, Crystal and Neil Lazarus (eds) (2002), *Marxism, Modernity, and Postcolonial Studies*, Cambridge: Cambridge University Press.
A collection of essays especially useful for how different contributors elucidate the connections between Marxism and postcolonial discourse around the topic of modernity.

Boehmer, Elleke and Steven Matthews [1999] (2011), 'Modernism and Colonialism', in Michael Levelson (ed.), *The Cambridge Companion to Modernism*, 2nd edn, Cambridge: Cambridge University Press, pp. 284–300.
The essay provides a very useful update on current trends in academic debates about the significance of colonial developments to the narrative of modernism.

Booth, Howard J. and Nigel Rigby (eds) (2000), *Modernism and Empire*, Manchester: Manchester University Press.
One of the first compilations whose individual contributions address the interface between empire and specific modernist texts.

Childs, Peter (2007), *Modernism and the Post-Colonial: Literature and Empire 1885–1930*, New York: Continuum.
A survey of the same interface as that covered by the Booth and Rigby collection but with the advantage of single-author coherence over the period that links late Victorian literature to early twentieth-century writing.

Doyle, Laura and Laura Winkiel (eds) (2005), *Geomodernisms: Race, Modernism, Modernity*, Bloomington: Indiana University Press.
A large collection of essays, with a variety of approaches to the relation between race and modernism on a global scale, as a corrective to narrower accounts of modernism.

Esty, Jed (2012), *Unseasonable Youth: Modernism, Colonialism, and the Fiction of Development*, New York: Oxford University Press.
A lively account of the *Bildungsroman* from English novelists of the period in which modernism and colonialism overlap, which provides the author an opportunity for a range of insights into the contradictions inherent to plots of development and progress, in empires as well as in individual lives.

Gikandi, Simon (1996), *Maps of Englishness: Writing Identity in the Culture of Colonialism*, New York: Columbia University Press.
Exceptionally perceptive account of how conceptions of Englishness have interacted with colonial culture from the mid-nineteenth to the twentieth century.

Marx, John (2005), *The Modernist Novel and the Decline of Empire*, Cambridge: Cambridge University Press.
An interesting argument that links the decline of Britain as an imperial power to the global spread of English modernist writing.

Modernism/Modernity 13.3 (Sept. 2006), Special Issue: 'Modernism and Transnationalisms'.
A fascinating and scholarly collection of articles devoted to the idea of modernity in relation to specific instances of modernist practice.

Modern Language Quarterly 73.3 (Sept. 2012), Special Issue: 'Peripheral Realisms'.
An excellent sampling of the latest interventions on the debate concerning modernism and realism, which suggests that the tide has turned away from prioritising the role of experimental writing in the literatures of alternative modernities.

Moses, Michael Valdez, Richard Begam, Maria DiBattista and Declan Kiberd (eds) (2007), *Modernism and Colonialism: British and Irish Literature, 1899–1939*, Durham, NC: Duke University Press.
A recent collection on the interrelations between modernism and empire, with sections devoted to modernist authors and topics specific to Britain, Ireland and Scotland, and a concluding section on postcolonial writing.

Index